"Catching Up"

Vladislav L. Inozemtsev

"Catching Up"

The Limits of Rapid Economic Development

Transaction Publishers
New Brunswick (U.S.A.) and London (U.K.)

Library of Congress Catalog Number: 2002020271
ISBN: 0-7658-0108-6 (cloth); 0-7658-0841-2 (paper)
Printed in the United States of America

Library of Congress Cataloging-in-Publication Data

Inozemtsev, Vladislav L. (Vladislav Leonidovich)
    Catching up : the limits of rapid economic development / Vladislav L. Inozemtsev.
    p. cm.
    Includes bibliographical references and index.
    ISBN 0-7658-0108-6 (alk. paper)
    1. Economic development. 2. Economic development—Case studies. 3. Economic policy—Case studies. I. Title.

HD75 .I547 2002
338.9—dc21   2002020271

Contents

Introduction to the American Edition   vii

1. The Concept of "Catching Up"   1
   Development in the Twentieth Century

2. Post-Industrial Trends and Prerequisites for the   27
   Crisis of the "Catching Up" Development Model

3. Internal Contradictions of the "Catching Up"   61
   Development Model

4. The Japanese Economic Miracle: A Manifest   81
   Success or a Strategic Setback?

5. Southeast Asia: From Boom to Crisis   109

6. China: Sharing the Fate of the Others or Going   137
   Its Distinctive Way?

7. Russia: Pipe Dreams and Realistic Objectives   161

Index   185

Introduction to the American Edition

The twentieth century has been the only one in Russia's millennial history to inspire in its nations as many fervent hopes as it ruthlessly thwarted. It has abounded in unheard-of upsurges, spectacular victories, tragical downfalls and humiliating defeats. The early 1900s saw Russia searching for a road of its own, suitable for it alone; over the decades that followed our country often aspired to decide the destinies of civilization—only to close the century at the crossroads facing, like the proverbial knight-errant of an old Russian fairy-tale, the fatal choice of equally disagreeable (if not disastrous) economic alternatives.

Russia's record of the past few years evokes a multitude of questions to which no unequivocal answers can be given. Historians are examining the military and political aspects of the past; sociologists are trying to gain an insight into the inner workings of Soviet society and its Russian successor; economists are matching the efficiency of the planned economy against the performance of what the end-of-the-century reforms have brought. In our book we shall attempt a diversion from an analysis of applied problems and consider the history of our country against the background of the economic and social evolution other nations of the modern world have undergone to date. Realizing that the Soviet Union and Russia have been and remain for our compatriots the only country they can call their motherland, we suggest that the problems of its development be compared with those of other nations which, along with us and by the same right, make up the texture of modern civilization. It is only in this case, I am deeply convinced, that this study will result not in an ideologized doctrine preaching the revival of great-power ambition but a concept putting Russia's place in the global economy of the twenty-first century into the right perspective, helping to define attainable objectives and to map out the optimal ways of attaining them.

Russia's history is not that of an economically and politically advanced nation; at the same time it is the history of a state which has repeatedly and quickly caught up with the neighbors it used to lag far behind. At the time when the Byzantine Empire came into being, the territory of what later was referred to as "Third Rome" was inhabited by semi-nomadic tribes, but towards the eleventh century large Russian cities sprang up there to became centers of Christian culture and, in some cases, even models of medieval democracy. At the end of the thirteenth century when St. Thomas and St. Francis scintillated in the West and was serfdom had been abolished in northern Italian states, Russian principalities were overridden and devasted by the Mongols, but it took Muscovy a mere two hundred years or so to become the largest state in Europe. In the seventeenth century when the foundations of the capitalist economy were being laid in European monarchies, when England, Spain and Portugal owned colonies on all continents and when scientific progress heralded the approach of the Kingdom of Reason, Russia remained a continental land cut off from all the seas, a country where the natural economy and the patriarchal social system reigned supreme; in the mid-eighteenth century, however, it became a leading European nation with developed industry and culture, a formidable army and navy, and a capital city which had risen, in all its metropolitan glory, from dreary marshlands on the Baltic coast. By the early 1860s, Russia found itself falling behind again; however, Western Europe had ceased to play the indisputably dominant role in the world by then, either. An epoch of uncertainty was setting in when "catching up" with those in the lead could no longer be a great power's political imperative.

In our opinion, the October coup was, besides everything else, a reaction of sorts to such a state of affairs; a new system of government was supposed to serve as a means of making Russia a leader of world progress. In terms of ideology, proclaiming such a change of status was no problem at all, but its confirmation in practice required impressive economic achievements and an efficient economic system that would set the standard for the rest of the world to measure up to. For the first time ever in its millennial history, the nation sought not to catch up with Western states, using the methods and technologies borrowed from them, but to attain a higher level of development and to create a qualitatively new economic and social environment.

On contact with harsh reality, however, these plans were bound to crumble—and did. To begin with, the notion that socialist society was in harmony with human nature and could be built up in no time on the basis of "War Communism" turned out to be an illusion. Within some three-odd years of taking over power, the Bolsheviks were compelled to change their tactics and to introduce NEP—the New Economic Policy. While promoting economic progress, NEP did not prevent restoration of the old ways, that is, it helped narrow down the gap but failed to give birth to a new social system. Since the late 1920s, undisguised violence and terror be came the main tool in "building socialism." The shift of emphasis brought impressive results but such inquisitional practices could not go on for too long; the enormous overstrain of World War II put off the crisis of the system but did not prevent it.

The ruthlessness of Stalin's rule was such that just the renunciation of its more odious forms triggered an impulse which propelled the nation forward in the 1960s. In that period, too, nothing was invented to serve as the groundwork for the new social system. Having come close to the industrialized countries' economic and technological performance indices, largely formal as they were, the nation entered a long period of stagnation which culminated in the collapse of the Soviet system. Thus the example of the Soviet Union showed the futility of the attempts to *outstrip the industrialized nations along the lines of building up an alternative social system.*

This, however, is a view of Russia's socio-economic development in retrospect, from the turn of the twenty-first century. Such a glance can be cast at a nation's past only from the present. Just a few decades ago, however, even the most unbiased observer could see an entirely different "historical landscape." Back in the mid-1960s it was easy to presume (and to put forward convincing arguments in favor of such a presumption) that the twentieth century had offered unheard-of opportunities to the once backward states and nations. The record of the previous century seemed to corroborate such a conclusion. Indeed, in the fourteenth—early twentieth century European history boiled down, with rare exceptions, to a continuous antagonism between alliances rallied around Britain and France; in the 1870s Prussia inflicted a defeat on France to become the center of an alliance of German states and, ultimately, Europe's No.1 power economically and militarily. This compelled the English and the

French to make a common cause against this new force. Having emerged from World War I, European nations were forced to take a back seat to the United States which had unquestionably become the world's most developed nation by the mid-1920's. Yet it took Germany a mere twenty years to regain its position whereupon it suddenly came up against a strong Russia which, at the beginning of the twentieth century, had not been reckoned with in a big world-wide game. World War II created new poles of global confrontation—the USSR and the USA, with former colonies becoming independent states and with war-ravaged Japan placing third and, in the 1970s, second among industrialized nations. Under the circumstances, the prospect of confrontation between the centers of the world economy were hard to predict.

Life sorted things out, though. There is no denying the fact that the modern world differs strikingly from what it used to be a hundred years ago, but it is perfectly obvious that neither the USSR, which broke up in 1991, nor fast-growing China or even Japan can possibly claim the lead the United States has taken. Yet, this is not the end of the story. European countries which many experts regarded as lagging behind the U.S. actually enjoy as high a standard of living and are as advanced technologically as the latter; actually, they have surpassed the U.S. in the quality of social services and are now evolving into the supranational European Union setting the rest of the world an example of the optimal organization of integration processes. On the other hand, Japan has been struggling with economic depression for a decade now to no avail; the nations of Southeast Asia, long regarded as the world economy's main "growth pole," are in the throes of a crisis; the Soviet Union has vanished into non-existence; the Latin American countries have fallen far behind (it ought to be borne in mind that in 1990 Argentina ranked as the world's seventh nation in terms of the volume of the gross national product); and most of the ex-colonies are dragging out a miserable existence.

Such dynamics and such a polarization of wealth and power have their varied and numerous causes. One thing is certain, however: one of the major causes was a dogged adherence to the "catching up" development doctrine which was a fetish for sociologists and politicians for most of the 20th century. The practice of the past centuries shows that the "catching up" development tactics can be successful given two musts. First of all, the nation trying to catch up with the leader could make a substantial headway only if the leader was at a higher level of *the same technological structure the pursuer belonged to.* Second, the "catching up" tactics can be effective only given an *adequate use of mobilization methods* all the way to direct coercion, if man is regarded as a mere tool of production. Consequently, the "catching up" development model has its limits.

This reasoning is logical enough and can be further clarified, if necessary. *On the one hand,* the "catching up" model of development cannot be used efficiently enough in a situation where the catching up party has no mastery of the leader's production techniques. Had any backward country acquired the converter process know-how in the middle of the last century, it would have stood a slim chance of ever putting it into practice. On the contrary, after European techniques of ordnance casting had spread to forged-ordnance making countries, the latter promptly used them to update their weapons. *On the other hand,* if the catching up country seeks to equal the leader's volume of coal production, the objective can be gained by mobilizing proles or raising coalminers' wages, even without large-scale technological modernization. When the objective is to create a new information product, it is only education obtained over decades and the worker's deeply ingrained aspiration for creative endeavor that can become the means of attaining it. What we have in the former case is a society agrarian by nature which can catch up with an industrialized society only by an all-out effort and using imported technologies; in the latter case, we see an industrialized society which is no longer in a position to catch up with a post-industrial one because the mobilization methods any "catching up" development model is based on by definition are not applicable to a free personality's creative work—the motive force of the post-industrial community. So, the *success of the "catching up" development model is confined to the limits of the system of industrial production.*

Today a new world economic order is taking shape. By opting for the evolutionary way of development, the United States and the European Union countries have guaranteed their people a high standard of living, which prepared them for accepting post-materialistic values. Although they have largely lost their mobilizing capacity, these nations have proved equal to producing, on an ever larger scale, new knowledge and new technologies—the basic production asset of the twenty-first century. Other countries' attempts at accelerated modernization have, indeed, led to a rise in their industrial potential but failed to produce a sustainable socio-economic system. These countries continue to depend on the Western world as a source of knowledge and as a market for their products, and decades of importing new technologies have not led to scientific breakthroughs of their own. The above cannot but suggest the conclusion that it is impossible to "catch up with" post-industrial nations by industrial methods, while mobilization–based construction of material requisites sufficient for launching post-industrial transformation causes mutations of the public mind which take more time to rectify than promoting economic progress does. In the context of the present-day reality, *the nations not belonging to post-industrial civilization at the moment may expect elements of the post-industrial system to crystallize out in their social order only given the immediate involvement of the leader nations in the process* (the eastern lands of reunified Germany are a case in point).

This conclusion will hardly go down well with those who would like to see Russia the leader of world progress in the coming century and are sure to arouse strong opposition from many quarters. In our book, therefore, we shall attempt to provide a rational explanation of why the "catching up" development doctrine—which, in various forms, has become one of the outgoing century's most popular social theories—no longer makes scientific and practical sense as we are approaching a new landmark in human history and ought, therefore, to be abandoned by Russia and the world at large.

1

The Concept of "Catching Up" Development in the Twentieth Century

The twentieth century was full of economic, social, and political revolutions. Never before had history witnessed such disparities in the economic development of countries and nations. Within decades, the image of the world changed repeatedly and radically: in the early twentieth century, the United States pushed Great Britain aside, emerging as the leading economic power; in a few years Germany came to dominate Europe and retained its position, on and off, until 1945; in the 1930s the USSR made a serious effort to become the second strongest economic player; during the Soviet-U.S. confrontation in the 1950s and 1960s, Japan made its historic breakthrough, forcing the Western powers to make way for her on the world's markets; finally, in recent years the countries of Southeast Asia and China made their bid to become economic leaders in the twenty-first century. As a result, "catching up" development came to be regarded almost as a universal economic paradigm to be adopted by economically less developed nations.

We do not believe that the concept of "catching up" development can be described as a complete or integral theory. Rather it is the product of an extremely complex synthesis of bourgeois views devoted to the propagation of capitalist social values and of Marxist ideas preaching the advantages of "distinctive" economic development. From the outset, this concept was highly politicized: it was directly linked to the objectives of the developed Western nations that dominated the world economy, of the newly independent Third World countries and of the Soviet bloc states that sought to spread their influence to various regions across the globe. This explains why within the concept of "catching up" development, elements of

1

universalism, promoted mostly by Western theorists, were oddly intertwined with propaganda of unique or distinctive types of economic progress—a brainchild of those national leaders who had only this uniqueness to take pride in. For these reasons, a review of the "catching up" development theories inevitably presents a somewhat eclectic picture, and emphasis on this or that study that contributed to the emergence of the concept will perforce be, to a certain extent, arbitrary.

Problems of accelerated development first became the subject of vigorous research back during the years of World War II, when the postwar global arrangements were discussed. The first major works in this field included "Problems of Industrialization of Eastern and Southeastern Europe,"[1] an article by P. Rosenstein-Rodan in the *Economic Journal* published in 1943, and E. Staley's book *World Economic Development: Effects on Advanced Industrial Countries*[2] which appeared a year later. In a few years, the problems theoretically formulated in these two studies drew the attention of economists and political figures when, in 1948-1949, the U.S. government launched its large-scale program for the economic rehabilitation of Western Europe known as the Marshall Plan.

Until the early 1950s, however, problems of accelerated development were, in fact, never considered with respect to countries of the periphery. The rehabilitation of the Western European economies and even the strictly U.S.-controlled economic rebuilding of Japan were generally designed to cope with the destructive aftermath of the war. These efforts did not reflect the application of a fundamentally new economic paradigm to less developed countries which mostly remained colonial at the time. The developing economies' actual rise, which combined theoretical and practical aspects of acceleration, began against the background of growing confrontation between the East and the West—the outbreak of hostilities first in Korea and then in Indochina and the upsurge of the liberation movements in Africa and Asia. The need for a new theory was chiefly connected with the operation of international organizations—at first the World Bank which, in 1948-1949, provided the initial major loans to Chile, Brazil, and Mexico, and then the United Nations which, in the early 1950s, set up specialized agencies to devise techniques of accelerated development for backward countries. In 1951, two expert commissions established by the U.N.—one to deal with "Measures for Economic Development of Under-Developed Countries" and the other, with "Measures for International Economic Stability"—published extensive reports that shaped the development of the new concept for the next decade.

Generally, the theory of accelerated development took shape in the 1940s and 1950s. W. Rostow lists P. Bauer, C. Clark, A. Hirschman, A. Lewis, G. Myrdal, R. Prebisch, P. Posenstein-Rodan, G. Singer, and J. Tinbergen among its founders and ideologues.[3] However, these researchers can hardly be treated as a group because many of them held diametrically opposed ideological positions. In assessing the then state of the concept, one can also firmly assert that in actual fact none of the theorists of accelerated modernization regarded it as a component of overall historical development or suggested a clear-cut system of assumptions about the kind of economic change that could lead agrarian countries to a radically new stage of economic progress.

From the 1960s, the concepts of accelerated development gradually became polarized depending on the ideological preferences of their authors. Some Western theorists preferred to promote development which required acceptance of the values of industrial society based on private enterprise and a market economy, while experts from the developing countries stressed government intervention in the economy, self-sufficient operation of the traditional industries, and planned economy elements. We hold that from that moment on, different theories of development should be considered as relatively independent from one another.

Theories of Accelerated Westernization

In the 1950s and 1960s, the industrial society concept spread increasingly and, for obvious reasons, most Western researchers were under the sway of the ideas of technological determinism. In the late 1950s, W. Rostow proposed the concept of stages of economic growth and singled out five stages in the economic history of each nation—traditional society, the preconditions for take-off, the take-off, the drive to maturity and the age of high mass consumption. He also acknowledged the possible onset of a sixth stage that he described as "beyond consumption." His definitions, however, were never made more specific.[4] According to Rostow, traditional society's "structure is developed within limited production functions, based on pre-Newtonian science and technology, and on pre-Newtonian attitudes toward the physical world." He held that the foremost parameters of the principal stages—the take-off and the drive to maturity—were levels of investment activity amounting to 5 to 10 and 10 to 20 percent of national income, respectively.[5] All other characteristics of any given stages were also strictly technological. In the 1960s, Herman Kahn, another prominent economist and futurologist, classifying societies by per capita income levels, divided the world's countries into five groups—pre-industrial, with an average per capita income of $50 to $200; partly industrialized, with an income of $200 to $600; industrial, at a level of $600 to $1,500; mass consumption (or developed industrial) societies, with a per capita indicator of $1,500 to $4,000, and, finally, post-industrial, averaging more than $4,000.[6] This was the technocratic approach at its purest because no other characteristics of a society except its economic development level were taken into account.

Within the context of this approach, Western theorists saw industrial development as an absolute value to which any ideological paradigm could be sacrificed. Their confidence was obviously strengthened by the fact that in the 1950s and 1960s, the Soviet Union made a tangible bid for leadership in technological progress and was quickly catching up with the United States, while Japan was emerging as a dangerous competitor and capturing traditional markets for U.S. and European goods. At that time, many experts in the West agreed that the United States and the USSR represented two models of an essentially integral industrial society, and "there was general optimism with respect to what could be accomplished by emphasizing planned investment in new physical capital utilizing reserves of surplus labor, adopting import-substitution industrialization policies... and central planning."[7] That was when the ideas of convergence of Western market economies and socialist-type economic systems gained popularity. All this explains why the West regarded worldwide introduction of the Western development model as both possible and desirable.

For example, R. Aron emphasized that in the modern world, "in economic and social terms, all countries of all races at all latitudes claim to see one and the same objective reflected in essentially similar values.... Industrialization is inevitable, and it seeks to become universal."[8] It was, in fact, maintained that the less developed countries should do their utmost to embark on the road of industrial progress and more or less follow in the footsteps of the evolution of most Western nations. This development model was usually vaguely described as "modernization." Its adherents largely adopted the monolinear sociological theory of T. Parsons who reduced all social evolution to forward motion from a primitive and archaic state to modernity.[9] The fullest definition of modernization was offered in the 1960s by S. Eisenstadt: "Modernization," he said, "is a process of change toward those types of social, economic and political systems that developed in Western Europe and North America from the 17th to 19th century and then spread to other European countries and, in the 19th and twentieth centuries, to the South American, Asian and African continents."[10] A technocratic attitude is also clearly present in the views of C. Black who saw modernization as an effort to adapt traditional institutions to new functions stemming from the unprecedented growth of the role of the kind of knowledge that made it possible to control the environment. M. Levy, Jr., another researcher influenced by technocratic ideas, regarded modernization as a social revolution going as far as possible without destroying society itself.[11]

In the 1950s and 1960s, the most important aspects of the problems of modernization were, of course, economic, sociopolitical, and cultural.

In economic terms, modernization was seen as hinging on accelerated industrial development involving the use of new technologies and efficient energy sources, greater division of labor and the advancement of commodity and monetary markets. Such accelerated development was to apply to all sectors of the economy without exception, not just to individual export-oriented industries. Back in the early 1950s, R. Nurske said that "the general level of economic activity is raised and the size of the market enlarged [by means] of a frontal attack—a wave of capital investments in a number of different industries... through the application of capital over a wide range of activities."[12] However, the question of where such investment was to come from to assure such rapid growth remained open. Most experts held (quite properly, we believe), first, that the developing countries could not do without a significant influx of outside capital and, second, that on the way to a market economy they would have to pass through a typically early capitalist stage of acute social differentiation. The principal recommendations were therefore limited, on the one hand, to the need for a vigorous drive to attract foreign investment and, on the other, to the idea that savings had to be encouraged as much as possible, consumption was to be curtailed and ownership differences were to be accepted: as a result, a socially heterogeneous nation would be able to create its bourgeoisie.[13] Many researchers stressed the role of the state that was to focus investment flows in priority areas and encourage business initiative so as to increase industrial output. One should note that such modernization was designed not to create a centralized planned economy but to shape a Western-type market economy in which the leading role belonged to industrial corporations, banks, and trading and financial companies. These were to be as independent as possible from political and ideological factors; as a result, economic growth would become natural and self-sustained.[14]

The sociopolitical aspect of modernization was linked primarily to the emergence in the developing countries of a Western social model essentially dominated by the principles of individualism and market economics. This approach appeared so self-evident that many sociologists used the words "civilizing mission" and "Westernizing mission" interchangeably.[15] Significantly, J. Tinbergen held that rapid and sustainable development hinged, first, on the creation and maintenance of a monetary equilibrium, second, on prevention of mass unemployment, third, on efforts to avoid excessive differences in incomes and, fourth, on indirect government intervention in those areas that could not develop properly on the basis of private enterprise alone. "It must be clear that programming is not an alternative to common sense; it cannot replace common sense and it should not," he said.[16] Clearly, preference was expressed for the traditional market-economy techniques of self-regulation.

Obviously, in developing countries, such a mechanism can only function properly within a legal system assuring the individual's economic freedoms and rights. Therefore, Western experts maintained that in the social systems being forged on the periphery of the developed world, a person's social status should be based on one's individual qualities—skills, performance, education, and the like—and not on one's lineage or caste. In this connection, social modernization was seen as an effort to replace a hierarchy of subordination and vertical accountability with a partnership of equals based on mutual interest. In order to create a modern society, it was also essential to modify political relations so as to protect human rights, assure proper division of powers and freedom of speech, and involve the public as much as possible in the political process.[17] For the sake of fairness one should note that back in the 1960s, most theorists of modernization realized that full compliance with their recommendations was not feasible; subsequently, they kept repeating that it was important for a society undergoing modernization to create a government apparatus staffed by well-trained, competent and able administrators. It was also emphasized that, contrary to tradition, public servants should not be selected on the basis of their social background or personal connections.[18]

The cultural aspect of modernization was connected in the 1960s with a rationalization of human awareness on the basis of scientific knowledge and a rejection of behavior rooted in tradition; moreover, the formation of a new cultural stereotype was seen as central to the entire process of modernization.[19] However, the problem was raised simplistically and the recommendations for tackling it were simplistic, too. It was commonly held that secular education, the fight against illiteracy, religious tolerance, progress in communications and the dissemination of information, as well as large-scale cultural enlightenment would automatically promote acceptance of Western values. Few analysts could afford to go beyond technological determinism and assert that "the central objective of all the countries undergoing modernization is to step up the formation of human capital."[20] The practical record has shown that modernization encountered its biggest problems in its political and cultural aspects: this was where the concepts of modernization had to undergo the biggest adjustments, and some of them were the reverse of the initial logic underlying these concepts.

The theorists of modernization admitted that different countries required different techniques or methods of modernization and that the rates of modernization would not be the same everywhere. The argument was that in some countries, modernization would occur naturally, in response to society's inner needs, while in others modernization would be induced by more developed nations.[21] The list of factors impeding modernization included the sway of traditional social institutions, the reluctance of the ruling elites to share power and profits for the benefit of the nation, as well as illiteracy and widespread absence of a rational outlook. Many champions of accelerated modernization suggested, as a radical prescription, removal of these factors; they held that, first and foremost, the traditional sector was to be destroyed or changed.[22]

Modernization concepts clearly pointed the way for the countries that opted for "catching up" development, yet successful change called for a number of conditions most of which proved unfeasible. According to some researchers, specifically, G. Myrdal, the Western countries that have reached the post-industrial development level and are already enjoying obvious advantages in technology can destroy, with their cheap goods, the Third World's traditional industries. Meanwhile, cheap labor remains the only source of appeal to foreign investment in developing countries. Cheap labor implies an extremely low level of domestic savings and as such impedes effective progress.[23] Indeed, most theories of accelerated development assumed an initial impetus from the Western countries. However, the West itself saw no point in investing vast resources in Third World economies[24] (in contrast to the program for Western European economic rehabilitation or aid to Japan, South Korea, or Taiwan that were confronting the Communist threat in Southeast Asia). On the other hand, the Third World was not about to ape the countries it saw as colonial oppressors. Besides, the theories of accelerated or "catching up" development appeared in the West decades after the market and civil society had begun to work there in a civilized and sophisticated manner[25]; unfortunately therefore, the idea of Westernization proved to be alien to the developing nations themselves. Its implementation called (and still calls) on them to overcome enormous resistance; therefore it could not (and cannot) become popular with the Third World. Moreover, both the developing countries themselves and the leftists in the West expectedly charged that such concepts promoted the periphery's economic dependence.

Alternative Theories of Development

The followers of the modernization theory maintained that by emulating the West, the developing countries could assure their own economic and social progress. Simultaneously, however, different concepts were suggested. One of them followed up on the ideas published, during the first postwar years, by R. Prebisch, an Argentinian economists who held prominent posts in the U.N. Economic

Commission for Latin America and in UNCTAD.[26] This theory, seriously influenced by Marxism, ascribed Third World problems not so much to the uneven use of the advantages offered by economic growth as to the direct and blatant exploitation of the "periphery" by the countries of the "center." As A. Foster-Carter noted at the time, the term "underdevelopment" was used to stress the steady destruction by the Western world of the economies that were dependent on it.[27] In 1957, these views simultaneously prompted P. Baran in the United States and S. Furtado in Brazil to advance what was called the concept of "dependientismo" (from the Spanish word for "dependent").

Its adherents did not oppose the Third World's accelerated development, as such, but warned the "Westernizers" against using uniform modernization models which failed to accommodate the distinctive cultural features of the "catching up" countries.[28] The "dependientistas" charged that the theories of modernization ignored the social, political, and cultural aspects of the developing countries' past and present and that it was impossible to separate economic and social factors of development because "development in itself is a social process; besides, its purely economic aspects are marked by its internal social relations."[29]

Working on the concept of "dependent development" in the 1960s and 1970s were many talented researchers—S. Furtado, F. Cardoso and T. dos Santos of Brazil, E. Faletto of Argentina, A. Monteverde and O. Sunkel, a Russian emigre, of Mexico, P. Baran of the United States, S. Amin of Senegal, A.G. Frank, a German American, and a number of others. As we noted above, they ascribed the backward state of certain countries to the evolution of world capitalism. "I believe it was the inner contradictions of capitalism and the historical development of the capitalist system that made the countries of the periphery backward: their surplus product was appropriated by the colonial powers; this assured the latter's economic progress and gave rise to a steady process [of exploitation] which is still with us," said A.G.Frank.[30] He also emphasized that underdevelopment should not be seen simply as nondevelopment because this distinctive social and economic system was due to its ongoing exploitation by the leading world powers whose policies, on the one hand, shaped the developing countries' orientation on exports and, on the other, kept up a constant flight of these economies' surplus value to other regions. In this way, the growing exports of raw commodities and the imports of industrial goods (for the benefit of the West) kept reproducing the "vicious circle" that made it extremely difficult to boost economic development.[31] In the view of the "dependientistas," the biggest problem was not that it was impossible to create a dynamic sector of the Third World economies but that the social structure was shaped by dependence on the capitalist centers and the traditional foreign trade ties impeded development.

This school saw the economic situation in Asia, Africa, and Latin America not as an essential stage on the way to a developed industrial society but primarily as a result of the "invasion by modern capitalist enterprises into archaic social structures."[32] The theory of "dependientism" explained the reproduction of the developing countries' dependence on the major centers of economic power by the need for their continued financing from abroad. In the opinion of O. Sunkel, the growing share of raw commodities in the exports and of industrial goods in the imports, as well as the ever-present fiscal shortages combined to generate "the implacable necessity to obtain foreign financing... [that] is the crucial point in the mechanisms of dependence."[33] In this connection some of the "dependientistas" noted the developing countries' foreign debt (which skyrocketed throughout the 1980s): this, they believed, indicated an increasingly irreversible redistribution of added value in favor of the centers of world capitalism.

Among the "dependientistas," there were both serious scholars with excellent knowledge of history, sociology, and economics (such as I. Wallerstein) and relatively superficial researchers who declared their Marxist affiliation and tried to update some Marxist tenets (such as P. Baran). Small wonder that on a number of issues their positions differed considerably. In the opinion of I.Wallerstein, capitalism is developing naturally as a market-economy system, and therefore equally comprises both the exploited classes of the capitalist countries themselves and the countries of the "periphery" even though the strictly capitalist elements such as hired labor and nationwide commodity production are less developed there. Just as capitalist relations had spread to all social strata in Europe from the sixteenth to the nineteenth centuries, capitalism kept expanding toward the periphery.[34] Other "dependientistas" maintained that the great powers were only interested in the developing world because they saw it as a source of cheap raw commodities. Some of them oversimplified world history so much that in earnest explained Japan's success by the fact that the country had no natural resources and a small domestic market and was therefore "of no interest to the imperialist forces."[35]

The "dependientistas" criticized the modernization theory from several angles.[36] They claimed that the backwardness of today's "traditional societies" was due to the development of international capitalism. They argued that in order to develop rapidly, the backward countries should go their own way instead of using foreign capital and adopting Western cultural values. In their view, industrialization could not raise the developing countries to a qualitatively new level of economic progress. On the one hand, the orientation toward exports merely strengthened the international division of labor that had taken shape in the colonial era, with its "overwhelming dominance of the leading countries in labor productivity in all possible fields, which compels the states of the periphery to accept their role of suppliers of not too important goods such as exotic farm produce or raw materials they are naturally in a good position to offer."[37] On the other hand, even imports-substitution industrialization in most cases failed to affect the system of dependence because imports of technologies did not raise the productivity level above that of the developed countries and were therefore unable to put an end to underdevelopment.[38] The "dependientistas" therefore regarded accelerated development as a vicious circle which could not lead the developing countries to prosperity. As R.Prebisch said in the mid-1950s, "my diagnosis of the situation of the countries of Latin America was constructed on the basis of my criticism of the pattern of outward-oriented development, which I considered to be incapable of permitting the full development of those countries. My proposed development policy was oriented toward the establishment of a new pattern of development which would make it possible to overcome the limitations of the previous pattern."[39] Regrettably, one must admit that neither Prebisch nor his followers have succeeded in offering a feasible alternative.[40]

The "dependientistas" were particularly averse to the modernization theory advocates' claim that the developing countries should follow in the footsteps of Western Europe and North America, but more rapidly. The "dependientistas" said this would only help establish a worldwide U.S. hegemony and sap the developing economies, exacerbate social conflicts, destroy the environment and have the international monopolies (primarily U.S.-based) dominate the Third World countries.[41] Without denying the very possibility of industrial development in the backward countries, the "dependientistas" held that it would not produce any radical change and would merely serve to keep the developing countries backward and isolated from the post-industrial world.

The "dependientist" concept particularly stressed the unfairness of exchange in relations between the Third World and the industrial centers: the developed countries artificially depressed the prices of Third World commodities and inflated those of technologies and industrial articles imported by the developing nations. Also inflated were the charges for financial services, debt repayment, and so on. Unfairness was also seen in the fact that the same kind of investment (for example, in real estate development) generated far higher profits in the advanced countries than in the Third World, thus making the latter much less attractive to investors.[42] No matter how diverse they may appear at first sight, all these elements of the concept of "dependientism" indicate that already in the 1970s, many researchers were aware that it was impossible to "catch up" with the post-industrial world, irrespective of whether the effort was based on the use of Western investment or on self-sufficiency.

It was also noted that certain social groups in the developing countries themselves wanted their nations to remain backward. F. Cardoso referred to "an internal structural fragmentation connecting the most 'advanced' parts of their economies to the international capitalist system. Separate although subordinated to these advanced sectors, the backward economic and social sectors of the dependent countries then play the role of 'internal colonies.'"[43] Therefore, even the slow and uncertain economic progress of the developing countries, mostly in the export-oriented sectors with their close ties to the international monopolies, was incapable of "dragging" the entire economy through a process of change. It could only push the boundary of backwardness deeper into the national economy, thus making it "dual." Largely on the basis of these views, S. Amin asserted categorically in the mid-1970s that the "economies of the periphery are without any internal dynamism of their own."[44]

The "dependientistas" mostly criticized the theory of modernization but failed to indicate any ways toward creating developed systems with a market-economy infrastructure in the countries of Latin America, Africa and Asia. The failure to provide such an answer was all the more unusual in the 1970s, when the decades of colonial rule had long been past but the Third World economies showed no signs of improvement. Although they did preach proper attention to the distinctive social and cultural features of the periphery, the "dependientistas" in fact badly underrated the role of the human factor in economic and social processes and ignored the universal sociocultural aspects of social evolution. As a result, their recommendations for overcoming backwardness were reduced to minor, random and technical advice in the economic and political fields.

Essentially, the ideology of the "dependientistas" favored economic isolationism in an age of growing internationalization. According to S. Amin, "so long as the less developed country continues to be integrated in the world market, it remains helpless... [and] the possibilities of local accumulation are nil."[45] Therefore, the champions of the developing countries' "distinctive way" argued that export earnings should be used more frugally and effectively not so much to transform the industrial sector that linked these nations with the rest of the world but to modernize the traditional sectors and create a more updated infrastructure. The foremost objectives included self-sufficiency in resources, accelerated development of local industry, saturation of the domestic market reduction of imports and closer political integration of the Third World on the international scene so as to introduce the so-called new economic order.[46] In the 1970s, when the West was facing the energy crisis and commodity shortages, the demands of the Third World countries did sound seriously, yet today those years are remembered as a strange dream.

The more radical followers of the "dependientism" theory agreed on the need for structural change to expand the domestic market, yet they also suggested social democratic and even leftist socialist measures, such as more government intervention in the economy and less dependence on the centers of world capitalism.[47] Calls for a socialist revolution and for weaker ties with the West and the world market were also not unheard of.[48] In most cases, such calls were based on an obvious substitution of concepts and on the unfounded belief that "a modern economy with its high labor productivity inevitably underlies the socialist system."[49] No wonder that those adhering to such attitudes maintained that backwardness and dependence could only be ended by a socialist revolution which would allegedly open the way to "self-reliance," with the existing industries giving rise to economic growth primarily to satisfy national requirements.[50]

Such prescriptions highlight the limitations of the theory of "dependientism." Devised as an alternative to the concepts of modernization, it actually preached "modernization for internal consumption" and industrialization within a nation which did not permit either foreign competition or any other outside influence. The "dependientistas" proposed outdated solutions which had become a thing of the post in the developed countries, appealed to the social strata that represented the economic past, not future, and failed to accord proper attention to matters of education, science and culture. Therefore, the "dependientist" concepts did not and could not offer a realistic alternative to the theories of Westernization.

Post-Industrial Change and the Decline of "Catching up" Development Theories

The practical economic record of the 1970s-1990s showed clearly that the forecasts of the ideologues of "catching up" development came true only partially and that the advocates of Westernization proved much more accurate in their assumptions and calculations than the "dependientistas."

The main economic trends of the past three decades have noticeably narrowed the freedom of economic movement of the developing countries. The 1980s not only strengthened the conviction that both types of industrialism—capitalism and socialism—were fated to disappear from the world arena but also witnessed the collapse of the USSR which was seen as the only alternative to the Western economic model, something on which the developing countries could orient themselves. Post-industrial change radically reduced Western demand for the products of the periphery, pushing many developing countries to the brink of economic disaster. Human intellect and creative capabilities emerged as the foremost factor of economic progress. The technological revolution assured the Western powers of unprecedented prosperity—although, in the words of James K. Galbraith, "the number of winners in a winner-take-all lottery is necessarily a small fraction of those who would like to play... 'Technological revolution' is a game that only a few can win."[51] Therefore, in recent years many developing countries have concentrated on the manufacture of relatively simple mass products in demand on world markets—far from the worst of the possible development options.

Still, most of the Third World countries did feel the impact of the post-industrial world's growing self-sufficiency and the weaker demand for their traditional exports. The rising efficiency of production in the West meant that this was where the production not only of industrial items but also of farm produce proved to be more profitable. From the mid-1960s, North America accounted for the entire surplus of net grain exports;[52] the United States, Australia and South America are the leading exporters of meat and poultry. Today, the developing countries even feel like outcasts on the markets for their traditional exotic products: while in the mid-1960s Africa's share in the world output of palm oil reached 80 percent, it fell to 20 percent by the end of the 1980s. While Africa accounted for 60 to 80 percent of the world's peanut and peanut butter exports in the 1960s, in the mid-1980s this figure did not rise above 10 to 16 percent.[53] The developing countries have been dealt even more obvious blows on the market for raw commodities: they are facing more problems there because the costs of producing (not extracting) natural resources are in fact zero; therefore, their pricing is a subjective rather than an objective process. Meanwhile, the low value placed on the output of such industries is a consequence of the "relative power of social classes that conditions the functioning of the market; specifically, labor and capital are two powerful social classes, while resource owners... are not."[54] The 1990s saw the prices of raw commodities go down. Even the impressive industrial boom in Western Europe and the United States in the middle of the decade failed to reverse this trend. Between 1990 and mid-1999, the overall commodity index calculated by the *Economist* fell to almost 30 percent. Having become leaders in agricultural production, the developed nations imposed unfair trading prices in this field, too: the prices of the main staples—wheat, corn, and rice—increased by 29, 58, and 30 percent, respectively, from 1993 to 1996.[55] This means that the Third World's last chances of pressuring the "First World" are disappearing fast.

The developing countries' plight has never been more painful. While in the early nineteenth century, the gap between the economic potential of the center and the periphery was merely threefold[56] and the difference in average incomes was 30 to 50 percent,[57] today's dichotomy is estimated to be 50- to 72-fold.[58] In 1993, the world's GNP totaled $23 trillion, including $18 trillion generated in the developed nations and a mere $5 trillion in the developing countries where more than 80 percent of the population of the globe lived. The difference in the nominal incomes in the post-industrial countries and all other nations grew from $5,700 a year in 1960 to $15,400 in 1993. That is, the richest one-fifth of the human race appropriated 61 times more wealth than the poorest one-fifth,[59] although this figure was only 30 times back in 1960.[60] In early 1993, producing 1.4 percent of the world's GNP, the poorest one-fifth accounted for 0.98 percent of global savings and 0.95 percent of the total trade turnover.[61] Against this background, living standards in many developing countries have been falling: from 1985 to 1989, average per capita food production decreased in as many as 94(!) countries, average per capita income went down in 40 nations,[62] and 13 states now produce and consume less per capita food volumes than 30(!) years ago.[63] The increasingly widespread view that these economies are bankrupt leads to reductions in their share of foreign investment: from 1967 to 1990, this share fell from 30.6 to 18.9 percent of the total. This drop was particularly dramatic in the regions that are, with good reason, described as the "Fourth World"—from 17.5 to 7.3 percent in Latin America and from 5.3 to 2.1 percent in Africa.[64] These statistics not only highlight the economic ineffectiveness of the poorest regions but also indicate that the gap will keep widening.

However, the 1970s and 1980s not so much discredited the theories of "catching up" development as witnessed their revision. Although many researchers—specifically, B. Schneider—acknowledged the complete failure of all previous plans for having the nations of the periphery develop in Western ways,[65] it was clear that certain developing countries' efforts yielded quite successful and even fantastic results. In Southeast Asia, rapid economic growth did not conflict with but was rather largely rooted in the local sociocultural environment. This appeared to bear out the view of R. Bendix that he voiced back in 1967—that it was wrong to contrast tradition and modernity and that modernization did not necessarily destroy the existing social systems.[66] At about the same time, G. Myrdal said that "awareness of history and the search for national identity do not by themselves threaten or even conflict with commitment to the ideals of modernization."[67] As a result, the advocates of "catching up" development, on the one hand, *analyzed the significance of human capital* for accelerated economic progress and, on the other, *centered on the role of the state* in the transformation of traditional economic systems into modern industrial ones.

The *former* effort, as it turned out, produced no tangible results but was limited to general theoretical considerations arguing that at the close of the twentieth century, the world was becoming increasingly diverse, which called for a synthesis of universalism and the cultural distinctiveness of different nations.[68] Significantly, in discussing the human factor, the developing countries referred not so much to a higher intellectual level or promotion of creative individuality as to the immediate use of human capital so as to assure the advancement of the existing socioeconomic system. In other words, these countries identified human capital, albeit vaguely, not with something to be created according to the Western model but with what was on hand and had been created within this or that particular nation. Education was interpreted in an excessively broad cultural context. For example, the assertion that "the success of development implies, first and foremost, a strengthening of the human potential by education geared to the requirements of modernization" was accompanied by the reservation that "support for national culture aimed at preserving the nations' identity and reassert the authenticity of their development is not an excessive demand or a luxury but forms an integral element of motives for development and emerges as the basis of the specific choice that makes it possible to mobilize their energy."[69]

By the late 1980s, an "improved" concept of modernization had been formed. It provided for dynamic economic and social development which did not force the particular society to accept the industrial system values widespread in the West. The new concept no longer argued that each "catching up" country should go its own separate way but preached a distinctive synthesis of universalism and particularism. The need for such a combination was ascribed to the fact that an imbalance between modernity and tradition would doom the reforms and give rise to acute social conflicts. For example, in the opinion of A. Touraine, the world's survival depended on whether it would be possible to couple rationality and culture, modernity and national identity, development as a universal goal and the way of life as a choice of values, economic development and social reform.[70] J. Attali also spoke out for the need to reconcile rationality and spirituality in the modern world.[71] Recently, the advocates of this approach have been using the term "countermodernization" (to describe accelerated industrialization as practiced in the USSR during the 1930s-1960s and in some other socialist countries where rapid industrial development led to autarky and undermined market economy values) and even "antimodernization" (to denote a radical destruction of basic social values—something that obviously pushed the productive forces backward and revived primitive economic forms, the way it happened during the "cultural revolution" in China).[72] However, we believe that "modernization to bypass modernity" which the authors of the new concept preach testifies to the crisis of this view, just as the ideas of "post-modernity" indicate that it is pointless to juggle with post-modernist terms.[73]

The *latter* trend proved to be much more fruitful because from the outset, working on it were not theoretical sociologists but those who deal with practical economics and politics—primarily, in the Asian countries that sought to industrialize fast by using Western technologies and in this way achieve integration in the world economic system. Central to this approach was the use, in the course of industrial development, of the potential of the state that, in most developing countries, in fact remained the only social institution capable of implementing the necessary reform.

The term "developmental state" ("*hatten-shiko-kata-kokka*") was coined back in the 1970s, but it failed to gain currency in the English-speaking countries because the concept itself was in demand primarily in East Asia.[74] In the West, the first serious attempt to examine this system of views can be found in C. Johnson's book on industrial policy in Japan, published in 1982.[75] Central to the "developmental state" are the considerable concentration of economic power in the hands of the state apparatus, this apparatus' relative independence from the social processes, which enables it to intervene, as an "outsider," in economic and social affairs, and, finally, close ties between the state and the business community, the state playing the leading role.[76] In this case the state influences the economy by way of customs policies, differentiated interest rates, monopolist opportunities for certain groups of producers, incentives for imports of technologies and exports of finished products and a wide range of protectionist measures to keep the domestic market covered. Although the resulting economic system is highly bureaucratized and the methods of its management are very similar to those used in the socialist economy of the USSR, all developmental states nevertheless remain oriented on active interaction with the outside world. This interaction takes the form of large-scale imports of technologies and exports of finished products, efforts to attract foreign investment, the development of the stock market, and so on.

From the outset, the concept of the "developmental state" was linked with the theory of "catching up" development which was formulated by the Japanese economist K. Akimatsu in the 1930s and which was also known as the "flying geese vee formation" theory. The precept was that as technological progress advanced and spread beyond the boundaries of the developed nations, less developed countries would also be able to manufacture the finished product just as efficiently, using their own labor and the latest technological achievements. In other words, as the leading goose rises higher, it is confidently followed by the entire vee formation.[77] In the 1970s and 1980s, when Japan attained its impressive economic success, a modified version of this concept (naturally, with Japan as the "leader") was promoted by Japanese economists and sociologists throughout Southeast Asia.[78] To this day, Western analysts keep noting that Japan (and, to a lesser extent, South Korea) has demonstrated a unique example of the way a nation committed to "catching up" development reaches a point where, instead of following the leader, itself becomes the leader and has the adjacent countries emulate its progress.[79]

In subsequent chapters we will attempt to take a comprehensive view of the record of "catching up" development both in Japan and in other Southeast Asian countries. At this point however, let us note that both the Japanese and all other versions of the concept proved insufficient for the countries that opted for them to assure sustainable progress. Clearly dependent on the technological progress of the Western world, they concentrated excessively on the manufacture and export of mass-produced industrial goods. In the 1990s, the rates of the "catching up" countries' development slowed down noticeably, and in 1997-1998 the Asian financial crisis broke out and laid bare the limitations of this model as a whole. Although in recent years, most analysts have preferred to argue that this crisis was due to certain particular financial mistakes of the region's countries and can therefore be overcome soon, we believe—as we will try to prove—that the fundamental reason for the crisis lies in the untenable nature of the very theory of "catching up" development.

* * *

The twentieth century has seen both a number of practical attempts at accelerated development and a variety of theories suggesting different ways for the developing countries to end their age-old backwardness. Now that the next century has begun, it is becoming clear that socioeconomic realities do not fit into these theories; many of them have been proved to be mistaken. Again and again, these realities prompt the social scientists to devise a clearer picture of a just world and to formulate a more distinct question about the conditions in which this or that country can join the developed industrial economies.

As never before, the eve of the twenty-first century has placed the spotlight on the inevitable division, not inner unity of today's world. As the well-known sociologist and philosopher Z. Bauman noted two years ago, even when humanity was artificially divided into the opposite Western and Eastern blocs, into a capitalist system and a communist camp, individual parts of the world appeared much less isolated than they do today. "By dividing the worlds," he said, "the politicians created the illusion that it was whole"[80] by promoting the conviction that in the course of this confrontation, the foundations of a balance for the entire civilization would be forged. Following up on his view, we can now add that during the Cold War years, there existed two systems, each claiming to contain an independent (and sufficiently effective) economic paradigm, and the developing countries were free to adopt either model or to look for a path of their own. Now that the former socialist countries have lost their historical competition with capitalism and the developing countries (except those that sought vigorously to apply the achievements of the Western world) are lagging disastrously behind the leading post-industrial nations, the impression is that our deeply divided civilization is entering an era of dangerously exacerbating global contradictions. Today, "the idea of development [on one's own] appears to be no more than a ruin against the backdrop of the modern intellectual scene,"[81] and one can hardly hope that things will get any better during the next few decades.

Modern globalization has failed, in our opinion, to justify the hopes that were pinned on it. One cannot really expect, even in the future, any unity between the developed world which is benefiting from each new stage of technological and social progress and the developing countries whose position is mostly deteriorating steadily. Many experts note that the relations between these two groups demonstrate less and less interdependence which could in any way rally our civilization together; on the contrary, it is being divided into the increasingly "globalized" developed nations and the ever more "localized" poorest regions isolated from the finest achievements of civilization.[82] Viewed from this angle, the prospects of "catching up" development appear in fact exhausted to us. The sources of technological progress remain outside the Third World—yet only access to them can make any given country industrially developed. Natural wealth such as territorial or mineral resources which, in the past, could help relatively backward countries rise above their level are ceasing to be meaningful factors of production and cannot provide their owners with a new status. The inner contradictions of the very paradigm of "catching up" development (with which we will deal in detail below) and the self-sufficiency of the Western world which does not need the developing countries as the latter need the post-industrial powers—all this proves that the concept of "catching up" development, a product of rapid industrial progress, will inevitably be relegated to the past in the era of the information society. This "almost realized" dream of the twentieth century will have no place in the twenty-first.

Notes

1. See Rosenstein-Rodan, P. "Problems of Industrialization of Eastern and Southeastern Europe," *Economic Journal,* June-September, 1943, pp. 202-211.
2. See Staley, E. *World Economic Development: Effects on Advanced Industrial Countries,* International Labour Office, Montreal, 1944.
3. For details, see Rostow, W.W. *Theorists of Economic Growth from David Hume to the Present With a Perspective on the Next Century,* Oxford University Press, New York-Oxford, 1990, p. 385.
4. See Rostow, W.W. *The Stages of Economic Growth: A Non-Communist Manifesto,* 3rd ed., Cambridge University Press, Cambridge, 1995, pp. 4, 11-12.

5.   Rostow, W.W. *The Stages of Economic Growth*, pp. 4, 8-9.
6.   See Kahn, H., Wiener, A. "The Next Thirty-Three Years: A Framework for Specu-
     lation," *Daedalus*, Summer 1967, pp. 716-718.
7.   Meier, G.M. *Leading Issues in Economic Development*, 6th ed., Oxford University
     Press, New York, Oxford, 1995, p. 86.
8.   Aron, R. *Trois essais sur l'age industrielle*, Editions Gallimard, Paris, 1966, pp. 60,
     93.
9.   See Parsons, T. *The Evolution of Societies*, Prentice-Hall, Englewood Cliffs (N.J.),
     1977, p. 25.
10. Eisenstadt, S.N. *Modernization: Protest and Change,* Prentice-Hall, Englewood
     Cliffs (N.J.), 1966, p. 1.
11. See Black, C. *The Dynamics of Modernization: A Study in Comparative History,*
     Harper & Row, New York, 1966, pp. 7-8; Levy, M., Jr. *Modernization and the
     Structure of Societies: A Setting for International Affairs,* vols. 1-2, Princeton Uni-
     versity Press, Princeton (N.J.), 1966, p. 735.
12. Nurske, R. *Problems of Capital Formation in Underdeveloped Countries,* Basil
     Blackwell, Oxford, 1958, pp. 14, 13.
13. See Bettelheim, Ch. *Planification et croissance accélérée,* Maspero, Paris, 1964, p.
     30.
14. See Levy, M., Jr. *Modernization and the Structure of Societies,* pp. 518-519.
15. See Laue, Th. von. *The World Revolution of Westernization: The Twentieth Century
     in Global Perspective,* Oxford University Press, New York-Oxford, 1987, p. 323.
16. See Tinbergen, J. *The Design of Development,* Johns Hopkins University Press,
     Baltimore, 1958, pp. 65, 9.
17. See Eisenstadt, S.N. "Post-Traditional Societies and the Continuity and Recon-
     struction of Tradition," in Eisenstadt, S.N. (ed.) *Post-Traditional Societies,* Basic
     Books, New York, 1972, p. 7; Eisenstadt, S.N. *Tradition, Change, and Modernity,*
     Basic Books, New York, 1973, p. 26.
18. See Levy, M., Jr. *Modernization and the Structure of Societies,* pp. 440-454.
19. See Eisenstadt, S.N. *Modernization: Protest and Change,* p. 5.
20. Harbison, F.H. "Human Resources Development Planning in Modernising Econo-
     mies," in Meier, G. (ed.) *Leading Issues in Development Economics: Selected
     Materials and Commentary,* Oxford University Press, New York, 1964, p. 273.
21. See Hoselitz, B. *Sociological Aspects of Economic Growth,* Free Press, Glencoe
     (Ill.), 1960, pp. 97-109; Eisenstadt, S.N. *Modernization: Protest and Change,* pp.
     67, 72.
22. See Higgins, B. *Economic Development: Problems, Principles, and Policies,* 2nd
     ed., W. W. Norton, New York, 1968, pp. 17-20, 296-305.
23. G. Myrdal's concept of the "vicious circle" in relations between the post-industrial
     world and the developing countries is considered by D.K. Fieldhouse in Fieldhouse,
     D.K. *The West and the Third World. Trade, Colonialism, Dependence and Devel-
     opment,* Blackwell Publishers, Oxford-Malden (Mass.), 1999, pp. 54-56.
24. This is borne out, among other things, by the fact that neither politicians nor fellow
     economists supported Myrdal's calls for much greater aid to the developing coun-
     tries and even for an international system of additional taxation which could finance
     such aid (see Myrdal, G. *The Challenge of World Poverty: A World Anti-Poverty
     Program in Outline,* Pantheon Books, New York, 1970, p. 365).
25. See Arndt, H.W. *Economic Development: The History of an Idea,* University of
     Chicago Press, Chicago-London, 1987, p. 165.
26. See Prebisch, R. "Growth, Disequilibrium, and Disparities: Interpretation of the
     Process of Economic Development," in *Economic Survey of Latin America,* New
     York, 1949, pp. 49-65ff.

27. See Foster-Carter, A. "Neo-Marxist Approaches to Development and Underdevelopment," in Kadt, E. de, Williams, G. (eds.) *Sociology and Development,* London, 1974, p. 80.

28. See Furtado C. *Teoria e Politica do Desenvolvimento Economico,* 6-a ed., Sao Paulo, 1977, pp. 96-97.

29. See Cardoso, F.H., Faletto, E. *Dependencia y desarrollo en America Latina: Ensayo de interpretacion sociologica,*13-a ed., Mexico, 1977, p. 11.

30. Frank, A.G. *Capitalism and Underdevelopment in Latin America,* London-New York, 1967, p. 3.

31. See Frank, A.G. *Capitalism and Underdevelopment in Latin America,* p. 11.

32. Furtado, C. *Desenvolvimento e Subdesenvolvimento,* Fundo de Cultura, Rio de Janeiro, 1961, p. 180.

33. Sunkel, O. "National Development Policy and External Dependence in Latin America," *Journal of Developmental Studies,* October, 1969, p. 31.

34. For details, see Wallerstein, I. "The Present State of the Debate on World Inequality," in Wallerstein, I. (ed.) *World Inequality: Origins and Perspectives on The World System,* Black Rose Books Ltd., Montreal, 1975, pp. 12-28.

35. Baran, P. *The Political Economy of Growth,* [Publisher's details should be added] New York, 1957, p. 294.

36. The differences between the "dependientistas" and the champions of the modernization theory are discussed in greater detail in Isbister, J. *Promises Not Kept: The Betrayal of Social Change in the Third World,* 4th ed., Kumarian Press, West Hartwood (Conn.), 1998, pp. 50-57.

37. Amin, S. *Unequal Development,* Harvester Press, Sussex, 1979, p. 200.

38. See Cockcroft, J.D., Frank, A.G., Johnson, D.L. *Dependence and Underdevelopment: Latin America's Political Economy,* Doubleday Anchor, Garden City (N.Y.), 1972, pp. xii-xiii.

39. Cited in: Meier, G.M., Seers, D. (eds.) *Pioneers in Development,* Oxford University Press, New York-Oxford, 1984, p. 177.

40. See Lal, D. *The Poverty of "Development Economics,"* MIT Press, Cambridge (Mass.), 1985.

41. See Furtado, C. *Hegemonia dos Estados Unidos e Subdesenvolvimento da America Latina,* 3-a ed., Fundo de Cultura, Rio de Janeiro, 1978, pp. 35-42.

42. For details, see Meier, G.M. *Leading Issues in Economic Development,* p. 108.

43. Cardoso, F.H. "Dependent Capitalist Development in Latin America," *New Left Review,* July, 1972, p. 90.

44. Amin, S. *Unequal Development: An Essay on the Social Formations of Peripheral Capitalism,* Zed Books, London, 1976, p. 179.

45. Amin, S. *Accumulation on a World Scale,* Penguin Books, Harmondsworth, 1976, p. 131.

46. See Furtado, C. "Dependencia externa y teoria economica," *El trimestre economico* (Mexico), no. 2, 1971, pp. 318-321, 327-330.

47. See Garcia, A. *Atraso y dependencia en America Latina: Hacia una teoria latinoamerica de desarrollo,* Buenos Aires, 1972, pp. 111-112.

48. For a more detailed discussion of such views, see Fieldhouse, D.K. *The West and the Third World,* pp. 55-57.

49. Amin, S. *Neo-Colonialism in West Africa,* Penguin Books, Harmondsworth, 1973, p. 384.

50. See Frank, A.G. *Capitalism and Underdevelopment in Latin America,* pp. 118-120; Amin, S. *L'accumulation à l'échelle mondiale: critique de la théorie de la sous-développement,* Presses Universitaire de France, Paris, 1970, pp. 38-44.

51. See Galbraith, James K. *Created Unequal. The Crisis in American Pay,* Free Press, New York, 1998, p. 164.

52. See Daly, H. E. *Steady-State Economics,* 2nd ed., Earthscan Publications Ltd., London, 1992, p. 10.

53. See Grilli, E. *The European Community and the Developing Countries,* Cambridge University Press, Cambridge, 1993, p. 173.

54. See Daly, H. E. *Steady-State Economics,* p. 109.

55. Calculated from Brown, L. R., Flavin, Ch., French, H. et al., *State of the World 1998. A Worldwatch Institute Report on Progress Toward a Sustainable Society,* Earthscan Publications Ltd., New York-London, 1998, pp. 16, 17, 94; see also: *Economist,* July 5, 1997, p. 104.

56. See Plender, J. *A Stake in the Future. The Stakeholding Solution,* Nicholas Brealey Publishing, London, 1997, p. 223.

57. See Cohen, D. *The Wealth of the World and the Poverty of Nations,* Cambridge (Mass.)-London, 1998, p. 17.

58. See Plender, J. *A Stake in the Future: The Stakeholding Solution,* p. 223; Cohen, D. *The Wealth of the World and the Poverty of Nations,* p. 17.

59. See Brown, L. R., Renner, M., Flavin, Ch. et al. *Vital Signs 1997-1998. The Environmental Trends That Are Shaping Our Future,* Earthscan Publications Ltd., London, 1997, p. 116.

60. See Ayres, R. U. *Turning Point. An End to the Growth Paradigm,* Earthscan Publications Ltd., London, 1998, p. 125.

61. Calculated from: Sandler, T. *Global Challenges. An Approach to Environmental, Political and Economic Problems,* Cambridge University Press, Cambridge, 1997, p. 183.

62. See Meadows, D. H., Meadows, D. L., Randers, J. *Beyond the Limits: Global Collapse or a Sustainable Future?* Earthscan Publications Ltd., London, 1992, p. 5.

63. See Caufield, C. *Masters of Illusion. The World Bank and the Poverty of Nations,* Macmillan, London, 1997, p. 332.

64. See Dunning, J. H. *The Globalisation of Business,* Allen & Unwinn, London, 1993, pp. 288, 290.

65. See Schneider, B. *The Barefoot Revolution. A Report to the Club of Rome,* IT Publications, London, 1988, pp. 1-7.

66. See Bendix, R. "Tradition and Modernity Reconsidered," *Comparative Studies in Society and History* (The Hague), no. 3, 1967, pp. 326-329.

67. Myrdal, G. *Today's Problems of the Third World.* Abridged translation from the English, Moscow, 1972, p. 132 (in Russian).

68. See Abdel-Malek, A. *The Project on Socio-Cultural Development Alternatives in a Changing World: Report on the Formative Stage* (May 1978-December 1979), Tokyo, 1980, pp. 4-5, 18-19, 24-25, 51-53.

69. Abdel-Malek, A., Huynh Cao, Tri, Rosier, B., Le Thanh, Khoi. *Clés pour une stratégie nouvelle du developpement,* Paris, 1984, p. 15.

70. See Touraine, A. "Modernity and Cultural Specificities," Modernity and Identity: A Simposium. Culture, Economy and Development, *International Social Science Journal,* Paris, November, 1988, p. 451.

71. See Attali, J. *Lignes d'horizon,* Paris, 1990, pp. 65-66.

72. See Touraine, A., Hartmann, J., Hakiki-Talahite, F. et al. *Quel emploi pour les jeunes? Vers des strategies novatrices,* Odile Jacob, Paris, 1988, p. 46.

73. For details, see Inozemtsev, V. L. "Post-Modernism Today: An End to Social Forms or Degradation of Sociology?" *Voprosy filosofii,* no. 9, 1998, pp. 27-37 (in Russian).

74. For details, see Dore, R. *Flexible Rigidities: Industrial Policy and Structural Adjustment in the Japanese Economy, 1970-1980,* Stanford University Press, Stanford (Cal.), 1986, pp. 1-6.

75. See Johnson, Ch. *MITI and the Japanese Miracle: The Growth of Industrial Policy, 1925-1975,* Stanford University Press, Stanford (Cal.), 1982.

76. See Kohli, A. "Where Do High-Growth Political Economies Come From? The Japanese Lineage of Korea's 'Developmental State,'" Woo-Cumings, M. (ed.) *The Developmental State,* Cornell University Press, Ithaca (N.Y.)-London, 1999, pp. 132-133.

77. Only one of K. Akamatsu's basic works was translated into English in the 1960s (see Akamatsu, K. "A Historical Pattern of Economic Growth in Developing Countries," *The Developing Economies,* no. 1, 1962).

78. See Hatch, W., Yamamura, K. *Asia in Japan's Embrace. Building a Regional Production Alliance,* Cambridge University Press, Cambridge (U.K.)-New York, 1996, pp. 27-28.

79. See Murphy, R. T. "Japan's Economic Crisis," *New Left Review,* Second Series, no. 1, 2000, p. 32.

80. Bauman, Z. *Globalization: The Human Consequences,* Columbia University Press, New York, 1998, p. 58.

81. Edwards, M. *Future Positive. International Cooperation in the 21st Century,* Earthscan Publications Ltd., London, 1999, p. 19.

82. See Beck, U. *What Is Globalization?* Polity Press, in association with Blackwell Publishers Ltd., Cambridge (U.K.)-Oxford, 2000, pp. 57, 55.

2

Post-Industrial Trends and Prerequisites for the Crisis of the "Catching Up" Development Model

Even a brief look at the modernization theories presented in the previous chapter will show their obvious limitations. Before I proceed to analyzing their basic flaws, I might as well mention the "trump cards" played by the adherents of the "catching up" development doctrine, namely, the possibility of using monopoly rights to certain types of resources or the possibility of drawing extensively on other nations' technological advances and making a more efficient use of them than the countries of origin do. The idea of self-sustaining modernization is objectively embodied in communist practices because it inevitably calls for an actually all-out mobilization of a nation's powers and presupposes its overt or covert isolation from the outside world. The record of the Soviet Union is the most convincing illustration of the in efficiency of this way of development. Thus, any "catching up" development strategy depends on using unique—objective or subjective—potentialities of a given country for optimizing economic industrialization.

In itself, such a practice is perfectly understandable and justified at certain junctures of history. There is no ignoring the fact, however, that the specific resources which go into a rapid development of industrial production are finite, as a rule. Mineral resources are running short, their world market prices are anything but stable, and the sectors which, under certain conditions, provided an impetus to industrial progress may end up being a drag on it. In developing countries, labor is cheap but it is not going to stay that way forever; amid a continued raise in the standard of living, labor costs are tending upwards to levels characteristic of more advanced nations. Consequently, neither natural resources, nor cheap labor can be relied upon for a breakthrough to the post-industrial heights because the accelerated accumulation they bring has natural limits and is not self-sustainable.

A nation can assume a firm lead in the modern world only given such unique conditions of production and such a monopoly characteristic that are capable of self-reproduction and that undermine the inner powers of society by their self-reproduction. For as long as a nation's monopoly resource has no such specific features or requires social overexertion to maintain it, this nation's leading positions can easily be challenged. History offers relevant examples galore. At the height of the Middle Ages, for instance, Venice was the most powerful European state of all, with a budget three times as large as France's, because it had trade routes between Europe and Levant under its control. No sooner had Holland and Britain set up large trading companies of their own, however, than the grandeur of Venice became a thing of the past. Processing English wool into fabrics which had a ready market on the continent made Holland one the wealthiest states in Europe. As soon as the English had built up a network of textile mills of their own, Holland found itself all but crowded out of that niche, and well down the list of Europe's rich nations. Spain and Portugal offer a different example. They had to pay a dear price for having discovered the New World and flooded Europe with gold—that unprecedented achievement cost them unprecedented depopulation. The Latin American colonies of their countries won their freedom nearly two centuries ago, while their former parent-states degraded into the backyard of Europe and remained such for centuries.

The nation's intellectual potential and its citizens' emancipation are the only source of its stable prosperity, and I shall repeatedly emphasize this below. The twentieth century has borne this statement out on many occasions. Whereas in the eighteenth and nineteenth centuries Britain came out on top owing to the achievements of experimental science—some of them arrived at naturally, and others, by chance—Germany took over the lead in the industrialized world at the beginning of the twentieth century thanks to new industries only, such as chemistry and electrical engineering, where the use of theoretical rather than empirical knowledge was the pledge of success. The United States' leadership in the middle of the century was due to its breakthroughs in the sphere of information technologies where theoretical knowledge was used not for the manufacturing of new products but for generating new knowledge. These aspects of Western societies' progress have repeatedly received penetrating analysis.[1]

Thus, in a situation where information and knowledge become an immediate productive force there emerges the monopoly resource featuring previously unknown qualities and characteristics. On the one hand, the assimilation of information and knowledge serves as a prerequisite for the production of new knowledge, while their alienation does not detract from the available amount of this resource; therefore, it becomes inexhaustible, which radically changes the nature of the missions and objectives facing mankind and forms a new system of motivations. On the other hand, the access to this resource remains limited because knowledge is distinguished from most industrial boons by its rarity and unreproducibility, while the expenses involved in creating it are out of all proportion to the results obtained; therefore, the value of knowledge is regulated by the laws governing the prices of monopoly boons, and its possessors find themselves in an exclusive position with regard to the people around them. It should be stressed that the rise of the society in which knowledge and information are the most important productive assets calls for the maximum advancement of every individual, that is, it opens up new vistas turning man from a "cogwheel" of the industrial machine into a free individual and makes the progress of the social whole a derivative from individual accomplishments of the persons making it up. The resultant social system turns out to be the most dynamic one ever, and this alone dashes the hopes of the developing and industrialized countries for a successful realization of the "catching up" development strategy.

The Rise of Post-Industrial Society and the Foundations of Its Stability

Much has been said and written about the early stages of post-industrial society, therefore we shall concentrate not so much on reproducing the process of its formation as on tracing the logic of this process.

The important thing here is to look into the inner connections between the industrial and post-industrial types of development, to discern the moment of inversion which marked the outset of the former regularities giving way to new ones. Progress of scientific knowledge ought to be recognized as the axis that both of these forms of social organization rotate on. It is precisely the said progress that conditioned an uninterrupted and accelerating rise in demand for skilled workers and the formation on that basis of a new social group—the "intellectual class" which came to account for an ever larger share of national wealth. Let us place it in this context: the rise of the society cultivating essentially post-materialistic motivations of human activity and the corresponding system of values proceeded, up to a point, on the basis of realizing perfectly utilitarian interests.

This alone explains a steady rise in industrial workers' qualification standards throughout almost all the twentieth century. To illustrate, whereas in 1890 only seven percent of American youths aged between fourteen and seventeen went to school, in the postwar years the figure topped 90 percent.[2] In 1940, less than 15 percent of high-school leaders aged eighteen to twenty-one went on to college; by the year 1993, the figure rose to 62 percent.[3] Such a "thirst for knowledge" was worthily rewarded: beginning with the mid-1970s, real incomes of college graduates began to grow against the background of the living standards stagnation and decline among non-college-educated persons. Over the period of 1978-1987 alone, the incomes of the latter fell 4 percent, while that of college graduates rose 48 percent.[4] Nevertheless, a free society running on competition encourages those who achieve outstanding results against the general background. Therefore, as soon as college graduates began to fill up this "general background" in the labor market, those having earned degrees or were distinguished by their unique abilities came to be valued most. In 1987-1993, college graduates' average pay cut constituted over 2 percent;[5] in the meantime, those holding B.Sc. or D.Sc. degrees received 30 and nearly 50 percent raises, respectively.[6] Experts of that caliber, however, seek not only large incomes but personal advancement as well and, consequently, the new social group they belong to develops a system of motivations essentially different from that centering on personal gain. From the moment the intellectual elite turned into the dominating class of Western societies, social transformations took on an irreversible character.

It would hardly be an exaggeration to say that the intellectual class now constitutes the top stratum of Western societies. This is evidenced by a wealth of facts. Whereas at the beginning of the twentieth century only 10 percent of the U.S. industrial company

CEOs had a college education, today holders of doctorates make up over 60 percent of America's managerial personnel. Among those constituting 1 percent of the wealthiest Americans (whose share in U.S. national wealth has increased from 19 to 39 percent over the past twenty years alone[7]), only every fifteenth makes money as profit on capital invested while more than half hold administrative posts in large companies, almost a third are practicing lawyers and physicians, the rest being professionals, university professors and instructors included.[8] Four out of every five contemporary American millionaires are self-made men who have built up their fortunes practically from scratch rather than multiplied the assets they inherited.[9] Another important thing is that the members of the intellectual class display a firm commitment to the values they have selected; whereas in 1980 only 30 percent of young people coming from $67,000-a-year families had a college education, today this index amounts to 80 percent.[10]

Knowledge-based societies are taking shape in modern Western countries, and this process could not but have its effect on the distribution of wealth not only within these countries but worldwide as well. At present, 20 percent of the planet's population residing in the developed states account for 86 percent of the gross world product;[11] back in the mid-1990s, seven post-industrial powers possessed among them 80.4 percent of the world's computer technology, accounted for 90.5 percent of high-tech production[12] and controlled 97 percent of the world's registered patents[13] (notably, 80 percent of the patents issued in developing countries also belonged to citizens of the post-industrial world[14]). By that time, the West controlled more than four-fifths of the world services market with a total volume of business exceeding $1 trillion in 1992.[15] Over the period of 1986-1995, the U.S. intellectual property export volume grew 3.5 times, and the favorable balance of trade in this sphere topped $ 20 billion; by 1995, the United States had accounted for 72 percent of the world's information services and data processing market[16] with a current capacity of over $95 billion.[17]

Funds invested in knowledge-intensive industries have been returning a truly fantastic profit over the past few decades (from 1960 to 1999 it averaged 45 percent a year, as investment in shares yielded, on balance, a mere 13.34 percent a year[18]), hence the influx of funds to the appropriate breakthrough projects. In 1995, U.S. direct investment in revolutionary technologies constituted $6.4 billion; in 1997, the figure rose to 11.5 billion; and by 1999, to 35.5 billion.[19] Investment funds financing venture projects drew even more generous injections, increasing from about $9 billion in 1995 to $56 billion in 1999. In the first quarter of 2000 alone, they attracted $22.7 billion. As to the annual average yield on this investment, it soared from 2 percent a year in 1990 to 20 percent in 1993; 34 percent in 1996; and 147(!) percent in 1999.[20] Over the past decade, U.S. institutional and private investors spent an average of about $240 billion a year on R&D while private companies put about $30 billion[21] into upgrading their employees' educational standards—an equivalent of the appropriations made for all lines of research in Russia, China, South Korea, and Taiwan taken together. In 1997-1999, the United States appropriated $635 billion a year, or double the military spending figure,[22] for the promotion of all forms of education. Such generosity paid off; improved higher educational facilities alone were responsible for a quarter of the entire U.S. gross national product increment in the twentieth century.[23]

The result was an unprecedented technological breakaway of the industrialized world from all the other nations. Today the United States accounts for 44 percent of the world's R&D spending as against Latin America's and Asia's 1 percent[24]; the United States has 126,200 R&D workers per one million of the population compared with the world's average of 23,400, at the most.[25] In 1997, U.S. citizens constituted almost three-fourths of the world's Internet users, the total share of Americans, Canadians, and West Europeans in that index exceeding 96 percent.[26] This factor is of utmost importance considering that in 1998 the industry built around that global web contributed over $236 billion[27] to the world gross product—an amount comparable with Russia's entire GNP in the same year. Technological progress has been accelerating steadily over the past decade; since the onset of the automobile era, it took thirty-five years before every fourth American family came to own a car; for the PC, the mobile phone and e-mail, such time intervals constitute eighteen, thirteen, and seven years, respectively.[28]

In our opinion, this technological breakaway has to do with ever-growing differences in general economic indices characterizing the progress made by various regions of the planet—a fact which has become distinctly manifest since with the mid-1970s. The 1993 world gross product was generally estimated at $24 trillion, of which 19 trillion dollars' worth was created in the post-industrial states and only five trillion dollars' worth by all the developing countries with a population amounting to 80 percent the world's total. Accordingly, the difference in people's nominal annual incomes increased from $5,700 in 1960 to $15,400 in 1993 and $19,200 in 1999; consequently, one-fifth of mankind on one pole of development appropriated thirty times more wealth than the remaining four-fifths on the other pole;[29] sixty-one times[30] more in 1993; and an appalling seventy-four times[31] more in 1999. Notably, this is going on in a situation where real incomes of the world's poorest countries have actually stagnated over the past 120(!) years,[32] and the extrapolation of this dynamics gives certain researches reason to claim that by the mid-twenty-first century the gap may widen 350-fold.[33] According to a U.N. commission, the world's wealthiest 358 persons own as much money as the planet's 2.3 billion poor,[34] while the 400 biggest transnational corporations are in control of two-thirds of all the basic production assets now in existence.[35] In 1975-1995, the share of the world's wealth possessed by 20 percent of the industrialized nations' citizens grew from 70 to 82.7 percent,[36] while the share of the Third World's poorest 20 percent shrank from 2.3 to 1.4 percent[37] and the chances of that situation improving look slim.

As we can see, the rise of post-industrial society had materialistic causes behind it until a certain moment. In the meantime, sociologists have long discovered that "as welfare standards go up, the need to acquire still more good things of life loses its urgency with problems of combining security and freedom, justice and responsibility coming to the forefront."[38] Under present conditions, the profit-gaining motive which used to reign supreme in the industrialized West before, has receded to the background,[39] the prospect of fast professional advancement, valued so highly in the 1980s, no longer looks attractive enough to many, especially if advancement means spending less time with one's family or giving up one's pet hobbies.[40] One prefers to concentrate on becoming a new and better self tomorrow than one is today;[41] the emphasis has shifted to self-improvement, which A. Maslow refers to as the ultimate value.[42] Western sociologists are increasingly inclined to see these processes as the emergence of post-materialistic motivations.

Post-materialistic motivations are slow to take shape and are not a linear function of affluence. A person rid of the necessity to seek means of satisfying his material needs gets an opportunity, to create and cultivate human needs[43] in all their diversity. This does not, mean, however, an immediate and automatic actual domination of the new system of values on the scale of the social whole. "More often than not," R. Inglehart points out, "post-materialists are those who have enjoyed all the material goods since early in life, which largely explains their arrival at post-materialism";[44] now, people who have always craved business success are much less likely to accept the post-materialistic ideals because "once selected, values come to stay."[45] Thus, the transition to the post-materialist system of motivations which goes on as generations succeed one another is bringing the outlines of the intellectual class into ever sharper focus.

On the basis of market exchange, society is redistributing an ever-larger proportion of national wealth in favor of the intellectual elite year in and year out. This means the removal of the last obstacles to the progress of a society based on a meritocratic hierarchy and post-materialistic values. The intellectuals' most important mission is to produce new knowledge, and because the latter is, by nature, in-alienable from its creator (objectivized knowledge ceases to be such and becomes information), the production process turns into "inter-relationships between individuals in the course of which either party fulfills himself as a subject"[46] and loses the character of interaction with a transformed natural environment thus becoming "an inter-play of humans,"[47] as D. Bell put it. From that moment on, it is not savings invested in production at the expense of routine consumption, as was the case in the industrial epoch, but, on the contrary, the very consumption of non-material assets that becomes the foundation for the progress of production, and post-industrial society gains a firm foothold for steady self-reproducing headway. Therefore, the Western nations' dynamism comes neither from the need for an answer to any external challenge, nor from inner contradictions of post-industrial society; it embodies the emancipated potential of a creative personality, man's awareness of himself as "the measure of all things" (to quote Karl Marx) under the conditions of the information economy.[48] This, in our opinion, is the best guarantee against this type of development being stopped or reversed. It is definitely more comprehensive than the industrial model; therefore, the nations adhering to the "catching up" development doctrine and giving top priority to accelerated industrialization are on a wrong track—catching up with the post-industrial world using industrial methods is a hopeless task.

It ought to be borne in mind, though, that developing nations and new industrial states have repeatedly exerted serious influence on the character of post-industrial society's formation processes; therefore, a brief outline of the Western world's development over the past three decades may be of some interest in the context of our study.

Post-Industrial Society: Stages of Development

The rise of post-industrial society is usually referred to as a process which had its start in the late 1950s and which is still continuing. Over that period, however, the Western world's economic history has witnessed dramatic events dividing it into several stages: the first stage which commenced in 1973 and ended, on the whole, in the early 1980s; the second stage (1981/82–1989); and the third stage whose onset can be traced back to 1992 and which is not over yet.[49]

In the 1950s and the 1960s, industrial society had its heyday in the Western world. The United States and other countries made unprecedented economic progress amid a stable market situation (to illustrate, from 1946 to 1954, the U.S. gross national product increased at an average rate of 4.7 percent a year; consumer spending rose 38 percent over the decade; the level of unemployment dropped to four percent of the able-bodied population, and the of rate inflation never exceeded 2 percent a year[50]). Development proceeded against the background of a rapid restructuring of the economy: whereas in 1955 the U.S. manufacturing and construction industries employed up to 34.7 percent of the nation's aggregate manpower and accounted for about 34.5 percent of the GNP[51] (with Germany, Britain, and France showing somewhat higher figures: 41.2 and 47.4; 44.4 and 42.1; 30.4 and 43.2 percent, respectively),[52] by 1970 this proportion diminished to 27.2 percent.[53] Sociologists started talking about the birth of a services-based society.

The situation did not cancel industrial laws, however. Most of the services were of a pronouncedly subject-object rather than subject-subject character, while rapid economic progress made for a marked rise in the consumption of basic raw materials, giving a superficial observer the impression that Western society remained an industrial one by nature.

It is against this background that the first stage of post-industrial society's development began. Let us take, by way of illustration, the 1973 oil shock as its point of departure, and the confrontation between industrialized nations and commodity-exporting countries as its content. Regarding themselves as the monopolists in the raw materials market, developing countries first made an attempt at a gradual price rise (in the period of 1965-1970, for example, the price of oil went up 15 percent; coal, 20; silver, 40; nickel, 60; and copper, over 70 percent[54]) and then, acting on cartel agreements, inflated the prices several times over. Changes in commodity prices were so substantial that the total worth of oil arriving at the American market jumped from $5 billion in 1972 to $48 billion in 1975, with the volume of deliveries diminishing somewhat.[55] One of the worst economic crises ever struck: in the United States, prices rose 8.7 percent in 1973, and 23.3 percent in 1974,[56] unemployment reached 9 percent of the able-bodied population, the Dow Jones index dropped almost to a half over the period of January 1973 to December 1974, and industrial production fell nearly 15 percent.[57] Characteristically, a decline in demand spurred the price rise on instead of stopping it. That was due to the developing countries' heavy dependence on export earnings (oil exports accounted for 94 percent and 96 percent of Iran's and Saudi Arabia's currency proceeds, respectively; Zambia depended on copper for 93 percent of its export earnings; Mauritania, on iron ore for 78 percent; Guinea, on bauxite for 77 percent,[58] etc.). Over fifteen years, from 1975 to 1980, the price of a ton of bituminous coal rose from $38.5 to $45.3; of iron ore, from $22.8 to $28.1; of timber, from $61.8 to $137; of copper, from $1,320 to $2,200; of nickel, from $4,560 to $6,500; of tin, from $6,860 to $16,750; of silver, from $1.42 to $ 6.62 per 10 g; and of gold, from $56.8 to $214.4.[59] By July 1, 1980, the oil price jumped to an all-time high of $34.73[60] (over $60 a barrel in current prices[61]). A disaster seemed imminent.

Using the achievements of technological progress, however, the West prevented the establishment of the "new world economic order" the developing countries insisted on in 1976. The 1970s were the period of the most radical restructuring the United States and

Western Europe had ever undergone in the twentieth century. In 1973-1978, oil consumption in the United States diminished at the rate of 2.7 percent a year per unit of industrial production value; in Canada, 3.5 percent; in Italy, 3.8 percent; in Germany and Great Britain, 4.8 percent; and in Japan, 5.7 percent while demand for oil in 1979 became as elastic as that for most consumer goods for the first time ever.[62] In 1973-1985, the OECD member-states' gross national product increased 32 percent, and their energy consumption, a mere 5 percent;[63] over the same period, the energy resources utilization efficiency factor increased more than 40 percent in the United States.[64] Against the background of the gross product increasing more than 25 percent in 1975-1987, American agriculture cut energy consumption by a factor of 1.65,[65] and as to ferrous metals, the U.S. economy is using less of them now than it did in 1960.[66] Over 20 years, from 1976 to 1996, the federal government assigned a total of about $60 billion to subsidize the development of improved energy resources utilization technologies[67] thus speeding up the progress of non-materials-intensive industries and cutting back on inefficient production facilities. In the United States, the share of transport in the total GNP diminished 21 percent; of agriculture, 19 percent; and of construction, by nearly a third in 1970-1983, while the share of the services sphere increase nearly 5 percent; trade, 7.4 percent; and telecommunications, over 60 percent.[68] What's more, experts predict that by the year 2010 renewable sources will meet about 10 percent of the United States energy requirements, which means the beginning of a new revolution in power engineering.[69] Towards the year 1996, the gross product of the U.S. mining industry was 25 percent up on the 1947 level; of construction, 44 percent; of the manufacturing industry, 156 percent; while the relevant index for the information and telecommunications sectors amounted to 625 percent.[70] As a result, the prices of natural resources started tending downwards since the mid-1980s, hitting an all-time low for 150 years[71] in 1997-1998 and coming close to the level of outlays necessary for their production, while the developing countries, burdened with enormous debts, had ceased to play any substantial role in the world economy by the early 1990s.

At the same time, the mass production opportunities opened up by the import of technologies and cheap manpower turned into an important competition factor in the 1970s. It was exactly in that period that the nations which had opted for the "catching up" development model did best.

The second stage of post-industrial tendencies' development began with the coming to office, in 1979-1981, of right-wing conservative governments in Great Britain, the United States and Germany which launched reforms aimed at encouraging free commercial enterprise. The most characteristic feature of that stage was the struggle between post-industrial powers and new industrial nations.

Throughout the 1970s and the 1980s, high technologies were used primarily for making the production of material goods cheaper, and the information sector did not become the basis of post-industrial economies yet. Having combined the use of scientific advances with the advantages offered by mass production lines manned by cheap labor, Asian countries took the lead in the world economy for the time being.

Japan was the main rival of the United States and Europe at that time. By the mid-1980s, it produced 81 percent of the world's motorcycles, 80.7 percent domestic video systems and about 66 percent photocopiers,[72] by 1982, Japanese companies controlled up to 60 percent of the American NC machine-tool market.[73] Over the period of 1973-1986, the U.S. share in the world production of goods and services diminished from 23.1 to 21.4 percent, and the E.C. share, from 25.7 to 22.9 percent, while Japan's grew from 7.2 to 7.7 percent.[74] American companies' positions worsened accordingly. Whereas in 1971, 280 of the world's 500 largest transnational corporations were American, by 1991, the figure dropped to only 157;[75] by that time, Japan actually caught up with the United States in this respect possessing 345 largest transnationals out of 1,000 (as against the America' 353);[76] at the end of the 1980s it owned the twenty-four largest banks, with seventeen of such banks left in the E.C. and a mere five in North America; nine of the ten largest service companies also represented the Land of the Rising Sun.[77] At the end of the 1980s, the Japanese "economic miracle" showed how far a country professing the paradigm of industrialization can go amidst neighbors belonging to the post-industrial world. The "new industrial countries" of Southeast Asia followed in Japan's wake.

The West's response to that challenge consisted, as had been the case before, in promoting the progress of new technologies, eliminating inefficient production units, and assuring the survival of the fittest. This response found its embodiment in Reagan's reforms which, on the one hand, mobilized the inner sources of accumulation to the utmost and, on the other, drew an unprecedented influx of foreign investment. The July 1, 1981 tax reduction saved Americans nearly 27 percent of all the taxes they paid in the 1980-1981 fiscal year[78] and helped the corporations save funds equivalent to 58 percent of all the expenditures involved in the retooling of the U.S. manufacturing industry in the mid-1980s.[79] In 1981 and 1982, the Federal Reserve System brought the official annual interest rate close to 20 percent for the first time ever, which promptly reduced the annual rate of inflation from 9 to 4.5 percent[80] and stabilized the yield on investment in long-term government bonds at 8.1-8.2 percent which was almost thirty times the late-1970s figure.[81]

The measures brought immediate results. As early as 1981, private savings amounted to 9.4 percent of available incomes—the postwar period's highest.[82] In 1983-1989, the aggregate investment constituted a steady 18 percent of the GNP[83] while investment in fixed assets ballooned at an average rate of 12.3 percent a year compared to a mere 1.3 percent during the Carter presidency; productivity in the national economy as a whole increased at the rate of 1.2 percent a year (3.6 percent in industry) in 1981-1984 as against 0.2 and 1 percent, respectively, under the previous administration.[84] Notably, this result was achieved in a situation where the U.S. savings-to-GNP ratio was one-fifth of the Japanese figure.[85] Restructuring continued at an accelerating rate: in 1975-1990, the share of those employed in the American industry diminished from 25 to 18 percent of the total workforce while over the previous fifteen years it had declined by a mere 2 percent—from 27 to 25 percent; in 1982-1992, the share of material assets in American companies' book cost dwindled from 62 to 38 percent whereas the share of information products and intellectual capital increased from 37 to 61 percent.[86]

These efforts made it possible to stop Japanese expansion towards the late 1980s. Geared to a rapid rise in exports and fueled by financial speculations, the Japanese economy was in no position to keep its balance in an increasingly competitive environment. The real U.S. balance deficit in trade with Japan went down to the acceptable figure of 10-15 percent, while the overstatement of Japanese asset prices led to a collapse in 1989 with the result that the Nikkei index lost two-thirds of its value and economic growth rate slowed down to zero. At the same time, the United States itself, where information technologies accounted for about three-quarters of the industry-created value added, began to demonstrate an entirely new type of the economic growth which made the Western world's impressive successes possible over the past decade.

As already indicated above, the third stage of the post-industrial nations' development began in 1992. From that moment on, all the Western nations entered a period of a steady growth of the information sector of the economy that formed the basis of economic progress. It is safe to claim that this stage is marked by the invulnerability of the post-industrial world whose progress rests on a firm inner foundation.

The economic boom of 1992-2000, the longest one ever in U.S. history, heralded the stage of the Western nations' development at which they function as mature post-industrial systems. Experts estimate that in the 1980s over 70 percent of their gross national product growth was induced by a rise in the workers' educational standard, the spread of information technologies and other circumstances normally placed into the category of intangibles, rather than by material factors alone.[87] The worth of the services exported by the industrialized countries reached almost $900 billion while in the rest of the world's regions this index did not exceed $200 billion.[88] Since 1991, when the expenditures on the acquisition of information and information technologies amounted to $112 billion in the United States to top the spending on fixed assets ($107 billion),[89] the gap between these two indices has been growing by an average of $25 million a year.[90] In 1995, almost 43 percent of the GNP came from public health, scientific research, the education sphere, and software production.[91] Over the past three years, the sectors producing information goods accounted for one-third of the US GNP growth and for 37 percent of all the newly created jobs.[92] About 28 percent of the foreign trade earnings have been payments for technologies or profits derived from their use; in the United States, patent export proceeds surpass the expenditures on acquiring similar assets abroad more than fourfold.[93] As intangible assets are gaining in importance, the capitalization of U.S. companies is growing at an unprecedented pace: the Dow Jones index has almost quadrupled over the past six years, while the increment in the market value of shares over the period of 1998-1999 alone made American citizens $10 trillion richer.

Today the GNP growth rates are rising in most post-industrial countries, and the U.S. leadership in the world economy is becoming unquestionable. Whereas in 1989-1995 the U.S. economy's average annual growth rate constituted 1.9 percent, in 1996-1998 it amounted to 3.9 percent;[94] in 1999, to 4.2 percent,[95] and in the first quarter of 2000, to 5.4 percent,[96] and the trend looks steady enough. Whereas in 1973-1994, productivity in the American economy rose 1.4 percent a year on the average, in 1995-1999 this index constituted 2.9 percent.[97] Whereas in the third quarter of 1999 capital investment increased 10.2 percent relative to the corresponding period of 1998, in the first quarter of 2000 it soared to 25.2 percent relative to the first quarter of 1999, which fact promises a 7.5 percent GNP increase before the year 2000 is out.[98] Notably, this impetuous economic growth is accompanied by a steady reduction in the savings rate which became negative (-0.2 percent a year)[99] in September 1998, for the first time since 1959 (or even since 1938 considering its dynamics over 1998 as a whole). Private savings dropped below the zero mark back at the end of 1997 and hit an all-time low at the beginning of 2000 (-4.8 percent),[100] which signifies an extremely fast rise in demand in practically all the sectors of the economy. Accordingly, unemployment went down to 3.9 percent of the U.S. able-bodied population in April, 2000, which is the lowest level over the past thirty years.[101] In the meantime, economic growth obviously remains impervious to external shocks (such as the 1997 Asian crisis and the 1998 Russian default); consequently, the current steady upward climb may yet go on for years to come.

To sum up, the current economic situation in the post-industrial world is characterized by a number of entirely new circumstances. First of all, the raw material and resource restrictions of economic grown have been removed, and emphasis in consumer demand has shifted dramatically from conventional mass-manufactured goods to information assets. Second, an ever larger proportion of the population is seeking employment in sectors producing high-tech goods and services thus reducing dependence on the countries which remain industrial commodity manufacturing producers. And finally, economic growth assumes a new quality, with the cultivation by people of their own abilities becoming the most effective form of accumulation and with the human being, his knowledge and talents, becoming the most profitable investment media.

Under the circumstances, the Western nations' demand for raw materials and manufactured goods offered by countries at the industrial stage of development is declining sharply. As we have already pointed out, the "catching up" development strategy is based on the import of technologies and the export of manufactured goods to the developed countries as a means of drawing hard currency in the "catching up" economies to maintain their economic growth. Consequently, the growing "closeness" of the Western world is becoming a major obstacle to implementing the "catching up" development model.

Self-Sufficiency of Western Civilization

The modern post-industrial economic system is based on the production and consumption of knowledge. This fact, along with the much-talked-about "globalization" of information flows, leads to the growing isolation of the Western countries from the rest of the world—a development which receives considerably less attention.

The expansion of the knowledge-based economy has, first of all, radically diminished the industrialized countries' demand for material elements of production—raw materials and feedstock, especially—and, second, brought about a cardinal change in man's attitude to his environment and made a stable ecological balance possible. As a result, the West has found itself potentially free to reduce the intensity of economic interaction with other states and nations.

Today the possibilities for a rational utilization of raw materials, let alone replacing depletable natural resources by man-made materials, are more extensive than ever. The copper cable laid across the Atlantic Ocean floor in 1996 could carry 138 parallel telephone calls; the fiberoptic cable installed in the early 1990s is capable of serving 1.5 subscribers simultaneously;[102] the share of materials and energy costs in the overall spending on copper cable production amounted to 80 percent; in case of the fiberoptic cable, the figure does not exceed 10 percent.[103] According to a Sprint company forecast, by 2002, the transatlantic telephone communication service cost will go down to one-seventeenth of the 1998 figure making it possible to slash long-distance telephone call charges by almost 85 percent.[104] The range of industries dispensing with the use of rare resources keeps broadening: in the 1980s, the Kodak corporation took out a patent for a silver-free photography technique; the Ford Motor Company announced the introduction of catalysts operating on a platinum substitute; chip manufacturers do not use gold contacts and conductors any longer.[105] In 1991-1997, the mass of manufactured goods represented in American exports in terms of their one dollar's worth dwindled to less than a half,[106] while in 1967-1988 the index decreased by a mere 43 percent.[107] Over the next thirty years, the OECD member states are expected to reduce their natural resources requirements per $100 of the national income earned ten times over, that is, 31 kg as against 300 kg in 1996.[108] One can say that the technological revolution has practically eliminated the problem of an early depletion of mineral and energy resources; as a result, the post-industrial countries are now living in a new world, the world of unlimited resources.[109]

Owing to such changes, the ecological situation in the West has been improving steadily over the past twenty-plus years. Lately, the E.U. countries have been contributing from 4.2 to 8.4 percent of their GDP to environment conservation programs, and this trend is steadily tending upwards.[110] Modern technologies remove from production waste and exhaust fumes up to two-thirds of their NO_2 and three-quarters of their SO_2 contents;[111] as a result, the share of North American countries in the global amount of pollutant discharges into the atmosphere is likely to decrease from 26.7 percent today to 21. 9 percent by the year 2010.[112] In 1996, the United States became the world's only country to stop the production of ozone destroying substances,[113] and the share of the OECD member states in the volume of the carbon dioxide discharges into the atmosphere worldwide has remained practically stable over the past thirty years.[114] Most European countries put 0.5 to one percent of their gross national product, that is, about 60 billion dollars a year, into the promotion of international environment protection programs.[115]

At the same time, the development of the post-industrial economy, first of all, raised the degree of its self-sufficiency and, second, rerouted trade and investment flows from the Third World to the highly industrialized countries. As a result, the Western world has actually become closed upon itself.

Owing to secondary raw materials recycling technologies, the post-industrial world currently controls no fewer resources than the developing countries do. In the mid-1990s, the United States recovered from waste 70 million tons of steel, 3.5 million tons of aluminum, 1.45 million tons of copper, one million tons of tin, 22.5 thousand tons of titanium and a wealth of other mineral raw materials; the share of recovered materials in the overall consumption of raw materials constituted, in the above-mentioned categories, 68.5; 40.0; 38.6; 61.5 and 49.0 percent, respectively.[116] In the meantime, the main centers of industrial production also remain concentrated in the post-industrial countries, and in the 1990s, the sales of cheap Asian manufactured appliances in U.S. and European markets began to decline and the supply of high-quality domestic products, to grow.[117] Today's Texas, where farmers earn higher incomes than their counterparts elsewhere across the world, produces cheaper wheat than Nigeria, while even official statistics show that Dutch farmers' labor productivity is 100 times that of Russian ones. Over the past few decades, the post-industrial countries have become the biggest exporters of not only manufactured goods but also of farm products, such as peanuts and soybeans, which were traditionally imported from the poorest African and Asian countries.

As a result, the fast-growing volumes of commodity flows are becoming concentrated within the limits of the post-industrial world. Whereas in 1953 the more advanced industrial powers supplied to their peers 38 percent of their total exports, in 1963 the figure rose to 49 percent; in 1973, to 54 percent; and in 1990 it amounted to 76 percent.[118] Another example: in 1959, African countries' accounted for 28.2 percent of France's export deliveries and 20.3 percent of its imports; by the mid-1980s, the figures were 7.8 and 5.9 percent, respectively.[119] On the other hand, two-way commodity and investment flows between the E.C. and the U.S. increased fivefold over the past thirty years and topped $1 trillion in 1990.[120] The result was that in 1997 only 5 percent of the commodity flows originating from or arriving at the territory of one of the OECD member-states passed by this group of countries,[121] and the post-industrial nations are now importing from the developing world goods and services worth no more than 1.2 percent of their aggregate GNP.[122] It is noteworthy that although there do exist imbalances in the trade between individual post-industrial countries, on the whole the trade between the G-7 countries and the rest of the world is quite well-balanced: with exports being worth over $5 trillion in 1999, the unfavorable balance of trade constituted a mere $28 billion, that is, slightly over 0.5

percent of the export volume or less than 0.1 percent of the industrialized countries' GNP.[123]

Considering the attempts sometimes made to overestimate the importance of the economies of new industrialized nations' one should bear in mind, first of all, the scale of their re-export operations (if the latter are left out of account it will look as if the mass of commodities China supplied to the world market at the end of 1996 was worth less than Belgium's)[124] and, second, the fact that the U.S. unfavorable balance of trade that analysts are talking so much about is of no decisive importance for as long as most of the settlements are made in U.S. dollars.[125] On the whole, the fact that in 1959-1994 international trade grew thrice as fast as the world gross product did, on the average, but only twice as fast as in the United States,[126] speaks for the post-industrial economies' self-sufficiency; as a result, the United States' export-to-GNP ratio was one-third that of Britain 150 years ago, that is, in the 1840s. If we trace the comparative dynamics of this index over the period of 1913-1987, we shall see that for the U.K. it grew only by 0.6 percent points (from 14.7 to 15.3 percent of the GNP); the corresponding figures being 1.5 percent (from 10.9 to12.4) for Canada; 1.8 percent (from 4.1 to 6.3 percent) for the United States; and 6.6 percent (from 22.3 to 28.9 percent) for Switzerland.[127]

For the Western industrialized nations in general, it has grown by 2.5 percentage points (from 11.7 to 14.3 percent of the GNP)[128] over the past 100 years—a fact which does not quite agree with all the rhetoric about "globalization" that has become current of late. As a result, experts are coming to the conclusion that from 10[129] to 18[130] percent of the goods and services produced worldwide are offered for sale in international markets; this confirms the view that "the allegation about capitalism being more transnational now than it used to be before 1914 can be called in question, with good reason, in many respects."[131]

Despite the formal indications characterizing the openness of the European countries' economies (for example, their aggregate turnover, made up 39.8 percent of world exports and 38.9 percent of wold imports[132] in 1994, and the ratio of the arithmetical mean of export and import volume to the GNP amounted to 23 percent)[133] most of the commodity flows remained restricted to the E.U. limits. In the early 1990s, for example, the proportion of the goods exchanged between the E.U. member states constituted 66 percent of the total, or 73.8 percent if Norway, Sweden, and Switzerland, who are not formally affiliated with the E.U., are counted in; for comparison, the share of the commodities supplied by Japan to Asian countries reached 30.1 percent during the same period, while the share of the U.S. deliveries to North and South American countries constituted 32.9 percent).[134]

As a result, it turns out that the volume of the E.U. exports actually coincides with the corresponding U.S. figure.[135]

The movements of world investment flows shows similar trends. Over the 1980s, the volume of direct foreign investment grew at a rate of about 20 percent a year, which was four times the international trade growth rate. Within the period of 1981-1985, the average annual volume of direct foreign investment amounted to about $98 billion; over the four years that followed it went up to $323 billion and climbed higher up to a record-high level of $440 billion[136] in 1997. By the mid-1990s, the overall volume of direct foreign investment increased more than thirty-two times over compared with the 1970 figure while the volume of exports grew a mere 16.5 times.[137] As a result, international capital cross-flows (including those connected with the purchases of foreign securities, currency and various derivative financial instruments) exceed commodity flows more than sixty times today,[138] and the volume of the world gross product, twelve to thirteen times (M. Castells estimates the overall worth of such transactions at $360 trillion as of 1997).[139]

The economic system born of this investment ranks as the world's second in the amount of the gross product it turns out: as early as the beginning of the 1990s, plants owned by non-residents produced a 4.4 trillion dollars' worth of goods and services, which exceeded the volume of world trade estimated at $3.8 trillion[140] and was comparable in scale with the American GNP worth about $6 trillion then. Most of the world's investment resources is obviously concentrated in post-industrial countries. As of April 20, 2000, the aggregate capitalization of the companies listed at the leading U.S. and E.U. stock exchanges of New York, London, Paris, Frankfurt, Milan, Amsterdam, Paris, Stockholm, and Madrid topped $25 trillion.[141] It is small wonder, therefore, that as early as the beginning of the 1990s, the U.S., the U.K., Germany and Canada accounted for 81 percent of all the direct foreign investment.[142]

Much less attention is usually paid to the fact of fundamental importance that most investment flows are also localized within the post-industrial world. In 1990, just five countries—the United States, Great Britain, Japan, France, and Germany—were responsible for 75.3 percent of direct foreign investment exports and for 76 percent of its imports worldwide. What is more, its share keeps growing owing to a steady increase in the volume of investment resources in leading post-industrial countries, the United States above all. In1992, the U.S. took over from Japan the lead in the volume of foreign investments by almost tripling it in 1992-1995, with Great Britain and Germany placing second and third. In the 1980s, the post-industrial countries accounted for about 94, and in the 1990s, for about 90 percent of all direct foreign investment, while the share of the developing countries remained under 10 percent.[143]

Naturally, most of the investment goes to the countries in a class with the donor nations in the level of basic economic performance indices. In 1996, for example, only seven countries—Great Britain, Japan, Canada, France, Germany, Switzerland, and the Netherlands, accounted among them for 85 percent of all the foreign investment made in the United States. In 1996 and 1997, European transnational corporations channeled $107 billion into purchasing American companies; in 1998 and at the beginning of 1999, the amount increased to $280 billion, with the leaders of U.S. industry, suchas Chrysler, Amoco, and Airtouch Communications, featuring among the Europeans' larger acquisitions.[144] The same holds true for the United States itself which placed about a third of its total foreign investment in Europe[145] and has by now increased the share of its aggregate investment in the E.U. nations to 60 percent (with Asian countries accounting for no more than 8 and Mexico, for less than 3 percent of U.S. investment in foreign countries).[146] The developing countries' share in the overall volume of world capital investment was shrinking steadily (from 25 percent in the 1970s to 17 percent in the 1980s).[147] As a result, the reciprocal investment of the United States, Europe, and Japan in one another and, besides, in Singapore, China, Malaysia, Indonesia, Thailand, Hong Kong, and Taiwan were accounted for 94 percent of the total volume of direct foreign investment;[148] whereas the countries not affiliated with the OECD of received no more than 5 percent foreign investments.[149] In the 1990s, corporations registered in one of the nerve centers of the post-industrial world—the U.S., the E.U. or Japan—accounted for over 90 percent of all investment made in the form of mergers and takeovers.[150]

Moreover, even amid the ongoing internationalization of the economies and a steady increase in the share of moneys invested by private individuals in stocks and other securities (in 1997, households' assets in stocks and securities exceeded the value of their real estate holdings for the first time in U.S. history),[151] most investors prefer to invest in national corporate debentures. Thus, 95 percent of the stocks and 97 percent of the bonds owned by Americans today have been issued by U.S. companies, with foreigners owning a mere 6 percent of the American stocks traded on the market and 14 percent of corporate bonds.[152] On the whole, despite the growing interpenetration of the post-industrial economies, in the mid-1990s, foreign investors possessed no more than 10 percent of the securities listed at the leading Western stock exchanges[153] (a recent update puts the figure at 11.2 percent).[154] Be that as it may, today's situation differs strikingly from that in 1913 when nobody talked about globalization yet but when about 60 percent of all the securities listed at the London Stock Exchange had been floated by foreign issuers.[155]

Before I conclude this chapter, I must say a few words about the phenomenon of human as well as financial flows "closing upon themselves" within the more advanced world. Significantly, it was not the post-industrial but industrial epoch that saw the most active migration of the population between countries of near-equal economic development levels and, moreover, emigration from more advanced to less-advanced countries. In the second half of the nineteenth century alone, more than 60 million Europeans immigrated to the United States, Canada, Australia, or colonies of European powers.[156] In 1870-1910, it was largely European immigrants who increased the U.S. population 17 percent and the U.S. aggregate workforce 24 percent.[157] Accordingly, Europe's population decreased more than 12 percent in 1850–1930 as against the figure 1900.[158] On the contrary, in the post-industrial epoch, as living standards are rising and information exchange methods improving, there is no intensive migration within the bounds of the post-industrial world, which is particularly true of Europe where, with no restrictions imposed on the freedom of movement, only 2 percent of the workforce seek and find employment outside the national borders (except for a relatively backward Portugal where the figure is over 10 percent).[159] At the same time, tensions on the advanced world's outer boundaries are mounting as immigrants from poorer countries, urged on by purely economic considerations, seek to partake of the blessings of Western civilization.

It is important to note in this context that modern migration processes are marked by a steadily widening gap between the immigrants' and the hosts' educational and cultural standards. At the end of the 1980s, most immigrants to the U.S. came from ten countries—Mexico, the Philippines, Korea, Cuba, India, China, the Dominican Republic, Vietnam, Jamaica, and Haiti.[160] In 1995, the standard of education of a legal immigrant was inferior to that of an average statistical American by a factor of four.[161] In the mid-1990s, the number of foreign workers who had arrived in the E.U. countries from the outside amounted to over 10 million or to about 11 percent of their total workforce,[162] which equaled the share of the unemployed in the population of Europe's leading countries. Prepared to work for pay not exceeding 55-70 percent of the Europeans' average wage rate in analogous job categories,[163] immigrants create competition in the labor market. As a result, anti-immigrant feelings are growing in the United States and in the E.U. countries. In 1998, these feelings were shared by 27.3 percent of the French, 39.6 percent of the Germans and 41 percent of the Belgians.[164] Politicians speculating on ethnic problems are becoming ever more popular and there is reason to presume that their coming to power in Austria as members of the coalition government in February 2000 will stir their kindred spirits elsewhere in Europe into more vigorous action. The rumor about strict restrictions to be imposed on the employment of foreign labor in the United States and the E.U. within the next few decades[165] is not far removed from reality because such restrictions would be quite in line with the post-industrial world's trend to "close upon itself" which has become strongly manifest over the past few years.

* * *

Summing up, let me point out once again that the rise and development of post-industrial society has accelerated world economic progress to an unprecedentedly high rate in the last third of the twentieth century. Over four decades, from 1960 to 2000, the West has maintained higher GNP per capital growth rates than the developing countries, despite the success scored by the East Asian economies.[166] In the 1990s, the lead became still more obvious as the U.S. economic growth doubled that of Japan.[167] There is reason to believe that this trend will firmly persist in the near future: in 1999, international financial institutions repeatedly adjusted upward their forecasts concerning the U.S. and E.U. economic growth rates. According to these forecasts, the U.S. growth rate will constitute 4.4 percent in 2000 and 3.0 percent in 2001, and that of the E.U. member-states, 3.2 and 3.1 percent, respectively, while the Japanese economy will continue to stagnate.[168] The impressive progress being made by the post-industrial nations will lead to an ever great lag of those remaining in the industrial phase of development (let alone those in the pre-industrial phase). We see three principal causes for the growth of such disproportions.

First of all, the turning of scientific knowledge into an immediate production resource has, on the other hand, made the developing world, which is in need of new technologies, more dependent on the post-industrial countries where the production of such technologies is concentrated today and, on the other hand, produced new models of reproduction which maximize the consumption of information and knowledge and speed up the post-industrial society's strengthening and development processes. That compelled the developing countries to curtail their domestic consumption for the sake of accumulating material resources necessary for acquiring new technologies; conversely, the character of post-industrial scientific and technological progress urged Western society to broaden consumption to the utmost and to cut the share of accumulation in the national income. In the meantime, developing countries exchanged their non-reproducible natural resources or products embodying the efforts of thousands of people for new technologies. As to the post-industrial world, it supplies high technology and knowledge-intensive products without detriment to the amount of resources left at its disposal. The exchange of products of work for products of creative endeavor, of industrial goods for knowledge—this is what underlies, in the final analysis, the split in modern civilization which has clearly manifested itself on the eve of the twenty-first century.

Second, the shift of emphasis from the consumption of mass-produced creature comforts to the consumption of services and information, a decline in the requirements for natural resources and energy, and an ever more extensive use of recoverable resources and man-made materials—all this is the result of the modern scientific and technological revolution which has radically reduced the demand for the agrarian and industrial countries' products. As a result, the market for their goods is narrowing down, and they are running short of the funds necessary to buy the latest technologies on which their future actually depends. The nations seeking to "catch up" with the post-industrial world have found themselves in a situation where they have nothing to offer it by way of an equal and mutually beneficial exchange.

Third, having gone through its formative stage and entered the period of internal stability, the post-industrial nations have established themselves as the most attractive investment media all along the line. In 1999, the prices of the shares issued by the U.S. high-technology companies rose over 80 percent, something which is incommensurate with the indices of the developing markets characterized, apart from sporadically high yields, by steadily excessive risks, political and social instability. An analysis of the biggest corporations' investment policy in 1996-2000 cannot but lead one to the conclusion that the developing countries are now being looked upon as assembly shops for international monopolies, as nations incapable of independent development and not unappealing for major portfolio investors.

An analysis of the processes under way in the world throughout the past decade has led most Western analysts to most unambiguous conclusions. Proceeding from the view that the 1990s have been, on the whole, a period of competition between the American and Asian capitalist systems and between the developed and "catching up" countries, A. Giddens states, for example, that that the victory of American capitalism leads to "the further spread of globalization processes meeting the American interests in particular and the interests of the Western model of capitalism in general."[169] P. Volcker is of the opinion that on the eve of the twenty-first century, the U.S. remains the only player of real influence in the international business sphere.[170] T. Friedman claims that the "onward globalization calls for a stable structure of international power" and that "no nation can do more than the U.S. for building it up"[171]. M. Hardt and A. Negri go even further than that. "The United States," they write, "is the only nation capable of maintaining justice in relations between countries and nations by acting not from its narrow national motives but in the name of international law."[172] Today such categorical statements may be disputed, and even disagreed with on some point or other, but rejecting this position outright would not make sense, to my mind.

On the eve of the twenty-first century the countries following the road of "catching up" development have discovered that this road has not led them to their coveted objective. Individual external circumstances and a set of accidental factors which interfered with their steady progress are hardly to blame for that. This is precisely why we are now proceeding to examine the most important contradictions inherent in the "catching up" development model of whatever form.

Notes

1.   See Drucker, P.F. *Post-Capitalist Society,* Harper Business, New York, 1993, pp. 19-21; Thurow, L. *Creating Wealth: The New Rules for Individuals, Companies, and Countries in a Knowledge-Based Economy,* Nicholas Brealey Publishing, London, 1999, pp. 19-20, et al.
2.   See Bellah, R. N., Madsen, R., Sullivan, W. M., Swidler, A., Tipton, S. M. *The Good Society,* Vintage Books, New York, 1992, p. 146.
3.   See Mandel, M. J. *The High-Risk Society: Peril and Promise in the New Economy,* Times Books/Random House, New York, 1996, p. 43.
4.   Winslow, Ch. D., Bramer, W. L. *FutureWork: Putting Knowledge to Work in the Knowledge Economy,* Free Press, New York-Toronto, 1994, p. 230.
5.   See Madrick, J. *The End of Affluence: The Causes and Consequences of America's Economic Dilemma,* Random House, New York, 1995, p. 110.
6.   See Judy, R. W., D'Amico, C. *Workforce 2020: Work and Workers in the 21st Century,* Hudson Institute, Indianapolis (Ind.), 1997, p. 63.
7.   See Nelson, J. I. *Post-Industrial Capitalism: Exploring Economic Inequality in America,* Sage Publications, Thousand Oaks-London, 1995, pp. 8-9.
8.   See Frank, R. H., Cook, P. J. *The Winner-Take-All Society: Why the Few at the Top Get So Much More Than the Rest of Us,* Penguin Books, London, 1996, pp. 88.
9.   See Dent, H. S., Jr. *The Roaring 2000s,* Simon & Schuster, New York, 1998, p. 280.
10.   See *Economist,* February 8, 1997, p. 57.
11.   See *Human Development Report 1998,* Oxford University Press for the United Nations Development Programme, Oxford-New York, 1998, p. 2.
12.   See Braun, Ch.-F. von. *The Innovation War: Industrial R&D :. the Arms Race of the 90s,* Prentice Hall PTR, Upper Saddle River (N.J.), 1997, p. 57.
13.   See Friedman, T. L. *The Lexus and the Olive Tree,* Anchor Books, New York, 2000, p. 319.
14.   See *Human Development Report 1999,* Oxford University Press for the United Nations Development Programme, Oxford-New York, 1999, p. 3.

15. See Rosecrance, R. *The Rise of the Virtual State: Wealth and Power in the Coming Century,* Basic Books, New York, 1999, p. 188.
16. See Toynbee, P. "Who's Afraid of Global Culture?" in Hutton, W., Giddens, A. (eds.) *On the Edge: Living with Global Capitalism,* Jonathan Cape, London, 2000, p. 206.
17. See *World Economic and Social Survey 1996,* United Nations Publication, New York, 1996, p. 283.
18. See Sherer, P. M. "Venture Capital Is Hedge Tool," *Wall Street Journal Europe,* March 24-25, 2000, p. 24.
19. See Preston, H. H. "Internet Spurs Rumblings of a Venture-Capital Revolution," *International Herald Tribune,* March 25-26, 2000, p. 118.
20. See *Economist,* May 27, 2000, p. 85.
21. See Davidow, W. H., Malone, M. S. *The Virtual Corporation: Structuring and Revitalizing the Corporation for the 21st Century,* Harper Business, New York, 1992, p. 189.
22. See Miklethwait, J., Wooldridge, A. *A Future Perfect: The Challenge and Hidden Promise of Globalization,* Crown Business, New York, 2000, p. 92.
23. See *Knowledge for Development: World Development Report 1998/1999,* Oxford University Press, Washington (D.C.)-Oxford, 1999, p. 20.
24. See Brown, L. R., Renner, M., Flavin, Ch. et al. *Vital Signs 1997-1998: The Environmental Trends That Are Shaping Our Future,* Earthscan Publications Ltd., London, 1997, p. 112.
25. See Castells, M. *The Information Age: Economy, Society and Culture,* vol. 1: The Rise of the Network Society, Blackwell Publishers, Malden (Mass.)-Oxford (U.K.), 1996, p. 108.
26. See Rosensweig, J. A. *Winning the Global Game: A Strategy for Linking People and Profits,* Free Press, New York, 1998, p. 37.
27. See Perkins, A. B., Perkins, M. C. *The Internet Bubble,* Harper Business, New York, 1999, p. 5.
28. See *Business Week,* European Edition, April 10, 2000, p. 72.
29. See Ayres, R. U. *Turning Point: An End to the Growth Paradigm,* Earthscan Publications Ltd., London, 1998, p. 125; for details see Sandler, T. *Global Challenges: An Approach to Environmental, Political, and Economic Problems,* Cambridge University Press, Cambridge, 1997, p. 20.
30. See Brown, L. R., Renner, M., Flavin, Ch. et al. *Vital Signs 1997-1998,* p. 116.
31. See Miklethwait, J., Wooldridge, A. *A Future Perfect: The Challenge and Hidden Promise of Globalization,* p. 257.
32. See *Human Development Report 1999,* p. 38.
33. See Adams, N. A. *Worlds Apart: The North-South Divide and the International System,* Zed Books, Atlantic Highlands (N.J.)-London, 1997, p. 238.
34. See Bauman, Z. *Globalization: The Human Consequences,* Columbia University Press, New York, 1998, p. 70.
35. See Robinson, W. I. *Promoting Polyarchy: Globalization, U.S. Intervention, and Hegemony,* Cambridge, 1998, p. 384.
36. See Porter, G., Brown, J. W. *Global Environmental Politics,* 2nd ed., Westview Press, Boulder (Colo.), 1996, pp. 109-110.
37. See Ayres, R. U. *Turning Point: An End to the Growth Paradigm,* p. 125.
38. Hicks, J. *Wealth and Welfare,* Pergamon Press, Oxford, 1981, pp. 138-139.
39. See Chatfield, Ch. A. *The Trust Factor: The Art of Doing Business in the Twenty-first Century,* Sunstone Press, Santa Fe (N.M.), 1997, pp. 54-55.
40. See Rifkin, J. *The End of Work,* New York, 1995, p. 233.

41. See Nuernberger, Ph. "Mastering the Creative Process," *Futurist,* no. 4, 1984, vol. XVIII, p. 36.

42. See Maslow, A. H. *Motivation and Personality,* Harper & Row, New York, 1970.

43. See Toffler, A. *Future Shock,* Random House, New York, 1970, pp. 220-221.

44. Inglehart, R. *Culture Shift in Advanced Industrial Society,* Princeton University Press, Princeton (N.J.), 1990, p. 171.

45. Boyett, J. H., Conn, H. P. *Maximum Performance Management,* Capstone, Oxford, 1995, p. 32.

46. Touraine, A. *Critique de la modernité,* Fayard, Paris, 1992, p. 354.

47. For details, see Bell, D. *The Cultural Contradictions of Capitalism,* Basic Books, New York, 1978, pp. 147-148.

48. See Davis, S., Meyer, C. *Future Wealth,* Harvard Business School Press, Boston (Mass.), 2000, p. 40.

49. For details, see Inozemtsev, V. L. *The Socio-Economic Problems of the 21st Century: An Attempt at an Unconventional Assessment,* Centre for Post-Industrial Researches, Moscow, 1999; Inozemtsev, V. L. *Civilization Split: The Available Prerequisites and Likely Consequences of the Post-Economic Revolution,* Academia-Nauka, Moscow, 1999, pp. 165-297; Inozemtsev, V. L. "Fin de siecle: Concerning the History of the Rise of the Post-Industrial Economic System (1973-2000)," *Svobodnaya mysl-XXI* (Free Thought-XXI), no. 7, 1999, pp. 3-27; no. 8, pp.19-42 (all in Russian).

50. See Baumohl, B. "The Best of Times?" *Time,* August 4, 1997, p. 42.

51. Calculated from: *National Income and Product Accounts, 1947-1965,* Government Printing Office, Washington (D.C.), 1967; *Yearbook of Labour Statistics, 1995,* ILO, Geneva, 1996.

52. Calculated from: *OECD: National Accounts Statistics: Detailed Tables. 1960-1970; Yearbook of Labour Statistics, 1995,* ILO, Geneva, 1996.

53. See Krugman, P. *Pop Internationalism,* MIT Press, Cambridge (Mass.)-London, 1998, p. 36.

54. Calculated from: *International Financial Statistics Yearbook,* Washington (D.C.), 1993, 1994, 1995, 1998.

55. See Hopkins, T. K., Wallerstein, E. et al. *The Age of Transition: Trajectory of the World-System 1945-2025,* Zed Books-Pluto Press, London and New Jersey-Australia (Leichhardt), 1996, p. 28.

56. See Bernstein, M. A. "Understanding American Economic Decline: The Contours of the Late-Twentieth-Century Experience," in Bernstein, M. A., Adler, D. E. (eds.) *Understanding American Economic Decline,* Cambridge University Press, Cambridge, 1994, p. 18.

57. See Fridson, M. S. *It Was a Very Good Year: Extraordinary Moments in Stock Market History,* John Wiley & Sons Inc., New York, 1998, p. 175.

58. See *Raw Materials Crisis of Modern Capitalism,* Nauka, Publishers, Moscow, 1980, p. 186 (in Russian).

59. Calculated from: *International Financial Statistics Yearbook,* 1993, 1994, 1995, 1998.

60. See Brockway, G. P. *Economists Can Be Bad for Your Health: Second Thoughts on the Dismal Science,* W.W. Norton & Company, New York-London, 1995, p. 51.

61. See Feldstein, M. (ed.) *American Economic Policy in the 1980s,* University of Chicago Press, Chicago-London, 1994, p. 87.

62. See Mitchell, K., Beck, P., Grubb, M. *The New Geopolitics of Energy,* Royal Institute of International Affairs, London, 1996, p. 42.

63.   See McRae, H. *The World in 2020: Power, Culture and Prosperity: A Vision of the Future,* HarperCollins Publishers, New York-London, 1994, p. 132.

64.   See Schwartz, P., Leyden, P., Hyatt, J. *The Long Boom: A Vision for the Coming Age of Prosperity,* Perseus Books, Reading (Mass.), 1999, p. 162.

65.   See Cleveland, C. J. "Natural Resource Scarcity and Economic Growth Revisited: Economic and Biophysical Perspectives," in Costanza, R. (ed.) *Ecological Economics: The Science and Management of Sustainability,* New York, 1991, pp. 308-309.

66.   See Thurow, L. *Head to Head: The Coming Economic Battle Among Japan, Europe, and America,* Warner Books, New York, 1993, p. 41.

67.   See Taylor, J., Van Doren, P. "Soft Energy Versus Hard Facts," in Bailey, R. (ed.) *Earth Report 2000: Revisiting the True State of the Planet,* McGraw-Hill, New York, 2000, p. 134.

68.   See *Problems of Energy Supply in Capitalist Countries in the Current Energy Situation,* Moscow, 1987, p. 24 (in Russian).

69.   See Mazarr, M. J. *Global Trends 2005: An Owner's Manual for the Next Decade,* St. Martin's Press, New York, 1999, p. 78.

70.   See Cox, W. M., Alm, R. *Myths of Rich and Poor: Why We're Better Off Than We Think,* Basic Books, New York, 1999, p. 145.

71.   See Castells, M. "Information Technology and Global Capitalism," in Hutton, W., Giggens, A. (eds.), *On the Edge,* p. 63.

72.   See Forester, T. *Silicon Samurai: How Japan Conquered the World's IT Industry,* Blackwell Business, Cambridge (Mass.)-Oxford, 1993, p. 147.

73.   See Kuttner, R. *The Economic Illusion: False Choices Between Prosperity and Social Justice,* University of Pennsylvania Press, Philadelphia, 1991, pp. 118-119

74.   See Castells, M. "The Informational Economy and the New International Division of Labor," in Carnoy, M., Castells, M., Cohen, S., Cardoso, F. H. *The New Global Economy in the Information Age,* Pennsylvania State University Press, University Park (Pa.), 1993, p. 25.

75.   See Greider, W. *One World, Ready or Not: The Manic Logic of Global Capitalism,* Simon & Schuster, New York, 1997, p. 22.

76.   See Sayer, A., Walker, R. *The New Social Economy: Reworking the Division of Labor,* Blackwell, Cambridge (Mass.)-Oxford (U.K.), 1994, p. 154.

77.   See Thurow, L. *Head to Head,* p. 30.

78.   See Niskanen, W. A. *Reaganomics: An Insider's Account of the Policies and the People,* Oxford University Press, New York-Oxford, 1988, p. 73.

79.   See Pilzer, P. Z. *Unlimited Wealth: The Theory and Practice of Economic Alchemy,* Crown Publishers, Inc., New York, 1990, p. 14.

80.   See Feldstein, M. *American Economic Policy in the 1980s,* p. 7.

81.   See Strange, S. *Casino Capitalism,* Manchester University Press, Manchester, 1997, p. 17.

82.   See Kiplinger, K. *World Boom Ahead: Why Business and Consumers Will Prosper,* Kiplinger Books, Washington (D.C.), 1998, p. 46.

83.   See Krugman, P. *Peddling Prosperity: Economic Sense and Nonsense in the Age of Diminishing Expectations,* W.W. Norton & Company, New York-London, 1994, p. 158.

84.   See Niskanen, W. A. *Reaganomics,* p. 234.

85.   See Krugman, P. *Pop Internationalism,* p. 100.

86.   See Shulman, S. *Owning the Future,* Houghton Mifflin Company, Boston-New York, 1999, p. 15.

87.   See *Knowledge for Development: World Development Report 1998/1999,* Oxford University Press for the World Bank, New York-Washington (D.C.), 1999, p. 19.

88. See *Entering the 21st Century: World Development Report 1999/2000,* Oxford University Press for the World Bank, Washington (D.C.)-Oxford, 2000, p. 64.
89. See Stewart, T. A. *Intellectual Capital: The New Wealth of Organizations,* Doubleday/Currency, New York-London, 1997, pp. 20-21.
90. See Roos, J., Roos, G., Edvinsson, L., Dragonetti, N. C., *Intellectual Capital: Navigating the New Business Landscape,* Macmillan Business, New York, 1997, p. 10.
91. See *Statistical Abstract of the United States. 1995,* Reference Press, Inc., Washington (D.C.), 1995, p. 411.
92. See Perkins, A. B., Perkins, M. C. *The Internet Bubble,* p. 6.
93. See Doremus, P. N. et al. *The Myth of the Global Corporation,* Princeton University Press, Princeton (N.J.), 1998, p. 103.
94. See Bluestone, B., Harrison, B. *Growing Prosperity: The Battle for Growth with Equity in the Twenty-First Century,* Houghton Mifflin Company, Boston-New York, 2000, p. 28.
95. See Martin, M. "A New Milestone in U.S. Expansion," *International Herald Tribune,* March 31, 2000, p. 1.
96. See *Economist,* April 29, 2000, p. 23.
97. See *Financial Times,* June 3-4, 2000, p. 6.
98. See Sanghera, S. "U.S. Growth Stronger in First Quarter," *Financial Times,* May 26, 2000, p. 7.
99. See Bluestone, B., Harrison, B. *Growing Prosperity,* p. 180.
100. See Wolf, M. "Greenspan Reaps the Whirlwind," *Financial Times,* May 24, 2000, p. 15.
101. See Berry, J. M. "U.S. Jobless Rate Falls to 3,9%," *International Herald Tribune,* May 6-7,2000, p. 1.
102. See Rosenberg, N. "Uncertainty and Technological Change," Landau, R., Taylor, T., Wright, G. (eds.) *The Mosaic of Economic Growth,* Stanford University Press, Stanford (Cal.), 1996, p. 336.
103. See Drucker, P. F. *The New Realities,* Butterworth-Heinemann, Oxford, 1996, p. 116.
104. See Kadlec, Ch. W. *Dow 100,000: Fact or Fiction?* New York Institute of Finance, New York, 1999, pp. 139-140.
105. See Pilzer, P. Z. *Unlimited Wealth,* p. 5.
106. See Kelly, K. *New Rules for the New Economy: Ten Radical Strategies for a Connected World,* Viking, New York, 1998, p. 3.
107. See Frank, R. H., Cook, P. J. *The Winner-Take-All Society,* p. 46.
108. See *World Resources 1998-1999,* Oxford University Press, New York-Oxford, 1998, p. 163.
109. See Pilzer, P. Z. *Unlimited Wealth,* p. 14.
110. Hampden-Turner, Ch., Trompenaars, F. *The Seven Cultures of Capitalism,* Judy Piatkus Publishers, London, 1994, p. 216.
111. See Meadows, D. H., Meadows, D. L., Randers, J. *Beyond the Limits: Global Collapse or a Sustainable Future?* Earthscan Publications Ltd., London, 1992, p. 181.
112. Calculated from: Mitchell, K., Beck Paris, Grubb, M. *The New Geopolitics of Energy,* p. 161.
113. See Brown, L. R., Renner, M., Flavin, Ch. et al. *Vital Signs 1997-1998,* p. 103.
114. See Brown, L. R., Flavin, Ch., French, H. et al. *State of the World 1998: A Worldwatch Institute Report on Progress Toward a Sustainable Society,* Earthscan Publications Ltd., New York-London, 1998, p. 114.

115. See Brown, L. R., Renner, M., Flavin, Ch. et al. *Vital Signs 1997-1998*, pp. 96, 108.
116. See Scarlett, L. "Doing More With Less," in Bailey, R. (ed.) *Earth Report 2000: Revisiting the True State of the Planet*, p. 57.
117. See Axtmann, R. "Globalization, Europe and the State: Introductory Reflections," in Axtmann, R. (ed.) *Globalization and Europe: Theoretical and Empirical Investigations,* Pinter, London-Washington (D.C.), 1998, pp. 2-3.
118. See Krugman, P. *Peddling Prosperity*, p. 231.
119. See Fieldhouse, D. K. *The West and the Third World: Trade, Colonialism, Dependence and Development,* Blackwell Publishers, Oxford-Malden (Mass.), 1999, pp. 102-103.
120. See Featherstone, K., Ginsberg, R. H. *The United States and the European Union in the 1990s: Partners in Transition,* Palgrave, New York, 1996, p. 115.
121. See Elliott, L., Atkinson, D. *The Age of Insecurity,* Verso, London-New York, 1998, p. 226.
122. See Krugman, P. "Does Third World Growth Hurt First World Prosperity?" in Ohmae, K. (ed.) *The Evolving Global Economy: Making Sense of the New World Order*, A Harvard Business Review Book, Boston (Mass.), 1995, p. 117.
123. See *World Economic Outlook: A Survey by the Staff of the International Monetary Fund. May 1999*, IMF, Publication Service, Washington (D.C.), 1999, p. 177.
124. See *Economist*, April 12, 1997, p. 119.
125. See Ohmae, K. *The Borderless World,* HarperCollins Publishers, London, 1994, pp. 138-139.
126. See Burtless, G., Lawrence, R. Z., Litan, R. E., Shapiro, R. J. *Globaphobia: Confronting Fears about Open Trade*, Brookings Institution, Washington (D.C.), 1998, p. 22.
127. See O'Rourke, K. H., Williamson, J. G. *Globalization and History: The Evolution of a Nineteenth-Century Atlantic Economy*, MIT Press, Cambridge (Mass.)-London, 1999, p. 30.
128. See Bairoch, P. "Globalization Myths and Realities: One Century of External Trade and Foreign Investment," in Boyer, R., Drache, D. (eds.) *States Against Markets: The Limits of Globalization*, Routledge, London-New York, 1996, p. 179.
129. See Mason, M. *Development and Disorder: A History of the Third World since 1945*, University Press of New England, Hanover-London, 1997, p. 443.
130. See Miklethwait, J., Wooldridge, A. *A Future Perfect: The Essentials of Globalization*, p. 121.
131. Mann, M. "As the Twentieth Century Ages," *New Left Review*, November-December, 1995, p. 117.
132. See Dent, Ch. M. *The European Economy: The Global Context*, Routledge, London-New York, 1997, p. 169.
133. See Jovanovic, M. N. *European Economic Integration: Limits and Prospects*, Routledge, London-New York, 1997, p. 243.
134. See Hirst, P., Thompson, G. "Globalization in Question: International Economic Relations and Forms of Public Governance," in Hollingsworth, J. R., Boyer, R. (eds.) *Contemporary Capitalism: The Embeddedness of Institutions*, Cambridge University Press, Cambridge, 1997, p. 355.
135. *World Economic Outlook: A Survey by the Staff of the International Monetary Fund, October 1997*, IMF, Publication Service, Washington (D.C.), 1997, pp. 51-54.
136. See Mazarr, M. J. *Global Trends 2005*, p. 161.
137. See *The World in 2020: Towards a New Global Age*, OECD Publications, Paris, 1997, p. 32.

138. See Sutherland, P. D. *Managing the International Economy in the Age of Globalisation*, The Per Jacobsson Foundation, Washington (D.C.), 1998, p. 5.
139. See Castells, M. *Information Technology and Global Capitalism*, pp. 60-61.
140. See Plender, J. *A Stake in the Future: The Stakeholding Solution*, Nicholas Brealey Publishing, London, 1997, p. 118.
141. See Boland, V. "Paris Exchange Seeks to Woo New Partners," *Financial Times*, April 26, 2000, p. 15.
142. See Weiss, L. *The Myth of the Powerless State: Governing the Economy in a Global Era*, Polity Press, Cambridge, 1998, p. 186.
143. See Collins, P. "Regional Trading Blocks and Foreign Direct Investment," in Dunning, J. H. (ed.) *Globalization, Trade and Foreign Direct Investment*, Elsevier Science Ltd., Kinglington (U.K.), 1998, pp. 31, 38.
144. See Castells, M. *Information Technology and Global Capitalism*, p. 54.
145. See Hopkins, T. K., Wallerstein, E. et al. *The Age of Transition*, p. 51.
146. See Burtless, G., Lawrence, R. Z., Litan, R. E., Shapiro, R. J. *Globaphobia*, pp. 36, 39, 29, 85, 86.
147. See Paterson, M. *Global Warming and Global Politics*, Routledge, London-New
148. See Heilbroner, R., Milberg, W. *The Making of Economic Society*, 10th ed., Prentice Hall, Upper Saddle River (N.J.), 1998, p. 159.
149. See Hirst, P., Thompson, G. *Globalization in Question: The International Economy and the Possibilities of Governance*, Cambridge, 1996, p. 53.
150. See Kobrin, S. J. "The Architecture of Globalization: State Sovereignty in a Networked Global Economy," in Dunning, J. H. (ed.) *Governments, Globalization, and International Business*, Oxford University Press, Oxford, 1997, p. 150.
151. See Castells, M. *Information Technology and Global Capitalism*, p. 54.
152. See Mazarr, M. J. *Global Trends 2005*, p. 172.
153. See Valladao, A. G. A. *The Twenty-First Century Will Be American*, Verso, London-New York, 1996, p. 104.
154. See *The World in 2020: Towards a New Global Age*, p. 52.
155. See Miklethwait, J., Wooldridge, A. *A Future Perfect: The Essentials of Globalization*, p. 5.
156. See Gilpin, R., with Gilpin, J. M. *The Challenge of Global Capitalism: The World Economy in the 21st Century*, Princeton University Press, Princeton (N.J.), 2000, p. 295.
157. See O'Rourke, K. H., Williamson, J. G. *Globalization and History*, p. 152.
158. See Arrighi, J., Silver, B. J. *Chaos and Governance in the Modern World System*, University of Minnesota Press, Minneapolis-London, 1999, p. 283.
159. See McRae, H. *The World in 2020*, p. 271.
160. See Lind, M. *The Next American Nation: The New Nationalism and the Fourth American Revolution*, Free Press Paperbacks/Simon & Schuster, New York, 1995, pp. 132-133.
161. See Burtless, G., Lawrence, R. Z., Litan, R. E., Shapiro, R. J. *Globaphobia*, pp. 86-87.
162. See Morgan, G. *Images of Organization*, Sage Publications, Thousand Oaks-London, 1997, p. 313.
163. See Pierson, Ch. *Beyond the Welfare State? The New Political Economy of Welfare*, Polity Press, Cambridge, 1995, pp. 87-88.
164. See *Newsweek*, Special Issue, November 1998-February 1999, p. 76.
165. See Rex, J. "Transnational Migrant Communities and the Modern Nation-State," in Axtmann, R. (ed.) *Globalization and Europe*, pp. 68-69.

166. See Ryrie, W. *First World, Third World*, St. Martin's Press, New York, 1995, p. 36.
167. See Cox, W. M., Alm, R. *Myths of Rich and Poor*, p. 92.
168. See Friedman, A. "IMF Lifts Forecast of Global Economy," *International Herald Tribune*, April 13, 2000, p. 1.
169. Hutton, W., Giddens, A. (eds.) *On the Edge: Living with Global Capitalism*, p. 41.
170. See Volcker, P. "The Sea of Global Finance," in Hutton, W., Giddens, A. (eds.) *On the Edge: Living with Global Capitalism*, p. 84.
171. See Friedman, T. L. *The Lexus and the Olive Tree*, p. 464.
172. See Hardt, M., Negri, A. *Empire*, Harvard University Press, Cambridge (Mass.)-London, 2000, p. 180.

3

Internal Contradictions of the "Catching Up" Development Model

By the end of the twentieth century it became obvious that the prosperity of Western societies based on liberal tradition is largely due to the natural course of their evolution. That explains the setbacks suffered by both socialist and developing countries that have never developed in a natural and self-sufficient way.

The twentieth century has witnessed the emergence of two types of the "catching up" development model. One of the models, strictly industrial, was adopted by the USSR in the 1930s; Germany in the 1930s and the 1940s; and the socialist countries in the 1950s and the 1960s. The other model reproduced, to some extent or other, features of the Western societies' post-industrial development; the latter model was adopted by Japan in the 1970s and the 1980s, and by the Southeast Asian countries in the 1980s and the 1990s. Inherent in either model was a fundamental conflict between self-sufficiency and naturalness of development which, far from generating constructive solutions, interfered with a successful accomplishment of the objectives set.

In the former case, the principle of self-reliance predominated (for ideological or political reasons, mostly), and a self-sufficient economy generated autarchy maintained by the toughening of authoritarian regimes. That involved the use of harsh mobilization measures which triggered either open protest or entailed social apathy, and ended up producing a backward and stagnant economy incapable of competing with market-oriented ones.

In the latter case, a certain degree of openness, combined with principles of accelerated development, and readiness to draw upon Western experience found its embodiment in wholesale technological and organizational borrowings and manifest gravitation of the nations in question towards external markets as capital suppliers and "insatiable" consumers of finished products. In this version of the model, a much more natural course of development which called for no harsh political pressure failed to make up, however, for a nation's dependence on external factors and slowness to respond to the post-industrial world's new development trends. Considering that the nations which adhered to the latter model have achieved considerable successes over the past decades, we shall concentrate here on the contradictions inherent in the "catching up" development pattern realized in Japan, Southeast Asia and China. In this Chapter we shall examine six such contradictions and the sets of circumstances that give rise to them.

The first of them consists in the patent one-sidedness of all the "catching up" countries' industrial development. For example, the Soviet bloc states or Nazi Germany were dominated by either the military sector or the heavy industry, neither of which had made the nation any better off despite's achievements. On the other hand, Japan and, to a still greater extent, Southeast Asian countries strongly emphasize engineering and electronics. Buying up American and European patents en masse, Japanese and Southeast Asian manufacturers boosted up the production of relatively inexpensive items of everyday use and flooded the Western countries' markets with them. As already indicated, Japan accounted, in the mid-1980s, for 82 percent of the world output of motorcycles; 80.7 percent, of home video systems; and about 66 percent of photocopiers,[1] which, however, does not tell the whole story about the Asian economies' narrow specialization. In the same period, the share of engineering in South Korea's overall industrial output reached more than 25 percent, and that of electronics, 17.8 percent;[2] these two sectors were responsible for more than 60 percent of South Korea' exports.[3] In Malaysia, the proportion of those employed in the electronic industry which constituted no more than 0.2 percent the total industrial workforce in 1970 swelled to 21 percent towards the late 1980s, and the share of that industry's products in the overall volume of exports topped 44 percent.[4] Taiwanese became the world's fifth biggest microprocessor manufacturer and the leading Taiwan companies' proceeds from their sales skyrocketed from all but zero in 1989 to $2.5 billion in 1993.[5] Whereas in 1970 the share of agriculture in the

GNP of South Korea, Thailand and Indonesia constituted 29.8; 30.2; and 35.0 percent, respectively, and was 3 to 7 percentage points larger than that of the industrial sector, in 1993 these indices attained the levels of 6.4; 12.2 and 17.6 percent, respectively, which is 40; 28 and 22 percent short of the industry's share.[6]

Such a progress of industrialization might have been regarded as successful had it not been for the obvious failure of those "catching up" nations' domestic markets to absorb their products. It is a well-known fact that at the end of the 1960s when no more than 165,000 passanger cars were found in South Korea, a plant with a rated output of 300,000 cars a year was put into operation there;[7] in the 1980s, Singapore's, Malaysia's and Hongkong's output of electronic equipment steadily exceeded those countries' domestic market demand for it 6 to 7 times over, while 60 to 70 percent of the immovables erected in those countries were acquired by foreign investors. It stands to reason that accelerated industrialization could not but demand that the "catching up" nations should concentrate on certain lines of business, but the likely negative side-effects of such a strategy are not to be ignored, either.

The second important set of circumstances is connected with the public underconsumption stemming from the industrial type of the "catching up" development model applied and putting up a practically insurmountable barrier to the rise of a capacious domestic market. It is common knowledge that the standard of living in developing countries which have opted for the "catching up" development strategy used to be low. As a rule, all of them decided for an accelerated industrial growth policy in a situation where the volume of the gross national product constituted $300 per capita a year, at the most. Whenever a new economic policy was adopted (in Malaysia, Singapore and Taiwan it happened at the end of the 1940s; in South Korea and Indonesia, in the early 1960s; in Thailand, in the late 1960s; in China, at the beginning of the 1980s; and in Vietnam and Laos, at the turn of the 1990s), this index did not exceed the level indicated. In Malaysia, it constituted no more than $ 300 in the early 1950s;[8] in war-ravaged Korea, about $100 at the end of the 1950s;[9] in Taiwan, $160 in the early 1960s;[10] in China, which embarked on the road of sweeping transformations in 1978, $ 280; and in Vietnam, the $220 mark was attained only in the mid-1980s.[11]

Such low income levels were a factor in launching accelerated industrialization which required measures to hold them down. In the mid-1990s, when in the more advanced countries an industrial worker earned from $12 to $30 an hour, in Korea and Singapore a highly skilled expert was salaried at the rate of no more than $7, and in Malaysia, $1.5 per hour. In China and India, workers were paid about $3, and Vietnam, no more than $1,5 a day[12] in the same period. In Thailand, Malaysia and Indonesia, real wages were actually frozen from the mid-1970s to the late 1980s;[13] even in a relatively more successful South Korea, average wages in industry constituted 15 percent of the Japanese and 11 percent of the US level in the late 1980s.[14] As a result, the per-capita GNP index in Thailand, Malaysia and Indonesia went down 7, 23 and 34 percent, respectively, compared to the analogous index computed for the G-7 countries.[15] The boom of the 1990s had no effect on the plight of those countries' population at large: in Thailand, for example, the incomes of the 10 percent top-income bracket tripled over that period, while the lowest-paid ten percent got no rise at all.[16] Most researchers concerned with problems of modern competition agree, however, that the "companies the *only* competitive advantage of which is low production costs do not dismiss executive managers of this or that sector from their posts too often".[17] This rule, in our view, fully applies to entire states rather than individual companies alone. The developing countries cannot gain a firm foothold on the post-industrial world's markets for the only reason that their economies are relatively primitive; and without securing a niche in the said markets, they can get no stimuli for further progress.

For all the apparent affluence of the East Asian countries and their upper class' high incomes (in 1996, for example, Singapore attained the world's highest per-capita GNP index; Indonesia, Malaysia, Thailand and the Philippines took the lead in Asia for the number of billionaires by mid-1997, each of these countries having twice as many of them as a higher developed and more densely populated South Korea,[18] and the people of Hongkong consumed more brandy and expensive wines and owned more cars and furniture, before that British colony reverted to China, than their aristocratic parent state with a 60-moillion population did),[19] the middle class, which is the mainstay of industrial nations, remained numerically small in Asia. As of the early 1990s, no more than four percent of the Indonesians identified themselves with the middle-class; in Thailand, the proportion of skilled workers, technicians, administrators and executive managers constituted no more than 7.6 of the population; in South Korea, the middle class accounted, according to various expert estimates, for 10.5 to slightly over 11 percent of the population.[20] So, the assertion that no country of Southeast Asia has a middle class of the kind which took shape in the 1960s to 1970s as the basis of the post-industrial nations' stability[21] appears to hold water, and Southeast Asia's lag behind the Western world remains enormous. If the annual income of $25,000 per family is taken as a welfare standard common to post-industrial countries, 79 percent of the world's 181 million families in this income bracket are found in the more developed countries, whereas their number, in the five leading new Asian "tigers"—China, South Korea, Taiwan, Indonesia and Thailand, whose aggregate population is six times that of the United States, does not exceed one-fourth of the number of such families found in the United States.[22] It is small wonder, therefore, that domestic demand in the newly-industrialized countries is fairly limited and there is no stable groundwork for their further economic progress.

The third set of circumstances which cannot be ignored within the framework of our analysis is connected with the predomination in the "catching up" economies of extensive development factors, which retards their economic progress substantially. We have already pointed out above that in the 1990s the post-industrial nations' steady advance proceeded against the background of their citizens' growing consumption of material and information goods, with the share of accumulation in national incomes shrinking continually. In Southeast Asia, a diametrically opposite trend is at work. The countries of that region have been compelled to channel a substantial proportion of their per capita gross national product, small as it is, into the development of production because industrial growth is unthinkable without a proportionate increase in the volume of the resources used. As a result, even at a relatively advanced stage of industrialization in the early 1990s, the share of savings in the gross national product amounted to 24 percent in Taiwan; 30 percent in Hongkong; 35 percent in Malaysia, Thailand and South Korea each; 37 percent in Indonesia; 47 percent in Singapore; and, at some observers' estimates, to an fantastic 50 percent in China.[23] As distinct from the rest of the world, South and East Asia remained the only regions where, over the period of 1965-1993, the share of savings in the gross national product markedly tended up rather than down (from 12 to 21 and from 22 to 35 percent, respectively).[24]

The way we see it, this tendency cannot be regarded as absolutely positive. There is no denying the need of large-scale investment in production facilities at the early stages of industrialization; it is over-emphasis on investment that may bring negative results. "Despite the fact that investment is more likely than not, the factor the most closely correlating with [the developing countries'] growth rates over the past four decades," the World Bank's experts point out, "it does not fully account for a spread in the said growth rates"[25] which remains quite considerable. Although they cannot very well qualify this or that country for entry into the industrialized nations' community, high accumulation rates are capable, nevertheless, of radically narrowing down the domestic market and depressing the popular consumption level, thus certainly retarding progress.

Low per capita incomes and high savings rates were not the only sources of an impressive industrial breakthrough achieved by the nations which had adopted the "catching up" development doctrine. As is the case in any agrarian country, developing industrial production demanded extra labor which was recruited from among peasants and artisans. An increase in the share of industrial production in the gross national product was accompanied, characteristically, by a proportional increase in the share of the active population employed in industrial sectors. In Singapore, this index increased from 27 to 51 percent[26] over the period of 1996-1990; in South Korea, from 22 to 48 percent from the early 1960s to the early 1990s; in Taiwan, from 17 percent in 1952 to 40 percent in 1993.[27] That was paralleled by a steady increase in the share of women in the total number of those employed and by the lengthening of the working day. As a result, industrial workers put in an average of almost 2,500 hours year in South Korea and Taiwan in the first half of the 1990s while in most European countries 1,500 hours a year was the statutory limit.[28] While contributing to the Southeast Asian countries' impressive achievements at the first stage of their industrial breakthrough, such a numerical expansion of the industrial working class made the local economies strongly dependent on low labor cost; as a consequence, the commencement of the per capita income rise in the mid-1990s cost those countries' economic systems their vital competitive advantage and landed them on the threshold of a crisis.[29]

All this goes to show that despite an extensive use of technological borrowings from post-industrial nations, the Asian economies developed using exclusively extensive methods until the 1997 crisis[30]. A comparison between the contributions of the productivity factor to the overall gross national product growth dynamics in various countries in the 1950s-1970s will show that in Taiwan only 2.6 percent of the annual GNP increment was achieved through an increase in productivity at the average growth rate of 9.4 percent; in South Korea, only 1.2 percent at the average GNP growth rate of 10.3 percent; in Singapore, a mere 0.2 percent at the annual growth rate of 8.7 percent; while in France these indices were 5.0 and 3.0 percent, respectively.[31] So, notwithstanding a number of fundamental differences between the nations which opted for the first, closed, or the second, relatively open to the outside world, "catching up" development models, the methods they used to accelerate industrial progress remained largely similar. Admittedly, therefore, P. Krugman's opinion to the effect that "the young industrial nations of Asia achieved high growth rates, just as the Soviet Union did in the 1950s, chiefly though an amazing mobilization of resources; their progress, just as that of the USSR in the high growth rate period, was stimulated, first and foremost, by an unprecedented increase in labor and capital inputs rather than by stepping up production efficiency"[32] discloses the basic difference between the post-industrial mode of development and the "catching up" development practice in a most objective way.

The fourth set of circumstances which further aggravated the problems facing the "catching up" countries has to do with the large-scale import of capital which accompanied this type of development from the very outset. Back in the 1950s and in the early 1960s, the United States rendered South Korea and Taiwan massive economic aid the amount of which constituted 5-6 and 10 percent of those countries' gross national product, respectively.[33] Later, the influx of foreign capital began to grow on a commercial basis and got to be so active (especially, the 1980s and early 1990s) that previous loans were returned from new ones, and investors bought up securities of East Asian companies often without taking the trouble of analyzing their financial status. As such, foreign investment should under no circumstances be regarded as a negative phenomenon; on the contrary, it is the most efficient means of transferring post-industrial production technologies to the Third World. In the countries which have opted for the "catching up" development model the expansion of foreign investment has often served to deepen their economic one-sidedness. From the very outset of its accelerated development period, Southeast Asia began to turn into international corporations' assembly shops: in the 1980s, South Korea's computer output increased twentyfold, but 95 percent of the computers it produced were manufactured under licenses; the cost of South Korean-made components did not exceed 15 percent, and all the software was imported.[34] The reverse side of foreign investment is the recipient countries' monstrous dependence on the supplies of components and technologies: by 1995, the imports of the ten Asian new industrial nations were worth $748 billion which was $12 billion in excess of the EU figure[35].

According to modern Western researchers, however, the laws governing economic progress are such that "for the Third World nations to catch up with the West, they will need the moneys by an order of magnitude larger than what they are actually capable of generating within themselves."[36] Therefore, the road taken by Southeast Asia, far from envisaging a gradual transition to self-reliance, called for ever larger supplementary investment, and its influx kept swelling up—for the time being. In 1987-1992 alone, the volume of direct foreign capital investment in the Malaysian economy increased almost ninefold;[37] in the Thai economy, twelvefold to fifteenfold;[38] and in the Indonesian economy, sixteenfold.[39] The influx of enormous funds to those countries (foreign investment growth rates steadily exceeded that of those gross national product in the 1980s and in the 1990s) actually obviated the need for raising production efficiency because the import of technological novelties kept increasing. The result was a decline in growth rates by the mid-1990s which passed unnoticed by most investors: foreign companies' direct investment in that region amounted to $93 billion in 1996 alone, growing more than threefold over the previous five years.[40]

Those "giddy successes" made many nations of the region overly confident of being on the right track—so much so that Japan, Singapore, Hong Kong and Taiwan, the leaders of the "catching up" development strategy, kept boosting their investment even after the riskiness of such practice had become only too obvious. In 1993, they accounted for 59.7 percent of foreign investment in Thailand while the U.S. share never rose above 20 percent; the corresponding figures for Malaysia were 62.2 and 11.6 (1994); and for Vietnam, 68.1 and 5.9 percent (as of the end of 1995). Moreover, whereas Japanese and Singapore investment in the region's countries grew at a rate of up to 30 percent a year in 1994-1996, American investment stagnated and even decreased (as was the case in Indonesia).[41] Money flows channeled into local stock markets grew at an incredible rate. Whereas in 1990 their volume did not exceed $2 billion, in 1990-1994 it totaled $42 billion.[42] As a result, in 1994 when the market capitalization of Chinese companies representing the country with a billion-plus population and a colossal economic potential amounted to about $44 billion, the corresponding index for Malaysia (population: 19 million) reached $200 billion or 300 percent of the GNP which was 2.5 times the G.B. and U.S. indices.[43] In the investment boom year of 1995, the market capitalization of Southeast Asian countries amounted to 58 percent of the developing world's total.[44]

That led to a considerable overestimation of all the national assets and contributed to an artificial rise in demand for land, immovables and durable consumer goods. Under the circumstances, the production efficiency problem receded to the background, with quantitative growth and production for production's sake, the expansion of which depended on supplementary investment, coming to the fore. Hence a vicious circle which had to be broken sooner or later. Notably, over the 1990s the composition of the investment made in developing countries underwent substantial changes: in 1996, despite the stock market boom, total capital investment in shares and commercial loans turned out to be smaller than direct foreign investment;[45] thus, the post-industrial West changed over from the policy of making speculatively high profits in developing markets to the expansion of production activities. From that moment on, industrial development of the East Asian nations largely turned into the development of the potential of Western companies operating in these countries.

The fifth group of factors determining the nonselfsufficiency of the "catching up" development pattern looks particularly important to us because they made the "catching up" nations dependent on the export of their products. The external market orientation concept has been and remains a cornerstone of the Asian industrialization model. In the meantime, this concept suffers from at least two fundamental flaws.

On the one hand, the nations professing this concept find themselves extremely sensitive to demand fluctuations in Western markets; a classical case in point is the aftermath of a sharp fall in the demand for raw material resources in the first half of the 1980s which hit hard most Third World economies[46] and gave the world economic system a new look at the close of the twentieth century. On the other hand, there comes the need for a harsh protectionist policy which may result not only in precipitous domestic price raises (in the late 1980s, for example, food prices in Japan were twenty times higher than those in the United States, on the average,[47] which cost Japanese consumers $40 billion a year)[48] but even in downright dumping intended to strengthen the positions of a country's goods in the post-industrial community's markets. In the 1990s, this policy ceased bearing fruit because keeping export sales volumes high demanded, first, extra investment (and low-yield one, into the bargain) and, second, added to the exporter's dependence on changes in the world market situation.

As a result, the "catching up" countries bring about a situation where their development parameters differ entirely from those of the countries they are trying to catch up with. Indeed, the post-industrial nations' exports constitute no more than 7 to 8 percent of their GNP; the corresponding index for China being 21.2 percent, for Indonesia, 21.9 percent; for the Philippines, 24.4 percent; for South Korea, 26.8; for Thailand, 30.2 percent; for Taiwan, 42.5 percent; for Malaysia, 78.8 percent. Hong Kong and Singapore merit special mention in this context: their exports amounted to fantastic 117.3 and 132.9 percent, respectively.[49] The absolutized principle of the developing economies' export orientation resulted in that South Korea and Taiwan owed their 42- and 47-percent economic growth indices, respectively, to American purchases of their manufactured products only;[50] U.S. imports were responsible for more than a half of Brazil's and almost 85 percent of Mexico' favorable balance of trade.[51] Plainly, the developing countries' dependence on the post-industrial world is assuming a strikingly disproportionate character. The share of those countries' exports supplied to the United States, Western Europe, and Japan fluctuates, as a rule, over the range of

45-60 percent while the share of developing countries' exports in the trade turnover of France and Italy constitutes 4.3 percent; of Germany, 5.5 percent; Great Britain, 7.7 percent; the United States, 16.3 percent; with Japan only maintaining this index at a much higher level: 30.4 percent.[52] It follows from the above that today the loss of developing markets would have been much less painful to the post-industrial countries than a reduction in goods deliveries to Europe and the US for the "catching up" nations. That was confirmed by the developments of the mid-1990s: in 1995, the volume of exports from South Korea increased more than 30 percent; from Malaysia, 26 percent; from China, 25 percent; and from Thailand, 23 percent; in 1996, the corresponding indices were: 4.2; 4.0; 1.5; and 0.5 percent, respectively.[53] At the same time, they remained heavily dependent on the supply of patents and standard components; this dependence resulted in industrial progress being financed at the expense of making up for the deficit with borrowed funds, which spelled an imminent crisis. By 1996, the Southeast Asian nations' current balance of payments deficit amounted to $36.5 billion, increasing more than 10 percent within the space of one year of which South Korea accounted for nearly two-thirds.[54]

By the mid-1990s, the record of the economic development of the "catching up" countries—be it Southeast Asian nations, Latin American states, or the transitional economies of Eastern Europe— had made it perfectly clear that they fully depended for their progress on the import of Western technologies and capital and on the export of their own products to post-industrial countries. Now even the apologists of the "catching up" development doctrine have come to realize that they could catch up with the post-industrial world only as fast and as far as that suited the latter itself.

And finally, the sixth set of circumstances important in the context of this chapter determines the "catching up" nations' absolute technological, intellectual and cultural dependence on the post-industrial world. All these countries have an unfavorable balance of trade in technologies with the West. A rudimentary middle class cannot serve as the basis for the formation of a social stratum in which education would be perceived as a significant value and the quest for creative work would be a pressing need, as is the case in post-industrial societies. Although in Japan or South Korea almost all children go to school today, this is rather a tribute to tradition without any underlying motive behind it; otherwise, how one would explain the fact that 60 percent of U.S. CEOs hold doctoral degrees while 30 percent of their Japanese counterparts have never gone to college.[55] In China and Indonesia, only 45 to 50, and in Thailand, less than 40 percent of the youth attend school.[56] Moreover, whereas in France 44 percent of students go on to college and in the United States this index amounts to 65 percent,[57] in Malaysia it does not rise above 12 percent[58] with the result that college students account for no more than 5 percent of the youth aged 20-24.[59]

The industrial model of progress rules out the possibility of investment in education being profitable; therefore, while in the United States, for example, the wages of men having no college education fell 12 percent in 1973-1987, in Japan high-school graduates boosted their incomes 13 percent,[60] with vocational competence improvement closing the list of the ten vital components of economic growth.[61] Having partaken of the values of the information society, gifted young people from developing countries give a decided preference to them; in the early 1990s, more than a quarter of South Korean, a third of Taiwanese and 95 (!) percent of Chinese students who had received their education abroad did not return home after graduation.[62] The cardinal objectives involved in the rise of post-industrial society—a radical improvement of living standards and the spread of scientific knowledge as a fundamental social value—have been set, at best, but far from accomplished in the newly industrial states today. One cannot but agree with F. Fukuyama's observation to the effect that "the experience of the Soviet Union, China and other socialist countries shows that centralized economic systems, effective enough to achieve a standard of industrialization conforming to the European model of the 1950s, proved altogether unequal to the task of creating an organism as complicated as the post-industrial economy in which information and innovation have a much more important role to play."[63] The source of economic breakthrough so efficiently used by the Western nations in the 1990s was left actually untapped by these countries.

Such are the basic explanations of why the "catching up" development model is not self-sufficient, contradictory, and incapable of delivering the nations adhering to it from under the post-industrial powers' control. Another important circumstance common to all the "catching up" countries stands by itself, as it were. It both ensues from, and determines all the six groups of circumstances named above; therefore, we should not put it in a class with them and study it out of context of each country's development. I mean a very special role played by the state which inevitably participates in any development mobilization scheme.

The importance of this factor was great enough to call for the coining of the term developmental state, made current in the West in the 1980s, which means a state professing and sustaining accelerated development. Toward the mid-1990s, however, it became obvious that theoretical construction built around this notion fails to provide the answers to many questions, including such fundamental ones as: which sectors of the economy gain most from within the framework of this model; which social strata should such a state lean upon; and finally, is it capable of effecting a transition to natural self-replicating development requiring no artificial stimulation?[64] Today most researchers are inclined to divide all the existing economic systems into three basic kinds: comprehensive, self-depending for whatever they need and generating technological innovations; transferring industrial production to other countries and specializing in exporting services and importing the results of material production and, finally, those capable of acting only as recipients of production facilities brought in from more advanced countries.[65] Over the past few years, however, the following school of thought has been confidently gaining ground: no matter how hard a state may try to speed up its economic progress, "no nation across the world has ever succeeded so far in accomplishing a genuine *advance* along the lines of carrying out individual *projects* (my italics.—*V. I.*);[66] we share the view that modern *post-industrial society* can take shape only along the lines of natural (harmonious, if you will) economic progress going on in parallel with changes in social attitudes and motivations for human activities and that, consequently, this society is *taking shape in an evolutionary way* and *cannot be built according to plans drawn up by the economic headquarters in advance.*

Historical experience shows that the state has interfered in economic affairs in various ways; it is precisely the state that initiated the "catching up" development doctrine and set the vital economic priorities; it is precisely the state that largely interferes in private companies' affairs using both restrictions and subsidies and arbitrarily emphasizing this or that industry or development program.[67]

Suffice it to recall that in the early 1960s Japan's Foreign Trade and Industry Ministry set up an association which incorporated such giants as Sony, Hitachi, Toshiba, NEC, and Mitsubishi and granted the new consortium an enormous low-interest credit, which marked the beginning of the Japanese computer industry.[68] It is precisely the state that encouraged underconsumption either by drawing funds from the public to the banks under its control or by triggering controllable inflation to reduce the public's purchasing power. In Indonesia, for example, minimum wages grew at a rate of 10 percent a year in 1990-1995 but their USD equivalent—30 cents per hour[69]—remained practically unchanged; in China, the situation is much the same. The state was largely responsible for extensive methods of industrial development professed in Asia. Suffice it to recall that the Korean government deliberately pursued the policy of subsidizing the largest companies despite their low performance efficiency: in the early 1980s, for example, more than 70 percent of all the credit resources were channeled into a few biggest corporations marked for their minimum profitability (in 1988, Samsung sold a 32 billion dollars' worth of its products making a profit of a mere $439 million, which corresponds to the profitability level of 1.5 percent); in Taiwan, credits for the production of export items were granted at half the interbank interest rate and at nearly a fourth of the credit market's accepted average.[70] While encouraging foreign investment, the state took measures to restrict free competition in the domestic market. Finally, the state has built up an enormous but inefficient bureaucratic machine (in relatively successful Japan, for instance, there are 170,000 farmers and 420,000 local-level managers and 90,000 Agriculture and Fisheries Ministry officials)[71] which often retards economic progress or poses an immediate threat to the country's economic security (suffice it to recall the establishment of a far-flung network of semi-government companies in Indonesia which permitted President Suharto's family to amass the largest fortune in Asia estimated at $40 billion).[72] The crisis which broke out in the region in 1997 revealed, first and foremost, the inefficiency and frailty of the statist model of industrial progress which had looked optimal just a few years before.

* * *

The foregoing cursory review of the more fundamental problems facing the nations which have opted for the "catching up" development model shows that even those of them which have made the most of it proved unequal to a number of vital tasks such as, especially: overcoming non-susceptibility to scientific and technological progress; establishing a research base of their own and changing over to the intensive type of economic progress; overcoming dependence on the capital and technology markets; learning to develop production without exporting their products on an ever larger scale; overcoming the backwardness of the social structure, lowering the savings rates which prevent the formation of the modern middle class; and finally, doing away with dependence on the intellectual potential found outside the limits of the industrially developing nations.

Two important circumstances are worthy of special note in this context.

First, various centers of the world economy have come to be more closely interdependent over the past decade, but this dependence is tending to be increasingly one-sided. The 1997 crisis was caused, mostly, by the developing countries' domestic problems such as production inefficiency; overvaluation of national currencies; weakness of the banking system; overbureaucratization; excessive short-term borrowing practice[73]—and, last but not least, by the fact that the post-industrial world had gained an unprecedented investor appeal. Many experts note that whereas previously capital gravitated toward the United States and Western Europe for reasons of their being relative secure against political uncertainty and catastrophic crises, today it is attracted by the obvious technological and economic leadership of those countries.[74] It is the emergence of an unprecedented technological gap between the First and Third Worlds and the rise of the new post-industrial economy in the West that have made the prospects for the "catching up" development model all but hopeless.[75]

Second, the successes achieved along the lines of "catching up" development look most dubious today. We cannot wholly accept the view taken by more radical researchers who maintain, in particular, that "globalization ... marks the limit to development, ... producing economic marginalization and political instability in the countries found beyond the triadic system [the United States, the EU and Japan.—V.I.]."[76] There is no denying, however, that "catching up" development does not, on the whole, narrow down the gap between the centers of the post-industrial world, on the one hand, and the peripheral regions, on the other. There emerge economic systems sometimes referred to as subordinated economies and commented upon as follows: "The assertion that subordinated economies make no progress does not mean that they are immune to change or incapable of growth; it implies that they remain subordinate with regard to the global system and, therefore, will never attain the much-coveted status of dominant and fully developed economic structures."[77] The record of the Southeast Asian countries is most indicative in this respect. In 1976, Hong Kong's and Singapore's GNP constituted $2,790 and $2,860 per capita; in Malaysia, the Philippines, Thailand, and Indonesia, the figures were $ 950; 410; 380 and 270, respectively. In 1996, on the eve of the crisis, the former two countries attained the GNP level of $21,600 and $23,400 per capita while the latter increased it to $3,520; 960; 2,210 and 880, respectively.[78] As we see, the nations which had been at a higher level of development a quarter of the century ago boosted their GNP eightfold, and the others, 3.6; 2.3; 5.9; and 3.6 times. No comment.

In conclusion, let me repeat: post-industrial society cannot be built; it can only be arrived at through evolutionary development proceeding on is own basis, its most important component being the liberation of the personality potential of its members who have attained high living standards. Where post-materialistic values are sacrificed to industrial development, no such society can see the light of day. The drama of the present-day situation is (as illustrated by the chapters which follow) that none of the countries capable of following the road of "catching up" development is unable to generate and control on its own the amounts of information and knowledge which Western European nations and the United States currently depend on for their advance, and that decades of borrowing new technologies produce no technological breakthroughs. It is impossible to catch up with post-industrial society using industrial methods; feverish attempts to lay the material groundwork for it induces mutations in the public mind which will take longer to put right than speeding up economic progress may take; such is the conclusion that ensues, to our mind, from research into the "catching up" development practice represented in its most explicit form by the record of Japan, newly industrial nations, and China.

Notes

1. See Forester, T. *Silicon Samurai. How Japan Conquered the World's IT Industry*, Blackwell Business, Cambridge (Mass.)-Oxford, 1993, p. 147.
2. See Hobday, M. *Innovation in East Asia: The Challange to Japan*, Edward Elgar, Cheltenham (U.K.)-Lyme (U.S.), 1997, pp. 31, 57.
3. See Bello, W., Rosenfeld, S. *Dragons in Distress: Asia's Miracle Economies in Crisis*, A Food First Book, San Francisco, 1990, p. 59.
4. See Robinson, R., Goodman, D. S. G. (eds.*) The New Rich in Asia: Mobile Phones, McDonald's and Middle-Class Revolution*, Routledge, London-New York, 1996, pp. 57-58.
5. See Yip, G. S. *Asian Advantage: Key Strategies for Winning in the Asia-Pacific Region*, Addison-Wesley, Reading (Mass.), 1998, p. 119.
6. See Islam, I., Chowdhury, A. *Asia-Pacific Economies: A Survey*, Routledge, London-New York, 1997 p. 8.
7. See Yergin, D., Stanislaw, J. *The Commanding Heights: The Battle Between Government and the Marketplace That Is Remaking the Modern World*, Simon & Schuster, New York, 1998, p. 170.
8. See Mahathir bin Mohammad. *The Way Forward*, Weidenfeld & Nicolson, London, 1998, p. 19.
9. See Yergin, D., Stanislaw, J. *The Commanding Heights*, p. 169.
10. See Robinson, R., Goodman, D. S. G. (eds.) *The New Rich in Asia*, p. 207.
11. See Murray, G. *Vietnam: Dawn of a New Market*, St. Martin's Press, New York, 1997, p. 2.
12. See Boyett, J. H., Boyett, J. T. *Behind Workplace 2000: Essential Strategies for the New American Corporation*, New York, 1996, p. xv; Garten, J. E. *The Big Ten: The Big Emerging Markets and How They Will Change Our Lives*, Basic Books, New York, 1997, p. 45; Naisbitt, J. *Megatrends Asia: The Eight Asian Megatrends that are Changing the World*, Nicholas Brealey Publishing, London, 1996, p. 110.
13. See Phongpaichit, P., Baker, Ch. *Thailand's Boom and Bust*, Silkworm Books, Chaing Mai (Thailand), 1998, pp. 31-32; McLeod, R. H., Garnaut, R. *East Asia in Crisis: From Being a Miracle to Needing One?* Routledge, London-New York, 1998, pp. 56-58.
14. See Bello, W., Rosenfeld, S. *Dragons in Distress*, p. 24.
15. See Palat, R. A. (ed.) *Pacific-Asia and the Future of the World System*, Westport (Conn.), 1993, pp. 77-78.
16. See Phongpaichit, P., Baker, Ch. *Thailand's Boom and Bust*, pp. 284-285.
17. Porter, M. E. *The Competitive Advantage of Nations*, Macmillan, Houndmills-London, 1990, p. 64.
18. See Hiscock, G. *Asia's Wealth Club*, Nicholas Brealey Publishing, London, 1997, pp. 107, 161.
19. See McRae, H. *The World in 2020: Power, Culture and Prosperity: A Vision of the Future*, Harper Collins Publishers, London, 1995, pp. 7, 20.
20. See Robinson, R., Goodman, D. S. G. (eds.). *The New Rich in Asia*, Routledge, London-New York, 1996, pp. 84, 143, 187.
21. See Rowen, H. S. "The Political and Social Foundations of the Rise of East Asia: An Overview," in Rowen, H. S. (ed.). *Behind East Asian Growth: The Political and Social Foundations of Prosperity*, Routledge, London-New York, 1998, p. 29.
22. See Morrison, I. *The Second Curve: Managing the Velocity of Change*, Nicholas Brealey Publishing, London, 1996, pp. 122-123, 167.

23. See Robinson, R., Goodman, D. S. G. (eds.). *The New Rich in Asia*, pp. 205, 161, 47, 135, 183, 77, 17.

24. For details see Kosai, Y., Takeuchi, F. "Japan's Influence on the East Asian Econo-mies," in Rowen H. S. (ed.). *Behing East Asian Growth*, p. 312.

25. See *Entering the 21st Century: World Development Report 1999/2000*, Oxford University Press for the World Bank ,Washington (D.C.)-Oxford, 2000, p. 15.

26. See Krugman, P. "The Myth of Asia's Miracle," *Foreign Affairs*, No. 6, 1994, p. 70.

27. See Islam, I., Chowdhury, A. *Asia-Pacific Economies: A Survey*, p. 31.

28. See Maddison, A. "Growth Acceleration and Slowdown in Historical and Com-parative Perspective," in Myers, R. H. (ed.). *The Wealth of Nations in the Twentieth Century: The Policies and Institutional Determinants of Economic Development*, Hoover Institution Press, Stanford (Cal.), 1996, p. 35.

29. See Vogel, E. F. *The Four Little Dragons: The Spread of Industrialization in East Asia*, Harvard University Press, Cambridge (Mass.)-London, 1991, p. 104.

30. For details see Islam, I., Chowdhury, A. *Asia-Pacific Economies: A Survey*, pp. 58-60.

31. See Cohen, D. *The Wealth of the World and the Poverty of Nations*, Cambridge (Mass.)-London, 1998, p. 24.

32. Krugman, P. "The Myth of Asia's Miracle," *Foreign Affairs*, no. 6, 1994, p. 70; for details see Krugman, P. *Pop Internationalism*, MIT Press, Cambridge (Mass.)-London, 1996, pp. 175-176.

33. See Vogel, E. F. *The Four Little Dragons*, p. 21.

34. See Bello, W., Rosenfeld, S. *Dragons in Distress*, pp. 152-153, 155.

35. See Plender, J. *A Stake in the Future: The Stakeholding Solution*, Nicholas Brealey Publishing, London, 1997, p. 224.

36. Fieldhouse, D. K. *The West and the Third World: Trade, Colonialism, Depen-dence, and Development*, Blackwell Publishers, Oxford-Malden (Mass.), 1999, p. 227.

37. See Islam, I., Chowdhury, A. *Asia-Pacific Economies: A Survey*, p. 230.

38. See McLeod, R. H., Garnaut, R. *East Asia in Crisis: From Being a Miracle to Needing One?* p. 50.

39. See Yip, G. S. *Asian Advantage*, p. 225; for details see *Economist*, July 26, 1997, Survey "Indonesia," p. 13.

40. See *Economist*, February 7, 1998, p. 142.

41. See Islam, I., Chowdhury, A. *Asia-Pacific Economies: A Survey*, pp. 203-205, 230-232, 259-260; Yip, G. S. *Asian Advantage*, pp. 65, 225; Murray, G. *Vietnam: Dawn Of a New Market*, p. 41.

42. See Islam, I., Chowdhury, A. *Asia-Pacific Economies: A Survey*, p. 56.

43. See Henderson, C. *Asia Falling: Making Sense of the Asian Crisis and Its After-math*, Business Week Books /McGraw-Hill, New York, 1999, p. 21.

44. See Mobius, M. *Mobius on Emerging Markets*, Pitman Publishing, London, 1996, p. 182.

45. For details see *The World in 2020: Towards a New Global Age*, OECD Publica-tions, Paris, 1997, p. 39.

46. For details see Adams, N. A. *Worlds Apart: The North-South Divide and the International System*, Zed Books, Atlantic Highlands (N.J.)-London, 1997, pp. 155-156.

47. See Kuttner, R. *The End of Laissez-Faire: National Purpose and the Global Economy After the Cold War*, University of Pennsylvania Press, Philadelphia, 1991, pp. 178-179.

48. See Ohmae, K. *The End of the Nation-State: The Rise of Regional Economies*, Free Press, New York, 1995, pp. 48-49, 98-99.
49. See Goldstein, M. *The Asian Financial Crisis: Causes, Cures, and Systemic Implications*, Institute for International Economics, Washington (D.C.), 1998, p. 27.
50. See Thurow, L. *Head to Head: The Coming Economic Battle Among Japan, Europe, and America*, Warner Books, New York, 1993, p. 62.
51. See Reich, R. B. *Tales of a New America: The Anxious Liberal's Guide to the Future*, Vintage Books, New York, 1987, p. 56.
52. See Goldstein, M. *The Asian Financial Crisis*, p. 22.
53. See Henderson, C. *Asia Falling*, p. 54; Goldstein, M. *The Asian Financial Crisis*, p. 16.
54. See Moody, K. *Workers in a Lean World: Unions in the International Economy*, Verso, London-New York, 1997, p. 13.
55. See Sakaiya, T. *What is Japan? Contradictions and Transformations*, Kodansha International, New York-Tokyo, 1993, p. 8.
56. See *Economist*, August 16, 1997, p. 47.
57. See McRae, H. *The World in 2020*, p. 77.
58. See *Economist*, August 16, 1997, p. 48.
59. See Snodgrass, D. R. "Education in Korea and Malaysia," in Rowen, H. S. (ed.) *Behind East Asian Growth: The Political and Social Foundations of Prosperity*, p. 176.
60. See Reich, R. B. *The Work of Nations: Preparing Ourselves to 21st Century Capitalism*, Vintage Books, New York, 1992, pp. 205-206.
61. See Katz, R. *Japan: The System That Soured: The Rise and Fall of Japanese Economic Miracle*, An East Gate Book, Armonk (N.Y.)-London, 1998, p. 135.
62. See Morrison, I. *The Second Curve*, pp. 17, 16.
63. Quated from: Koch, R. *The Third Revolution: Creating Unprecedented Wealth and Happiness for Everyone in the New Millennium*, Capstone, Oxford, 1998, p. 161.
64. See Pempel, T. J. "The Developmental Regime in a Changing World Economy," in Woo-Cumings, M. (ed.) *The Developmental State*, Cornell University Press, Ithaca (N.Y.)-London, 1999, pp. 144-145.
65. For details see Rosecrance, R. *The Rise of the Virtual State: Wealth and Power in the Coming Century*, Basic Books, New York, 1999, pp. 43-44.
66. Quated from: Edwards, M. *Future Positive: International Co-operation in the 21st Century*, Earthscan Publications Ltd., London, 1999, p. 70.
67. For details see Amsden, A. H. *Asia's Next Giant: South Korea and Late Industrialization*, Oxford University Press, New York-Oxford, 1989, p. 8.
68. See Kuttner, R. *The Economic Illusion: False Choices Between Prosperity and Social Justice*, University of Pennsylvania Press, Philadelphia, 1991, pp. 118-119.
69. See Yip, G. S. *Asian Advantage*, p. 241.
70. See Bello, W., Rosenfeld, S. *Dragons in Distress*, pp. 66, 242.
71. See Ohmae, K. *The End of the Nation-State*, pp. 48-49, 98-99.
72. See Mayer, M. "Suharto Family Values," *Newsweek*, May 18, 1998, p. 41.
73. For details see Gilpin, R., with Gilpin, J. M. *The Challenge of Global Capitalism: The World Economy in the 21st Century*, Princeton University Press, Princeton (N.J.), 2000, pp. 144-145.
74. See Rosecrance, R. *The Rise of the Virtual State*, p. 196.
75. See Schwartz, P., Leyden, P., Hyatt, J. *The Long Boom: A Vision for the Coming Age of Prosperity*, Perseus Books, Reading (Mass.), 1999, pp. 50-51.
76. Amoroso, B. *On Globalization: Capitalism in the 21st Century*, Macmillan, Houndmills-London, 1998, p. 52.

77. See Hardt, M., Negri, A. *Empire*, Harvard University Press, Cambridge (Mass.)-London, 2000, p. 283.
78. See Hamlin, M. A. *Asia's Best: The Myth and Reality of Asia's Most Successful Companies*, Prentice Hall/Simon & Schuster (Asia) Pte Ltd., Singapore-New York, 1998, p. 17.

4

The Japanese Economic Miracle: A Manifest Success or a Strategic Setback?

As one reviews the record of individual countries which have opted for the "catching up" development strategy, one cannot but admit that Japan's economic exploits are the most impressive ones. Having launched a sweeping reconstruction of its national economy in the late 1940s, under US military occupation, in the course of some three decades Japan developed into one of the world's leading industrialized nations thus setting the second precedent in history (after the USSR) of the economic superpower status being achieved through accelerated modernization. The third precedent (or the first one, to be exact) had been created by the United States in the evolutionary way.

Japan has gone the way of a model industrial country; devoid of natural resources and bled white by the war, it attained the pre-war level of production less than eight years after the last shot of that war had been fired, and maintained the average annual GNP growth rate at 9.4 percent and industrial production growth rate, at 13.1 percent for twenty years, from 1951 to 1972. Over the same period, productivity in Japan's industrial sector was rising at a rate of 9.7 percent, and wages, 10.2 percent a year.[1] The Japanese model of economic development stood an acid test in the oil crisis years of 1973-1974 when its balance of trade shrank from a favorable $7 billion in 1972 to the $5 billion deficit in 1974, entered the period of what seemed to be an unrestrained expansion as early as in the second half of the 1970s,[2] and by the mid-1980s the Japanese economy was universally recognized as the world's most promising one and boasted, by right, the world's top competitiveness index.

The proponents of the multipole world theory took heart from Japan's successes then and announced that Western cultural values were on the wane. Deliberately turning a blind eye on certain facts which did not quite fit into their conception, they regarded the triumphant advance of the Land of the Rising Sun as an evidence of the superiority of Confucian ideology and values over Protestant ethics.[3] Many researchers put Japan up as a striking example of making the most of human capital[4] amid a shortage of material and natural resources although it would make much more sense to presume that in a society which traditionally draws no line of distinction between *Gesellschaft* and *Gemeinschaft*[5] reliance on the human factor is impossible by definition. Be that as it may, most Western analysts tended to admit the uniqueness of Japan's record of economic progress and allowed for Japan getting the better of the United States economically. Such views persisted until the late 1980s when S. Huntington voiced his first misgivings about the self-sufficiency of the Japanese development model.[6] Even in 1991, I. Wallerstein wrote that the late-20th-century confrontation between Japan and the United States was a replica of the confrontation between the United States and Great Britain in the late 19th century;[7] the subsequent developments showed that a worse mistake could hardly have been committed then.

Why the Japanese model succeeded in the 1960s and1970s

Reforms of the Japanese economy were initiated in a situation where the country, like any other "catching up" nation, was at a low level of economic development: its per capita GNP did not exceed $3,500 which equals India's figure of the early 1990s. Within the space of fifteen years, by the time of the first "oil shock", the figure quadrupled to amount to $13,500[8] which remains unattainable for most Asian countries to this day. As a result, Japan became the world's second biggest industrial power, and the United States first found itself buying ever more from that country than it sold to it.[9]

The causes of such an impressive breakthrough lie in an efficient use of the mobilizing development system for the purpose of accelerated industrialization. On the one hand, measures were taken to buttress national producers. The government subsidized research projects, extended low-interest loans to corporations, helped maintain a high savings ratio and conducted an active protectionist policy.

In the end, all that materialized in financial-industrial syndicates the inefficiency of which was made up for by their size and by the scale of their government backing. On the other hand, the overall economic situation in the country was most favorable in the post-war decades. What with high production outlays in the United States and Europe, low prices of natural resources and relatively inexpensive technologies, Japan which had rather skilled and cheap enough manpower and which adhered to public effort mobilization traditions of long standing, had broad prospects ahead of it. It is noteworthy, however, that the main impulse to the economic breakthrough in Japan contained, in embryo, the inner contradictions of the "catching up" development strategy we have discussed in the previous chapter.

The first mobilization factor was an extremely high level of investments the share of which in the GNP never went below 35 percent. Their sources were quite conventional. By freezing wages and stimulating industrialists, the government maintained private investments, throughout the period of 1955-1970, at a level of 10 percent of the GNP while over the same period corporate investments grew from 7 to over 20 percent of the GNP. That resulted in high growth rates from which it could be inferred, by extrapolation, that Japan would surpass the United States in the per capita GNP index in 1985 and in the overall volume of industrial production, in 1998.[10] Such a policy, however, was fraught with a serious danger: artificial investment pumping resulted in production efficiency no longer being taken into account, and the yield on the capital invested which amounted to 34 percent in 1955, went down to 28 percent in1960, 18 percent in 1970, and 8 percent in 1980.[11] Whereas in 1950-1955, investment rate constituted 10.8 percent and the average annual GNP growth rate, 10.9 percent, in 1960-1965 the former index jumped to 18.5 percent and the latter one fell to 9.7 percent; in 1970-1975, investment rate decreased only slightly (to 17.8 percent) while growth rate fell almost by half (to 5.1 percent a year).[12]

Characteristically, the decline in efficiency only went to push investments further up, as was the case in the USSR over the same period. The growth was stimulated by restrictions imposed on the working men's incomes in three ways, at least. First, the share of wages proper in Japan's GNP, which is an important indicator of an economy's social orientation, remained a steady 15-17 percentage points short of the US figure (40 percent against 58 percent in the 1960s, and 52 percent against 64-67 percent in the 1970s[13]). Second, the average Japanese put in longer hours than his American and European counterparts did (in the 1980s, a Japanese worked 2,044 hours a day, i.e. 10 percent longer than an American, 20 percent longer than a Briton or a Frenchman and more than 30 percent longer than a German[14]). Third, corporations cashed in on protectionist measures, offering their products in the domestic market at inflated prices (at the end of the 1980s, US domestic electronic equipment cost 40 percent, and cars, almost 70 percent (!) less than Japanese makes[15]). The use of such actually extensive methods resulted in labor efficiency in Japan's heavy and electronic industries freezing at 65 percent the US level at the end of the 1980s following its steep rise in the 1960s and the 1970s (the relevant figures for the food industry and agriculture being 35 and 18 percent, respectively[16]). Therefore, capitalizing on individual companies' monopoly status became another source of building up investments. In 1950, the government introduced the practice of granting big corporations exclusive rights to purchase new technologies abroad. In 1951, the Toyo Rayon company received an exclusive right to purchase a nylon production technology (the next company to acquire this right had to wait its turn for three years); in 1958-1962, the license to produce polyethylene was granted to the Sumitomo, Mitsubishi and Mitsui companies (other companies received the license at the end of the 1960s). Foreign currency was available to the licensees from the Bank of Japan at a special exchange rate which meant a latent subsiding of investments in new technologies. That led to technologies in the 1950s accounting for 28 percent of the overall import volume, and for an unheard of 9 percent of the total investment.[17] As a result, a system of *keiretsu* monopolies—giant conglomerates which became centers of attraction for new investments through the banks and financial institutions under their control—emerged in the country. As we see, Japanese companies owed their fast growth to the accumulation of all funds—their own, borrowed and even public— meant for a massive investment in the sectors where they were initially guaranteed a monopoly status by the government.

The state's direct participation in the development and financing of strategic sectors was *the second factor in stimulating the country's impetuous industrial growth.* This strategy was masterminded by the

Japanese Ministry of International Trade and Industry (MITI) which actually subordinated industrial companies to itself and managed them efficiently enough to make Soviet Gosplan's performance look puny by comparison. The central government promoted the formation of companies capable of initiating new branches of the industry; Japan's other ministries were patterned after the MITI , and the relationships between the Ministry of Finance, on the one hand, and the Bank of Japan, commercial banks and financial companies, on the other, were suspiciously reminiscent of the relationships between the MITI and industrial giants.[18] In the 1950s, the government began to subsidize Japanese companies which preferred to purchase Japanese-made equipment, the amount of the subsidies constituting up to a half of the purchased equipment's worth. The authorities actively credited large companies, with centralized credits provided along the lines of the Japanese Bank for Development or the Bank of Japan accounting for up to a half of their borrowings until the mid-1970s. In most cases credits were granted at an interest rate 3 to 5 percentage points lower than the interbank average of the day.[19]

Such a policy was aimed chiefly at winning external markets because the influx of capital could be steadied only given a favorable balance of foreign trade. Being in possession of cheap production resources and having an access to large government credits, Japanese companies actively penetrated into other countries' markets using downright dumping. In the 1970s and 1980s, for example, steel prices in Japan were 30 percent higher than those charged in the world market, while polyethylene and other chemical industry products were overpriced 1.5 times and over.[20] The state resorted to protectionist measures to help its companies out of the predicament. Whereas in the United States only 6.6 percent of the GNP come from the industries now regarded as government-controlled, in Japan this index is 16.8 percent for the industry, 86 percent, for agriculture and 100 percent for the financial sphere, averaging 50.4 percent;[21] customs duties imposed on imports usually exceeded the latter's cost, and in case of imported American rice amounted to 800 percent[22]. It is small wonder, therefore, that government subsidies accounted for three-fourths of Japanese farmers' incomes.[23] As a result, Japan entered the 1990s with raw materials and capital goods prices (as estimated by the MITI) 30 percent higher than those in the United States; 19 percent higher than in Germany, and 46 percent higher than in South Korea. As to the prices of consumer goods and services, they were 51 percent higher in Japan than in the USA, 96 percent higher than in Germany, and 475 percent (!) higher than in South Korea.[24] The findings of a research conducted by the MITI in October 1989, revealed that 60 percent of the staple commodities were offered for sale in Japan at prices higher than those charged in the United States and Europe, and that 90 percent of imports were cheaper in their countries of origin than Japanese consumers had to pay for them.[25] Such protectionist policy cost the Japanese $110 billion a year—an amount constituting almost 4 percent of the country's GNP.[26]

The third constituent of the Japanese economy's swift progress was the booming of its export trade in commodities and capital alike. Whereas in 1950 Japan produced no more than 32,000 cars a year— as many as American automobile plants did in a day and a half (!)— by 1960 the output grew to 482,000 of which 39,000 were exported. In 1970, these indices already constituted 5.3 and 1.1 million cars a year. In 1974, Japan took over from the FRG as the world's leading car exporter, and in 1980, from the USA as the world's leading car manufacturer.[27] In the 1970s, export deliveries were responsible for 70 to 83 percent of the increment in the output of cars, seacraft and other engineering products.[28] Towards the early 1980s, the country had built up a gross national product surpassing those of the UK and France combined and constituting close to 55 percent of the United States'.[29]

The Japanese overestimated the Western market's potential for absorbing their products, however. While exporting 2.3 million cars a year to the United States at the end of the 1980s, Japanese companies set up production plants in the United States proper with an output capacity of another 2.5 million cars although the American market demanded no more than 10 million cars a year.[30] Japan's motor industry clearly set its sights on conquering the American market which accounted for 75 percent of its overall export sales.[31] Characteristically, the dynamics of the US trade deficit with Japan symmetrically reflected that of Japan's own trade surplus (in 1970, deficit amounted to $1 billion, and surplus, to $2 billion; in 1977, these figures were $8 billion and $11 billion; in 1983, 19 and 21; in 1985, 46 and 49[32]). That ought to have served as an unmistakable alarm signal alerting Japan to its growing dependence on the openness of the American economy and on the yen's exchange rate to the dollar, and to the fact that its economic progress was, slowly but steadily, becoming a function of circumstances beyond the powerful MITI's control. The overemphasis on export became one of the causes of the decline that followed.

As they were pondering new business tactics, Japanese entrepreneurs decided for increasing the export of capital, which was their worst mistake. Capital outflow from the country impeded competition in the domestic market and, as a result, maintained unnatural price proportions which interfered with making correct investment decisions. Since investments in the banking sector, trade and real estate transactions returned the highest yields in Japan itself, businessmen of the Land of the Rising Sun launched an attack on the analogous sectors in the United States and Europe. In the 1980s alone, they gained control over 11 percent of all banking assets on the US territory,[33] while in Europe their investments in the industry were smaller than those in immovables and trade and constituted a half of the total investments made in insurance and in the banking sector.[34] By 1985, "three-quarters of Japanese investments abroad were made in secure assets which were passive sources of income"[35] and returned no large yields either in the United States, or in Europe. This fact is of extraordinary importance because it showed, for the first time, that *an industrial country is incapable of making profitable investments in post-industrial economies.* As a result, the Japanese became increasingly active in Asian countries encouraging the latter to follow in their footsteps. In 1971, American investments in Southeast Asia constituted 36.4 percent of the total direct foreign investment in the region as against Japan's 15.4 percent. A few years later, the ratio leveled out, and towards the late 1980s Japanese investments in Asia were 2.5 times those of the United States.[36] In that region, Japan's traditional tactics of dumping, government subsidies and direct aid to Asian countries found fertile grounds. Characteristically, the main capital flow of $47 billion was channeled into the export-oriented sectors of Asian countries in the period of 1986-1993[37] and thus added to the Japanese economy's dependence on Western markets rather than insured it against such dependence. As a result, Asian countries received, in the mid-1990s, up to 45 percent of Japan's commodities exports (standard accessories, mostly) and 47 percent of its technologies export. Japanese financial institutions owned 25-40 percent of those countries' and their leading companies' debt securities.[38] The aftermaths of such a development of events are common knowledge.

In the meantime, the Japanese economy had its worst headaches in the period starting with the 1989 crisis. The country had achieved indisputable economic successes by then. Although Western experts stressed that its progress was largely artificial and pointed out the qualitative differences between the economic systems of Western societies and Japan, the former being capitalist regulatory states and the latter, a capitalist development state,[39] there was no denying its impressive achievements. Japan had offered the United States formidable competition in the world commodities and capital markets (in 1991, for example, 353 out of 1,000 largest transnational corporations were American, and 345, Japanese;[40] the country had 24 of the world's leading banks as compared with the European Union's 17 and North America's 5 and owned 9 of the 10 biggest service companies[41]) and secured a growing surplus in trade with the United States and Asian countries. Towards the end of the 1980s, at the peak of its economic might, Japan was responsible for 20 percent of all the advanced countries' direct foreign capital investments, and 25 percent of their equity capital. Its banks provided 50 percent of all short-term credits, and its industrial companies supplied to the market 55 percent of the total worth of corporate bonds.[42] For the most part, however, these figures reflected only the external aspect of Japan's successes achieved along the lines of accelerated industrialization. Mobilization mechanisms of economic development were patently and actively at work until the mid-1980s, and the nation was yet to prove its ability to hold the lead amid free competition and economic openness. Practice has shown that the secondary nature of Japan's economic progress became an insurmountable obstacle in the way of attaining this objective.

On the Threshold of a Crisis

The Japanese economic model maintained high growth rates for a long time using extensive methods. While actively borrowing the latest technological advances from the United States and Europe, the nation actually developed no technologies of its own: the balance of information and patents import/export remained unfavorable for over forty years. As we have already noted above, Japan's

development program emphasized industrialization and did not provide for investments in education; employees' loyalty to their company and their superiors was valued highly. Suffice it to note that
even in the 1980s about 43 percent of the workers had not changed
employers for over a decade at a stretch.[43] Seeking to boost capital
investments in material assets rather than in the human advancement potential, Japanese corporations actively borrowed from banks
which were responsible for more than a quarter of the total increment in world credit resources at the end of the 1980s.[44]

Pressure on the real estate and stocks market in the second half of
the 1980s triggered a boom which, as the subsequent developments
showed, spelt an end to the Japanese economic miracle. Over the
period of 1980-1987, the Nikkei index skyrocketed almost five-fold
remaining practically immune to the shattering knocks the stock
exchanges had taken in the United States and other Western countries late in 1987. As the year 1989 was drawing to a close, the aggregate estimated worth of the shares listed at the Tokyo Stock Exchange amounted to $5.2 trillion while the corresponding aggregate
index for all the three New York stock exchanges constituted $4.3
trillion, and for the London Stock Exchange, a mere $1.3 trillion.[45]
The real estate and land price rise was more impressive still: in 1990,
the overall worth of land was estimated by Japanese experts at almost ¥2,400 trillion, which is 5.6 times the worth of the gross national product,[46] while banks loans granted by way of funding development projects and real estate acquisitions grew at double the
rate of crediting for the economy as a whole over the second half of
the 1980s.[47] To illustrate the scale of these processes suffice it to
note that in those years the territory of Japan which constitutes about
three percent of the earth's surface cost more than the rest of the dry
land while the worth of the Tokyo real estate alone exceeded the
total worth of all the facilities ever built within the limits of the United
States.[48] Just to give you a notion of the price situation then: in 1990,
a $100 bill could not buy a land plot its size in central Tokyo.[49] The
government sought to make the most of the boom: in the early 1990s,
44 out of 47 prefectures received budgetary subsidies, with only
three prefectures, all of them within the bounds of Greater Tokyo,
being donors of funds.[50]

The irrationality of the situation became obvious amid a steady
decline in economic growth rates. In 1990, they still remained at the

level of about 5 percent, going down to 4 percent in 1991; 1 percent in 1992; and almost to zero in 1993.[51] As share and land prices could no longer be maintained by speculative expectations, the stock exchange index which had reached its all-time high of 38,915 points in 1989, plummeted all the way to about 20,000 by the end of 1990 and hit the local lowest of 15,000 in 1992;[52] nevertheless many experts considered it substantially overrated. Through the real estate prices kept growing *vis inertiae* till the winter of 1990/1991, they likewise went down more than by half by the winter of 1994/1995.[53] As a result, losses due to the depreciation of Japanese industrial companies' shares listed at the Tokyo Exchange ran into an unprecedented $2.6 trillion over the period of 1990-1994 alone when Japan's foreign currency reserves did not exceed $100 billion and when losses due to land and real estate prices fall topped $5,6 trillion.[54]

Naturally, industrial companies could no longer manipulate their financial resources as freely as they used to; many of the banks which had issued credits against real estate, land or securities encountered serious difficulties; rank-and-file citizens who had bought homes on an installment plan had to pay for them on the basis of the previous price and either to get rid of it, or to spend practically all of their incomes on interest payments.[55] At the same time, tax revenues shrank sharply because prior to the crisis the companies had paid taxes, *inter alia*, on their proceeds from the re-sales of securities, shares or land (in 1988, production as such accounted for only 40 percent of all budget revenues[56]). Despite the crisis, the Japanese government did not give up its policy of interfering in economic affairs; running up the state debt became, under the circumstances, the only means of securing new financial injections.

Government borrowing practice has a long history in Japan. In the early 1970s, at the first stage of massive industrialization, the state debt did not exceed ¥100 billion which constituted less than 10 percent of the GNP. Within a decade, however, it grew more than ten-fold to amount to almost 40 percent of the GNP;[57] the subsequent process of running up external and internal debts does not lend itself to explanation from the standpoint of common sense. The thing is that the Bank of Japan found itself to be the industrialized world's only central bank devoid of financial policy-making freedom and fully subordinate to the government.[58] Right after the crisis had broken out, the government demanded that the Bank of Japan should provide extra loans and guarantees necessary for a full-scale crediting of the real sector of the economy along the lines of the Ministry of International Trade and Industry. In 1992, when the economy plainly entered the phase of stagnation, the state debt amounted to 90 percent of the GNP,[59] and by early 1999 it amounted to 140 percent of the GNP.[60] It should be borne in mind that all these figures just indicate rather than reflect the real state of affairs. In the selfsame year of 1992, government guarantees on the debts of the railroads privatized in 1990 amounted to $270 billion, and agricultural subsidies, to almost $700 billion. Bank credits extended to industrial companies in 1992, added up to 262 percent of the GNP[61] and did not diminish at all since then. All that was made possible by the Bank of Japan not being really independent from the state, and the largest commercial banks, from the corporate networks they belonged to.

The Bank of Japan acted as a pocket bank of the Ministry of Finance: towards the mid-1990s the share of government bonds in its total assets approached an unheard-of 80 percent (!)[62]. Aware of high risks involved in raising commercial loans, the banks also showed an ever greater interest in government securities with the result that their rates of return, which amounted to 8 percent per annum in 1990, were now close to the zero mark. Such a state of affairs changed nothing, however, because having got a chance to borrow cheap, the government started using it on an ever larger scale and pumped more and more money into the real sector.

In an attempt to prevent a crisis, the government took a series of measures absolutely impermissible in a democratic market-oriented state. After the stock exchange index had dropped below the psychologically important 16,000-point mark in November 1992, the MITI functionaries "recommended" the managers of the leading insurance companies to float their spare cash in the stock market. The move increased the volume of business 80 percent and pushed the index 785 points up within one trading session. Later this category of investors became the most active market operator increasing its capital investments 18 percent a year, on the average, throughout the period of 1992-1995[63]. The government took vigorous action to stimulate export, to keep the favorable balance of trade with the United States at a high level, bore enormous unproductive expenses to finance public works, and established an extremely low general interest rate level which facilitated the crediting of enterprises. It looked as if those measures worked. The GNP growth rates resumed their upward climb, reaching 3.9 percent in 1996[64] (as against the 1990-1995 period's average of a mere 1.3 percent[65]), corporate profits rose (although over 60 percent of the rise came from credit rate reduction[66]), and the domestic market livened up somewhat.

All these temporary achievements of 1995-1996 were due, as a matter of fact, to the same government policy the preceding industrialization had been part of, the only difference being that the state's potentialities were actually exhausted this time. Over the previous decades it had failed to lay the groundwork for a system capable of making self-sustainable progress. Japan had achieved all its successes along the lines of Industrialization Without Enlightenment,[67] and this route, selected by the Land of the Rising Sun, differed entirely from the one old Europe had embarked upon. Under the circumstances, the state could only carry on its attempts to buttress the economy which continued to depend on still effective investments in other industrial Southeast Asian countries for the supply of extra resources. Those attempts, though, failed to assure a successful development.

Sic transit gloria mundi

The 1990s saw the end of the Japanese economic miracle. In 1991, Japan slid down from the top of the world's most competitive nations list to the fifth line in 1995, ninth in 1997, and 18th in 1998, falling behind all the European industrialized countries, Taiwan, Australia and New Zealand.[68] By 1995, Japan's proud domination in the world automobile market became a thing of the past, with the USA resuming the lead.[69] As distinct from the 1980s when the Americans went all out to draw foreign investments in their industry's retooling programs, they now opted for a cheap dollar policy sending the yen exchange rate up to a record-high 79 yen per dollar in 1995. As a result, Japan lost $50 billion in the first half of 1995 alone.[70] At the same time, American companies made their presence in the Japanese market more conspicuous by increasing their export volume 2.5 times—from $27 billion to $65 billion—over the 1986-1996 period.[71]

The Japanese government responded to the challenge by trying, for the first time, to stimulate demand rather than production which was supposed to harmonize the reproduction cycle in some degree. The paradox of this type of development which T. Sakayia aptly described not as *advanced* but as *ultimate* industrialism[72] consisted in that the efforts to stimulate consumer spending were of no avail because a substantial proportion of the "injected" funds was re-invested or put in lucrative projects abroad. Over the period of 1992-1997, annual domestic consumer spending figure remained practically unchanged (from ¥349,600 to ¥357,600 per family). The allocation in 1998, at the height of the Asian crisis, of an extra $123 billion for the development of the consumer market suppressed consumer spending (instead of boosting it) to ¥338,000 per family a year[73] (the lowest since the mid-1980s). Despite the Japanese government's titanic efforts, average household incomes did not increase since 1991, which gives observers reason to presume that consumer spending will stay at the 1996 level until the year 2005, at the earliest, while in the United States the corresponding index will grow no less than by a third over the same period.[74] In the past decade, the Japanese government has carried out the most sweeping demand-stimulating program in economic history which cost almost $1.2 trillion from August 1992 to April 2000; nevertheless, its economic growth proceeded at a rate of 1.7 percent a year.[75]

These phenomena are due mostly to growing unemployment (in the industry over 630,000 jobs were killed over the same years[76]) which reduced consumer spending and detracted from domestic savings. In turn, the rise in unemployment is connected with production cuts and small companies' bankruptcies the number of which ran into almost 110,000 in 1991-1997. No matter how hard the government tried to reduce unemployment, the latter grew at the rate of 10 percent a year in the period of 1992-1998;[77] right after the Asian crisis had struck, its level rose as high as the United States'[78] and surpassed it in November 1998 when 4.4 percent of Japan's able-bodied population found themselves out of work.[79] In 1999, the adverse trends persisted; by the spring of 2000, the army of the jobless swelled to 3.29 million or 4.9 percent of the able-bodied population.[80]

In the early 1990s, the Japanese government still had a chance of riding out the crisis through making its economy more open to the outside world and adopting Western values. Instead, the emphasis was placed on stepping up Japan's influence on the region the ruling regimes of which professed the "catching up" development strategy and reproduced, with slight modifications, Japan's record of the 1970s and 1980s.

The shift from the American market to the Asian one was accomplished by the Japanese with their characteristic efficiency and push. Whereas at the end of the 1980s Japanese investment funds had converted up to 60 percent of their assets into American securities, by 1994 the figure diminished to a fifth (13 percent); against this background, investments in the shares and securities issued by the Asian "tigers" grew from 18 to 75 percent.[81] In 1991, Japan exported a $96 billion worth of its products and services to Southeast Asia, or more than it did to the United States, with the volume of its export to that region increasing at the rate of 25 percent a year.[82] From 1990 to 1996, the number of Japanese banks having offices in Asian countries grew from 83 to 161, and the volume of credits channeled into those countries' economies reached $119 billion, or 43 percent of the Japanese banking system's aggregate capital[83] exceeding by almost 20 percent the credits extended to that region by the US, UK and German banks taken together.[84] Over the same period, Japanese exports to Southeast Asia were worth $170 billion a year, most of them going by early 1997 to the five countries worst hit by the financial crisis—Thailand, Indonesia, Malaysia, South Korea and the Philippines.[85]

Direct capital investments—made mostly by small- and medium-size companies seeking to raise their operating profits by any means—were growing at a still more turbulent rate; in 1990-1994, the share of such companies in direct foreign investments in Asian countries grew from 40 to 81.3 percent. By 1995, more than a half of all the companies set up in Asia with Japanese participation specialized in industrial production (the corresponding indices for the United States and the European Union were 31.6 and 20.7 percent).[86] Big corporations pursued the same policy. By 1996, the Mitsubishi concern made a $25 billion profit on export to Asia; a quarter of the Sony company's workforce was engaged in that sphere; in Thailand, Malaysia and Indonesia, Japanese companies provided employment for up to 7 percent of those countries' able-bodied population. As ever, banks and industrial companies sought to make speculative profit in the most "overheated" sectors of the market: notwithstanding the clearly inflated real estate prices in Southeast Asia, in 1996 Japanese investors spent more than $5.7 billion out of the $10-billion total investment in those countries on acquiring or building industrial and office blocks in Thailand, Malaysia, Indonesia and the Philippines.[87] All these facts and statistics go to show that no lessons have been learned from the development of the situation in Japan itself.

There being actually no links with the outside world in the form of foreign investments in the Japanese industry was an important factor in the deterioration of the economic situation in the country in the mid-1990s. The country's closeness was, in this particular case, an extremely negative factor because it interfered with obtaining objective information about changes taking place in the world markets and slowed down the responses to them by Japan's own producers. Failure by Japan to adopt new management methods common in the West in the early 1990s also played a role in that. In 1986, foreigners owned only one percent of Japanese companies' assets, and Western corporations' branches provided jobs for just 0.4 percent of the Japanese working people; the corresponding figures for the United States constituted 9 and 4 percent at the time.[88] In the early 1990s, Western investors owned only 14 percent of Japan's Canon company which had the largest share of foreign capital invested in it, and Sony was the only Japanese corporation to have foreigners on its Board of Directors.[89] Towards the end of 1992, Japanese investments abroad amounted to $246 billion while foreign investors put a mere $15.5 billion in the Japanese economy.[90] In 1995, there were $135 of foreign investments per capita in Japan as against $1,700 per each American, $2,200 per Frenchman and $3,400 per one resident of the United Kingdom[91].

In August 1997, a financial crisis broke out in Asia. Before we dwell on it in detail, it is worth noting that it was a carbon copy of the Japanese crisis of 1989-1993 which had dealt a shattering blow to the Japanese economy. In the second half of 1997 alone, Japanese banks' shares lost up to 40 percent of their pre-crisis value.[92] The stock exchange index dropped below 13,000 points with the result that investors lost at least $260 billion.[93] Two of Japan's twenty leading financial institutions—the Hokkaido Takushoku Bank and Yamaichi Securities—went bankrupt within months of the outbreak of the crisis in Asian countries.[94] Serious damage was done to the *keiretsu* giants: in 1997-1998 the two nerve centers of the Mitsubishi holding—financial (the Bank of Tokyo-Mitsubishi) and production

(Mitsubishi Motors)—sustained losses estimated at $6.7 billion and $900 million, respectively.[95] Preventing a financial collapse of the world's second-biggest economy required an all-out effort; most Japanese banks turned out to be actually insolvent.

Japan's financial problems which have come to light over the past few years can be traced back to the early 1990s. *The first* blow was dealt to the country's banking system by the stock market crash and by a sharp drop in land and real estate prices. It was partly cushioned by the attraction of extra funds to the stock market and also by sweeping public spending programs: in the period of 1991-1995 alone, the government allocated no less than $500 billion for the financing of the programs it had adopted. *The second* blow took place in 1995 following a rise of the yen against the US dollar which sent corporate profits and banks' revenues far down. It was then that the threat of a collapse first loomed up before the Japanese financial system and became imminent after the Japanese banks' bad debts exceeded, at the end of 1995, the total volume of their equity capital by more than 20 percent.[96] At that time the government rescued the banking system again by adopting a law whereby the deposits in all financial companies and banks were guaranteed by the state until March 31, 2001[97] which made it possible to slash deposit rates to a fantastic 0.34 percent per annum;[98] maximum taxation rates were also reduced to give large companies an extra chance to reimburse their bank debts. Finally, the government contributed some of its borrowed funds towards the readjustment of the banking system.[99] *The third* blow dealt by the Asian financial crisis was the most destructive of all owing largely to disregard for financial problems, dubious debt accrual in 1994-1998 and an ever larger scale of low-yield investment.

Such a state of affairs came also from an artificial suppression of interest rates which multiplied money mass and created an illusion that Japanese investors had unlimited resources. In 1995, Japan accounted for up to 60 percent of the world's net capital export using money which its bankers borrowed at practically zero interest rate. Considering the yen's depreciation from ¥ 79 per US dollar in 1995[100] to ¥ 147 per US dollar in October 1998, it is to be presumed that the yield of capital investment in the US or EU economy in yens converted into dollars first at the beginning and then at the end of the period could not, by definition, fall under 30 percent per annum.

In Japan proper, however, investors' incomes remained scanty. Whereas over the period of 1985-1993 investments in an average American pension fund returned a profit of 16.5 percent per annum, those in a Japanese fund brought only 5.5 percent.[101] This issue has always been and remains a social rather than a financial one because in the Land of the Rising Sun (where only 25 gainfully employed persons will be left per each 10 pensioners[102] by as early as the year 2010) the problem of public provision for the economic security and social welfare of the aging population is more acute than elsewhere across the world. Investments in the so-called postal savings deposits is a crying example of the state using depositors' spare funds because as of the early months of the year 2000 it would take 300 (!) years to double the amount deposited.[103] In the 1990s, however, Japanese investors, accustomed to domestic financial products, actually had no choice: in 1989 the Nikkei index reached 39,000 points while the Dow Jones index did not exceed 2,500; a decade later, the former fell 70 percent, and the latter rose almost 300 percent.[104] In case of financial companies, the situation was more dramatic still: from early 1987 to 1996 the worth of the mutual funds' assets increased 480 percent in the United States, 260 percent in Great Britain and a mere 13 percent (!) in Japan.[105]

Even in a situation like that, investment activities went beyond all reasonable limits. At the end of February 1997, when the symptoms of the Asian crisis were already very much in evidence, the total amount of the loans granted by Japanese banks to business companies topped $4.5 trillion (!); in the meantime, the analogous index of the American banking system, with its investment structure much less exposed to risk and its capitalized value being 2.5 times that of Japan's, did not exceed $2.8 trillion.[106]

Estimates of the Japanese banks' dubious debts vary. Some observers believe them to run into $3 trillion.[107] This amount, however, includes debts which no one expects to be ever repaid. At a more realistic estimate, Japanese banks' doubtful debts, which added up to ¥46 trillion in the autumn of 1995,[108] increased to ¥77-80 trillion by mid-1998 which is equivalent to $550-570 billion (some experts put the minimum amount for that period at $600 billion[109]). Now that the yen's exchange rate is ¥103-110 to the US dollar, the United States equivalent for these liabilities may range from $800 billion to $1 trillion[110] which constitutes about one-fifth of the GNP and over 60 percent of the budget revenues. Attempts at making up for this amount from government sources will hardly be successful because the practice of borrowing from the public has been stretched to the limit, and interest rates approaching the zero mark cannot be pushed any further down.

Today the Japanese economy is within a closed circle the elements of which are the diminishing of the gross national product, stagnant domestic consumption and, against this background, the lowering of interest rates which causes, on the one hand, a decline in production efficiency and, on the other, a steady growth of national debt. A simultaneous effect of all these negative factors on the national economy leads certain observers to the conclusion that the current recession "is the second greatest upheaval in the history of capitalism after the NY Stock Market Crash of 1929",[111] and it is easier to agree with this view than to find convincing arguments against it.

Economic "Baggage" for the New Generation

The last years of the outgoing century have, indeed, become the least favorable ones for the Japanese economy in the post-war epoch. It slowed down markedly in the early months of 1997, and the IMF revised its GNP growth rate projection, lowering it from 2.7 to 2.2 percent a year.[112] The Japanese government had nothing to show for its pains to stimulate its growth: in April and May the GNP decreased by a value corresponding to an 11.2-percent-a-year decline rate.[113] The second quarter of 1997 turned out to be the hardest since the time of the first oil shock. The GNP decreased 2.9 percent compared to the corresponding period of 1996; consumption fell 5.7 percent short of the previous quarter's level; industrial investments shrank 1.5 percent; and investments in real estate, 11.5 percent.[114] Although the situation stabilized, in a degree, by the summer of 1997, a new IMF projection, made public in August, put the Japanese economy's growth rate at 1.2 percent. A crisis which broke out in September-November dashed all hopes to the ground: in 1997 the country's GNP first decreased 1.4 percent and in 1998, another 2.3 percent. Over the past three years, starting with the second quarter of 1997, Japan's GNP closed only three quarters on the increase, diminishing over the other nine. In the second half of 1998, the GNP's quarterly reduction rate amounted to three percent, something unprecedented in the history of Japan's industrialization. As a result, its gross national product was 5.25 percent down from the maximum attained in the spring of 1997.[115] At the beginning of 2000 when the results of the GNP's reduction over the fourth quarter of 1999 were summed up, experts pointed out that gross national product continued to diminish at a rate of 5.5 percent, a year and consumer spending, 6.3 percent.[116] At alternative estimates made by the Japanese Economic Research Center, the country's GNP diminished at a rate equivalent to 7 percent a year at the end of 1999. The rest of the indices were also lamentable; meriting special attention is the decline in the demand for Japanese manufactured products abroad as a result of which Japan's export grew by a mere 1.5 percent in 1999, and its import, 6.8 percent.[117] At the beginning of 2000, the number of bankruptcies constituted 50 percent that of the corresponding period of 1999, and the country's financial instability compelled rating agencies to consider a reduction of its credit rating (until a few years ago, Japan was a major net creditor itself[118]).

The Japanese government is trying to emerge from the deepening economic crisis through more active crediting or even direct financing of industrial production. Throughout the period of 1990-1995, the Bank of Japan reduced the official discount rate on nine occasions as a result of which it went down from 6 to 0.5 percent and remains at this level since September 1995. Regardless of the West's persistent admonitions to abandon what has long come to be known as the zero interest rate policy, the Bank of Japan doggedly refuses to revise the strategy it has selected because it realizes that such a move would deal the last shattering blow to the economy.[119] However, the specific nature of the current situation is such, experts say, that even if the Bank of Japan sticks to this policy it will not be able to make an extra injection of money into the economy for the simple reason that the latter no longer needs it.[120] In the country which concentrated, for decades, on expanding production rather than on stepping up its efficiency, the share of production facilities non-competitive by world standards has reached 87 percent and a further increase in their number may paralyze the economy.[121] In our opinion, the situation can be remedied by devaluating the yen, pursuing a laissez-faire policy towards massive bankruptcies and opening the economy to foreign investors; however, the country's government lacks the political will necessary for the realization of such measures.

An increase in budget financing will add, of course, to Japan's public debt. Today many experts are of the opinion that the Land of the Rising Sun which redistributes about 40 percent of its gross national product along the channels of the state budget can always increase this share to 50-55 percent, that is to the level set in most of the advanced European states. This opportunity is perfectly realistic although there exist at least two circumstances preventing its use.

First of all, a unique situation has arisen in the currency adjustment sphere. On the one hand, a decline in consumer spending calls for a price reduction which may bring either zero inflation, or, which is more frequently the case, a steady deflation blocking economic growth. On the other hand, state budget deficit (its magnitude being fantastic not only by Western but by the current Russian standards as well: in the fiscal year of 2000 the budget constitutes Y84.98 trillion or almost $800 billion and the deficit amounts to 38.4 percent (!)[122]) leads to more borrowings and to a growing demand for the yen which permits no reduction in its exchange rate to world currencies (over the period of March 1999 to March 2000 the yen rose from 148 to 103 to the dollar and is at the historical maximum level against the Euro). The high yen exchange rate has resulted in a reduction of export, a rise in import and more government borrowings made for the purpose of supporting national producers.

Secondly, the increase in the public debt poses threat No.1 to Japan's national economy today. Towards the end of 1999 Japan took over from the United States as the world's leading issuer of government bonds (a dubious achievement). As of January 1, 2000, the value of the US Treasury bonds which circulated on the market totaled $ 3.28 trillion (Y352 trillion) or 40 percent of the country's GNP, their number decreasing 2 percent over the year 1999. On the other hand, the value of the Japanese government's bonds which circulated on the market rose 14 percent over the same year, reaching Y359 trillion ($3.293 trillion) which constituted about 100 percent of the GNP.[123] Many experts estimate today that by the year 2030 Japan's debt may reach 315 percent of its gross national product.[124] Already now, the servicing of the public debt costs the nation an unprecedented 22 percent of the total budget expenses—more than defense, social security and public education do in the aggregate.[125] As a matter of fact, the public debt surpasses formal estimates by far because it does not include municipal liabilities and numerous government guarantees. For example, already in 1996-1997 Japanese prefectures' local budget deficit indices were identical to the national government's today, and Greater Tokyo, once the chief donor of the nation, had run up a debt of almost $60 billion (80 percent of the regional GNP) by mid-1997.[126] Such examples abound.

In 1999-2000, the Japanese government took certain measures towards economic recovery which largely worked: the stock market index increased more than 50 percent with respect to its minimum value, topping, in January 2000, the psychologically important 20,000-point mark (only to drop 20-25 percent in April). The Southeast Asian countries' economies livened up a bit, making the prospects of a financial crash more remote, and a confident advance of the American economy capable of absorbing a substantial mass of imports, was an important factor in keeping Japanese producers in business. The country is now in for the acid test of liberalization and opening its market to Western investors. The first quarter of 1999 saw 417 takeovers of Japanese companies by Western capital, and in the first quarter of 2000 the number grew to 439. In the former case, the top ten takeover advisors included only two Japanese financial companies, and in the latter case, none at all.[127] By the summer of 2000 direct foreign investments in the Japanese economy (made chiefly in the form of local companies' takeovers) more than doubled as against the 1997 figures.[128] Nissan and Mitsubishi, Japan's largest motor companies, lost Y684 billion and Y23 billion, respectively, in the fiscal year of 1999/2000[129]—and were easily taken over by the French Renault and the German DaimlerChrysler which paid $5.3 billion[130] and $2.2 billion for them, respectively, while a year before Daimler had paid nearly $60 billion for Chrysler. As a result, Japanese managers themselves are pessimistic about the outlook for the national economy. Characteristically, while more than 70 percent of them have their doubts about Japan being in a position to offer America serious competition in the coming century, only 35 percent of their American counterparts think likewise.

On the eve of the 21st century, Japan is in a deep systemic crisis. Having suffered defeat in economic confrontation with the post-industrial world, it is coming under severe pressure from the industrial economies of Asia and is compelled to vie with China for the role of the regional superpower. In this new confrontation, Japan should hardly be considered more likely to win because it has already lost the advantages which industrial countries with their cheap manpower and borrowed technologies have over the post-industrial world. At the same time, it has not become a post-industrial country depending on non-material values for its further progress. The coming decades will show whether it can meet a new challenge and stay among the world's economic leaders.

* * *

The record of Japan's post-war economic progress is an ideal example of the "catching up" mode of development. Japan succeeded in making the most of the advantages ensuing from the position of a highly-developed industrial nation surrounded with post-industrial states in their formative stage, in securing an enormous influx of financial resources, and an unprecedented import of the latest technologies. According to A. Sen, a 1998 Nobel Prize winner in economics, Japan is the "only communistically organized nation which has achieved remarkable results".[131] At the same time, Japan's is the record of a nation which has attained one of the world's largest per capita GNP size indices, a very high standard of living and industrial technology but has never become a sustainable post-industrial power. This goes to show that the changeover from the industrial to the post-industrial model of development is determined not only by quantitative indices but, first and foremost, by subjective factors and cannot be effected by injunction. This also means that in a country which has set itself the aim of attaining the highest possible standard of industrial development, the public mind cannot switch to a different way of thinking—any more than an individual accustomed to material wellbeing since early in life can adopt a well-balanced system of non-materialistic motivations.

For all its impressive results, the Japanese model has demonstrated (and could not but demonstrate) the limits of the "catching up" mode of development. *First*, like any "catching up" economy the Japanese economic model took shape in a situation where industrial growth was achieved through relative underconsumption; consequently, there was no connection between a steady improvement of welfare standards and changing value preferences absolutely essential for the rise of a system of motivations characteristic of post-industrial society. Japan became the world's leading industrial power at the end of the 1980s, i.e. in the period when the industrial type of society was becoming a thing of the past and had ceased to be the aim of social progress.

Second, the "catching up" type of development certainly calls for a vigorous pumping of investments in the economy, which can be achieved, as a rule, only by a centralized coordination of efforts. While stimulating industrial growth, the government is compelled to cast about for capital investment reserves exceeding by far the amounts which can be reinvested at the accumulation rate common in the developed world. Investment assets can be obtained not only by squeezing consumption but also by stimulating export sales, which presupposes the reorientation of the economy to external markets – and cutting down on outlays, specifically by exporting capital to less developed countries which are bound to become the most dangerous rivals in future. The result is that behind the facade of no external borrowings and unprecedented credit expansion, there lurks an inefficient and most vulnerable economic system.

Third, Japan's record has shown that today's world economy cannot be dominated by a country which is not a prolific source of technological innovations and which has no favorable balance of trade with the rest of the world in patents, inventions, technologies and producer goods. The Japanese industry rose under conditions where the access to technologies was rather easy and further facilitated by the policy pursued by the Ministry of International Trade and the Industry. This largely explains obvious disregard for problems of education and research and the prevalence in society of values and traditions discouraging any manifestations of individualism which alone can bring scientific, technological and economic achievements adequate to the requirements of the coming century. Therefore, the limitations of the "catching up" development model became clearly discernible in the 1990s when information and knowledge became the main source of added value in advanced economies. That led to a radical change in the overall pattern of production expenses. The export of research projects and technologies became much more profitable than trade in consumer goods and other mass produced commodities. Japanese producers who satisfied mass consumer demand so successfully in Asia and America turned out to be incapable of offering products of interest to the "intellectual class" which is becoming the main social group determining demand and supply on the 21st-century markets.

In conclusion of this chapter, I must remark that all the differences and shortcomings of the Japanese "catching up" development model were particularly manifest in the Asian countries which copied the model in the 1980s . The next chapter will be devoted to a brief review of their past and of the so called Asian financial crisis which struck in 1997.

Notes

1. See McKinnon, R. I., Ohno, K. *Dollar and Yen: Resolving Economic Conflict between the United States and Japan*, MIT Press, Cambridge (Mass.)-London, 1997, pp. 75-76.
2. See Callon, S. *Divided Sun: MITI and the Breakdown of Japanese High-Tech Industrial Policy, 1975-1993*, Stanford University Press, Stanford (Cal.), 1995, p. 149.
3. See Hobsbawm, E. *On History*, Weidenfeld & Nicolson, London, 1997, p. 218.
4. See Becker, G. S. *Human Capital: A Theoretical and Empirical Analysis with Special Reference to Education*, 3rd ed., Chicago-London, 1993, p. 24.
5. See Hampden-Turner, Ch., Trompenaars, F. *The Seven Cultures of Capitalism: Value Systems for Creating Wealth in the United States, Britain, Japan, Germany, France, Sweden and the Netherlands*, Juldy Piatkus Publishers, London, 1994, p. 159; for details see Ohmae, K. *The Borderless World: Power and Strategy in the Global Marketplace*, Harper Collins Publishers, New York, 1994, pp. 17-18.
6. See Huntington, S. P. *The Third Wave: Democratization in the Late Twentieth Century*, Norman (Ok.)-London, 1991, p. 310.
7. See Wallerstein, I. *Geopolitics and Geoculture: Essays on the Changing World-System*, Cambridge University Press-Maison des Sciences de l'Homme, Cambridge, 1991, p. 20.
8. See Katz, R. *Japan: The System That Soured: The Rise and Fall of Japanese Economic Miracle*, An East Gate Book, Armonk (N.Y.)-London, 1998, p. 55.
9. See LaFeber, W. *The Clash: US-Japanese Relations throughout History*, W.W. Norton & Company, New York-London, 1997, p. 327.
10. See Krugman, P. *Pop Internationalism*, MIT Press, Cambridge (Mass.)-London, 1998, p. 179.
11. See Katz, R. *Japan: The System That Soured*, p. 71.
12. See Kosai, Y. *The Era of High-Speed Growth: Notes on the Postwar Japanese Economic System*, University of Tokyo Press, Tokyo, 1986, p. 5.
13. See Spulber, N. *The American Economy: The Struggle for Supremacy in the 21st Century*, Cambridge University Press, Cambridge, 1997, p. 93.
14. See Sakaiya, T. *What is Japan? Contradictions and Transformations*, Kodansha International, New York-Tokyo, 1993, p. 30.
15. See Kuttner, R. *The End of Laissez-Faire: National Purpose and the Global Economy After the Cold War*, University of Pennsylvania Press, Philadelphia (Pa.), 1991, pp. 178-179.
16. See Abramowitz, M., David, P. A. "Convergence and Deferred Catch-up: Productivity Leadership and the Waning of American Exceptionalism," in Landau, R.,

Taylor, T., Wright, G. (eds.) *The Mosaic of Economic Growth*, Stanford University Press, Stanford (Cal.), 1996, p. 33.

17. See Katz, R. *Japan: The System That Soured*, pp. 90, 89.

18. See Vogel, E. *Japan As Number One: Lessons for America*, Harvard University Press, Cambridge (Mass.)-London, 1979, pp. 78-79.

19. See Katz, R. *Japan: The System That Soured*, p. 154.

20. See Katz, R. *Japan: The System That Soured*, pp. 185-187.

21. See Hartcher, P. *The Ministry: How Japan's Most Powerful Institution Endangers World Markets*, Harvard Business School Press, Boston (Mass.), 1998, p. 192.

22. See Ohmae, K. *The End of the Nation-State: The Rise of Regional Economies*, Free Press, New York, 1995, pp. 48-49, 98-99.

23. See Johnson, Ch. *Japan: Who Governs? The Rise of the Developmental State*, W.W. Norton & Company, New York-London, 1995, p. 75.

24. See Tilton, M. C. "Regulatory Reform and Market Opening in Japan," in Carlile, L. E., Tilton, M. C. (eds.) *Is Japan Really Changing Its Ways? Regulatory Reform and the Japanese Economy*, Brookings Institution Press, Washington (D.C.), 1998, pp. 163-164.

25. See Johnson, Ch. *Japan: Who Governs?,* pp. 72-73.

26. See Fields, G., Katahira, H., Wind, J., Cunther, R. E. *Leveraging Japan: Marketing to the New Asia*, Jossey-Bass Publishers, San Francisco (Cal.), 2000, p. 186.

27. See Landes, D. S. *The Wealth and Poverty of Nations: Why Some Are So Rich and Some So Poor*, Little, Brown and Company, London, 1998, p. 483.

28. See Katz, R. *Japan: The System That Soured*, pp. 143-144.

29. See Kennedy, P. *The Rise and Fall of the Great Powers: Economic Change and Military Conflict from 1500 to 2000*, Fontana Press (An Imprint of HarperCollins Publishers), London, 1988, pp. 539-540.

30. See Ohmae, K. *The Borderless World*, pp. 49-50.

31. See Ohmae, K. *The Borderless World*, p. VIII.

32. See Callon, S. *Divided Sun*, p. 165, table 27.

33. See Barnet, R. J., Cavanagh, J. *Global Dreams: Imperial Corporations and the New World Order*, Touchstone/Simon & Schuster, New York, 1994, p. 405.

34. See Mason, M. "Historical Perspectives of Japanese Direct Investment in Europe," in Mason, M., Encarnation, D. (eds.) *Does Ownership Matters? Japanese Multunationals in Europe*, Clarendon Press, Oxford, 1995, p. 31.

35. See Krugman, P. *The Age of Diminishing Expectations*, MIT Press, Cambridge (Mass.)-London, 1998, p. 142.

36. See LaFeber, W. *The Clash*, pp. 366-367.

37. See Phongpaichit, P., Baker, Ch. *Thailand's Boom and Bust*, Silkworm Books, Chiang Mai (Thailand), 1998, p. 3.

38. See Henderson, C. *Asia Falling: Making Sense of the Asian Crisis and Its Aftermath*, Business Week Books, New York, 1999, p. 172.

39. See Johnson, Ch. *MITI and the Japanese Miracle: The Growth of Industrial Policy 1925-1975*, Stanford University Press, Stanford (Cal.), 1982, p. 19.

40. See Sayer, A., Walker, R. *The New Social Economy: Reworking the Division of Labor*, Blackwell, Cambridge (Mass.)-Oxford (UK), 1994, p. 154.

41. See Thurow, L. *Head to Head: The Coming Economic Battle Among Japan, Europe, and America*, Warner Books, New York, 1993, p. 30.

42. See Pempel, T. J. *Regime Shift: Comparative Dynamics of the Japanese Political Economy*, Cornell University Press, Ithaca (N.Y.)-London, 1998, p. 147.

43. See Gray, J. *False Dawn: The Delusions of Global Capitalism*, Granta Books, London, 1998, p. 173.

44. See Davidson, J. D., Lord William Rees-Mogg. *The Great Reckoning: Protect Yourself in the Coming Depression*, Touchstone/Simon & Schuster, New York, 1993, p. 161.

45. See Luttwak, E. *Turbo-Capitalism: Winners and Losers in the Global Economy*, Weidenfeld & Nicolson, London, 1998, p. 117.

46. See Hartcher, P. *The Ministry*, pp. 69-70

47. See Cargill, T. F., Hutchison, M. M., Ito, T. *The Political Economy of Japanese Monetary Policy*, MIT Press, Cambridge (Mass.)-London, 1997, p. 109.

48. See Dent, Ch. M. *The European Economy: The Global Context*, Routledge, London-New York, 1997, p. 147.

49. See Hayes, D. *Japan's Big Bang: The Deregulation and Revitalization of the Japanese Economy*, Tuttle Publishing, Boston (Mass.)-Tokyo, 2000, p. 42.

50. See Morton, C. *Beyond World Class*, Macmillan Business, Houndmills-London, 1998, p. 226.

51. See *Economist*, September 26, 1998, p. 24.

52. See *Economist*, September 25, 1993, p. 92.

53. See Cargill, T. F., Hutchison, M. M., Ito, T. *The Political Economy of Japanese Monetary Policy*, p. 91.

54. See Hartcher, P. *The Ministry*, p. 100.

55. See MacIntyre, D. "Spend, Japan, Spend," *Time*, April 20, 1998, p. 29.

56. See Hartcher, P. *The Ministry*, p. 68.

57. See Strange, S. *Mad Money*, Manchester University Press, Manchester, 1998, p. 148.

58. See Cargill, T. F., Hutchison, M. M., Ito, T. *The Political Economy of Japanese Monetary Policy*, p. 184.

59. See Ayres, R. U. *Turning Point: An End to the Growth Paradigm*, Earthscan Publications Ltd., London, 1998, p. 33.

60. See *Economist*, September 26, 1998, p. 27.

61. See Davidson, J. D., Lord William Rees-Mogg. *The Great Reckoning*, p. 155.

62. See Hayes, D. *Japan's Big Bang*, p. 7.

63. See Hartcher P. *The Ministry*, pp. 111, 113.

64. See *Economist*, June 20, 1998, p. 24.

65. See McLeod, R., Garnaut, R. (eds.) *East Asia in Crisis: From Being a Miracle to Needing One?* Routledge, London-New York, 1998, p. 22.

66. See *Economist*, April 11, 1998, p. 15.

67. See Cumings, B. *Parallax Visions: Making Sense of American-East Asian Relations at the End of the Century*, Duke University Press, Durham (N.C.)-London, 1999, p. 32.

68. See *Economist*, April 25, 1998, p. 122.

69. See Steers, R. M. *Made in Korea: Chung Ju Yung and the Rise of Hyundai*, Routledge, New York-London, 1999, p. 91.

70. See Hartcher, P. *The Ministry*, p. 174.

71. See Gough, L. *Asia Meltdown: The End of the Miracle?* Capstone, Oxford, 1998, p. 25.

72. Sakaiya, T. *What Is Japan?*, p. 264.

73. See MacIntyre, D. "Spend, Japan, Spend," *Time*, April 20, 1998, p. 30.

74. See Wehrfritz, G. "Shop Till You Drop—Please," *Newsweek*, November 30, 1998, p. 25.

75. See Abrahams, P. "Japan Gambles on Chance," *Financial Times*, April 3, 2000, p. 17.

76. See Powell, B., Kattoulas, V. "The Lost Decade," *Newsweek*, July 27, 1998, pp. 16-17.
77. See *Economist*, September 26, 1998, p. 24.
78. See *Economist*, June 20, 1998, p. 23.
79. See Kattoulas, V. "Midnight Run," *Newsweek*, January 11, 1999, p. 40.
80. See Strom, S. "Japanese Joblessness Hits a Record, but Government is Optimistic," *International Herald Tribune*, April 1-2, 2000, p. 1.
81. See Hartcher, P. *The Ministry*, p. 229.
82. See Cargill, T. F., Hutchison, M. M., Ito, T. *The Political Economy of Japanese Monetary Policy*, p. 87.
83. See Goldstein, M. *The Asian Financial Crisis: Causes, Cures and Systemic Implications*, Institute for International Economics, Washington (D.C.), 1998, p. 21.
84. See McLeod, R. H., Garnaut, R. (eds.) *East Asia in Crisis*, p. 275.
85. See *World Economic Outlook: A Survey by the Staff of the International Monetary Fund, May 1998*, IMF, Publication Service, Washington (D.C.), 1998, p. 44.
86. See Hatch, W., Yamamura, K. *Asia in Japan's Embrace: Building a Regional Production Alliance*, Cambridge University Press, Cambridge-New York, 1996, pp. 6-7.
87. See Spaeth, A. "Calling Japan," *Time*, February 16, 1998, pp. 37-38.
88. See Pempel, T. J. *Regime Shift*, p. 149.
89. See Grant, W. "Perspectives on Globalization and Economic Coordination," in Hollingsworth, J. R., Boyer, R. (eds.) *Contemporary Capitalism: The Embeddedness of Institutions*, Cambridge University Press, Cambridge, 1997, p. 324.
90. See Johnson, Ch. *Japan: Who Governs?*, p. 106.
91. See Pempel, T. J. *Regime Shift*, p. 149.
92. See *Economist*, June 27, 1998, p. 88.
93. See Gibney, F. "Stumbling Giants," *Time*, November 24, 1997, p. 55.
94. For details see *Economist*, November 29, 1997, pp. 85-87.
95. See *Economist*, May 9, 1998, p. 76; Gibney, F. "Is Japan About to Crumble?" *Time*, June 8, 1998, p. 30.
96. See Hartcher, P. *The Ministry*, p. 150.
97. See Ohmae, K. "Not Another Hashimoto, Please!" *Newsweek*, July 27, 1998, p. 19.
98. See "Japanese Finance. A Survey," *Economist*, June 27, 1998, p. S-8.
99. See *Economist*, August 30, 1997, p. 68.
100. For details see Soros, G. *The Crisis of Global Capitalism [Open Society Endangered]*, Little, Brown and Company, London, 1998, p. 189.
101. See Hartcher, P. *The Ministry*, p. 164.
102. See Mazarr, M. J. *Global Trends 2005: An Owner's Manual for the Next Decade*, St. Martin's Press, New York, 1999, p. 39.
103. See Bremner, B. "Nation of Risk-Takers?" *Business Week*, European Edition, May 8, 2000, p. 49.
104. See Davis, S., Meyer, C. *Future Wealth*, Harvard Business School Press, Boston (Mass.), 2000, pp. 153-154.
105. See *Japanese Finance: A Survey*, p. S-8.
106. See *Japanese Finance: A Survey*, p. S-6.
107. See Ohmae, K. "Not Another Hashimoto, Please!" *Newsweek*, July 27, 1998, p. 19.
108. See Cargill, T. F., Hutchison, M. M., Ito, T. *The Political Economy of Japanese Monetary Policy*, p. 118.
109. See Pempel, T. J. *Regime Shift*, p. 149.
110. See Cumings, B. "The Asian Crisis, Democracy, and the End of 'Late' Development," in Pempel, T. J. (ed.) *The Politics of the Asian Economic Crisis*, Cornell University Press, Ithaca (N.Y.)-London, 1999, p. 118.

111. An opinion of the economist P. Ormerod quoted from: Perkins, A. B., Perkins, M. C. *The Internet Bubble*, Harper Business, New York, 1999, p. 188.

112. See *Economist*, April 26, 1997, p. 79.

113. See Henderson, C. *Asia Falling*, p. 169.

114. See *Economist*, September 20, 1997, p. 101.

115. See *World Economic Outlook: A Survey by the Staff of the International Monetary Fund, May 1999.* IMF, Publication Service, Washington (D.C.), 1999, p. 15.

116. See Landers, P. "Japan's GDP Contracted 1.4% in Fourth Quarter of 1999," *Wall Street Journal Europe*, March 14, 2000, p. 3.

117. See *Nikkei Weekly*, March 6, 2000, p. 4.

118. See *Economist*, March 18, 2000, p. 75.

119. See *Economist*, March 18, 2000, p. 75; *Financial Times*, April 26, 2000, p. 4; for more details about interest rate dynamics in 1994-1999, see Murphy, R. T. "Japan's Economic Crisis," *New Left Review*, Second Series, January-February, 2000, p. 42.

120. See Ueda, K. "Why the Bank of Japan Can't Target Inflation," *Wall Street Journal Europe*, March 6, 2000, p. 10.

121. See Hamlin, M. A. *Asia's Best: The Myth and Reality of Asia's Most Successful Companies*, Prentice Hall/Simon & Schuster (Asia) Pte Ltd., Singapore-New York, 1998, p. 8.

122. See *Nikkei Weekly*, March 6, 2000, p. 4.

123. See Tett, J. "Japan Passes US as Top Issuer of Public Debt," *Financial Times*, March 4-5, 2000, p. 4.

124. See Hayes, D. *Japan's Big Bang*, p. 140.

125. See *Economist*, March 21, 1998, p. 26.

126. See *Business Week*, October 19, 1998, p. 30.

127. See Abrahams, P. "A Revolution is Well Under Way," *Financial Times*, May 8, 2000, Survey "Japanese Investment Banking," p. 1.

128. See D'Andrea Tyson, L. "Don't Look Now, But a New Japan Is Taking Shape," *Business Week*, European Edition, May 29, 2000, p. 14.

129. See Ono, Y. "Nissan Motor Posts a Large Net Loss for Latest Year," *Wall Street Journal Europe*, May 22, 2000, p. 7; Jaggi R. "Mitsubishi Motors Reports Loss of Y23bn," *Financial Times*, May 26, 2000, p. 24.

130. See Ernsberger, R., Jr. "On the Road to Regret?" *Newsweek*, March 29, 1999, p. 58.

131. See Sen, A. *Development as Freedom*, Oxford University Press, Oxford, 1999, p. 266.

5

Southeast Asia: From Boom to Crisis

In many ways, the record of the Southeast Asian nations is a classical example of the "catching up" type of development. First of all, as distinct from Japan which had already been a regional economic superpower before World War II, none of those nations had any industrial experience. Second, many of them had, for quite some time, been, under the influence of communist ideology or had developed "along socialist lines." Third, as they embarked on industrialization, they set themselves extremely ambitious aims such as going beyond the confines of the Third World and joining the world's community of industrialized countries. Fourth, in no part of the world had the process of industrialization ever received such a massive support in the shape of foreign investment and credit injections. And finally, never before had the market economy experienced a systemic crisis of industrial production like that of 1997 the aftermaths of which are felt to this day.

The Southeast Asian nations' recent history may serve as a graphic illustration of all the six groups of contradictions inherent in the "catching up" development model we discussed in Chapter Three: one-sidedness of the emergent economic system, predomination of extensive development factors, underconsumption of the middle class, a sweeping-scale import of capital and technologies, critical dependence on finished products' export to the post-industrial world, and a lag behind the latter in the spheres of scientific and technological progress and education. When analyzing these contradictions we have already illustrated them with statistics and facts of socioeconomic life of those nations, therefore we shall not repeat ourselves but concentrate, on the one hand, on the overall parameters of the Asian economies' development in the 1970-1980s and, on the other, on assessing the course and depth of the crisis that hit the region.

Yet, for all the features they have in common, the types of development of individual East Asian nations differ from one another substantially. They can be roughly divided into three categories, each producing its results and having its distinctive prospects.

Represented in the *first* category are countries which, having taken the line of industrialization in the 1960s, emphasized a high standard of living and technological self-reliance while gaining the status of Southeast Asia's financial and business centers and promoting foreign trade contacts. Having come up the closest to post-industrial society. those countries found themselves, in the end, developmentally dependent on the Western world, owing their successes to the west's need for them as financial outposts in Asia and islands of stability in that region. I mean, above all, Hongkong (a British colony until 1997), Singapore and Taiwan.

Falling into the *second* category are nations which have gone all the way to industrialization from a predominantly agrarian starting line through the overexploitation of their own people and an active attraction of foreign investment. All those nations—South Korea, Thailand, Malaysia, Indonesia and the Philippines, above all, became major exporters of their products to the world market in the 1980s and the 1990s only to fall a prey to the cataclysms now commonly referred to as the Asian crisis of 1997. As they are emerging from recession today, most of those nations still stick to the extensive industrialization policy.

The *third* type of progress, identified primarily with China, the region's most powerful nation economically, appears to be most controversial. While remaining at a very low level of economic development, the country has a large domestic market and is not too actively engaged in international business transactions; therefore, one can say that the main prerequisites for the 1997 Asian crisis are only in the embryo in China's economy today and, consequently, do not threaten large-scale economic upheavals as yet. In he meantime, the ambitiousness of China's policy, the complexity of social transformation and the extremely extensive nature of its economic progress remain factors which are not to be ignored in assessing the prospects for the further development of the People's Republic of China. One way or another, the specific nature of China's way and the widespread speculations to the effect that China may become a strategic partner of Russia in a "multipolar" world of the 21st century make it certainly worth our while to take a closer look, in the next chapter, at the course and first results of China's economic reforms.

Asian Countries' Industrialization in the 1970s-1990s

It was not simultaneously that the Asian countries began to lay the groundwork for the industrialization of their economies (in Malaysia, Singapore and Taiwan the beginnings of the industrialization process were very much in evidence as early as in the late 1940s, most other countries proceeded to industrialization in the 1960s, and socialist China, in the early 1980s); however, as we have already noted, most of them were at an extremely low development level. Combined with the availability of cheap manpower and a virtual absence of Western goods capable of competing with the products of national industry, that was the factor in stimulating economic growth the rate of which staggered economists' imagination worldwide for several decades.

Already in the 1970s, the first decade of industrialization in most Asian countries, the annual GNP growth rates constituted 7-8 percent in Thailand and Indonesia; 8.1 percent in Malaysia; 9.4-9.5 percent in Hongkong, South Korea and Singapore; and 10.2 percent in Taiwan.[1] In most of those countries they dick not drop below 7 percent even in the 1980s, in spite of a surge in the prices of oil and other raw materials and two crises which hit the world in the early- and late-1980s. Over the past twenty years, economic progress in the Asian region accounted for most of the overall increase in the developing countries' economic growth indices, as a result of which the share of the post-industrial powers in world production dropped from 72 percent in 1953 to 64 percent in 1985 and 59 percent in 1992.[2] In the period of 1991-1995, eight out of ten economies growing at rates of over 50 percent were concentrated in the Asia-Pacific Region, the growth indices for China and Indonesia constituting 135 and 124 percent, respectively.[3] By early 1996, China, Japan, India, Indonesia and South Korea were among the world's top dozen economies[4], and another four countries of the region, among the world's top twenty ones; Hongkong, Taiwan, Singapore, Malaysia and South Korea ranked with the world's top twenty nations for the volume of their commodity turnover (suffice it to say that Malaysia with its 19-million population turned over 20 percent more commodities than Russia and twice as much as India[5]). The East Asian region increased its contribution to the world GNP from no more than 4 percent in 1960 to 25 percent in 1991 and, according to statistical extrapolations, was capable of bringing it up to 30 percent by the year 2000[6]. In 1993, the World Bank announced the East Asian economic zone to be "the fourth pole of growth" along with the United States, Japan and Germany; according to its projections, Asia where the world's second- and third-largest economic empires are found, will approach the year 2020 having four out of five world's leading economies[7]; by then, the GNP of the Asian nations (minus Japan) will account for 25.8 percent the world's total, surpassing the GNP indices of North America (23.9 percent), the EU (22.1 percent) and Japan (11.3 percent).[8] Other forecasters go to absolutely fantastic lengths: they claim that the new Southeast Asian industrial states of will account for 57 percent of the world's production of goods and service by the year 2050 with the OECD member states, Japan included, left to content themselves with a mere 12 percent.[9]

In the sphere of mass industrial production, the countries of the East Asian region have become dangerous rivals of the post-industrial world and Japan. Over the period of 1980-1993, annual value-added growth rates in industry constituted 11 percent in Malaysia; 12 percent in Thailand; 12.6 percent in South Korea; and 15-16 percent in China.[10] The Asian "tigers" kept increasing their share in the world production of steel and rolled stock, audio- and video equipment, cars and semiconductors. By the early 1990s, Taiwan became the world's fifth biggest manufacturer of microprocessors, their sales proceeds received by the largest Taiwanese companies soaring from next to nothing in 1989 to $2.5 billion in 1993.[11] Over the same period, South Korea, Singapore, Taiwan and Hongkong exported, among them, over 45 billion dollars' worth of electronic equipment a year.[12] At the end of the 1980s, South Korea spent about 2.8 percent of its gross national product—or as much as Japan, as a matter of fact—on research and development, both basic and applied.[13] As a result of such impressive successes, South Korea, Taiwan, Hongkong and Singapore increased their GNP to over $10,000 per capita a year, i.e. came close to most industrialized countries in that respect, and built up currency reserves which were among the world's largest;[14] South Korea joined the Organization for Economic Cooperation and Development in 1996.

It should be borne in mind, however, that in the 1970s and 1980s, Southeast Asian nations owed the swiftness of their "catching up" development—as much as Japan had in the 1950s and the 1960s—to the emphasis on the export of their products to foreign markets. Because the average per capita income in most Southeast Asian countries remains quite low compared with Western Europe and the United States (for example, in Indonesia, on the eve of the crisis, an income of $260 a month put the earner in a class with the top-paid third of the population[15]), export has been and remains the basic means of assuring steady economic growth. In the 1960s and 1970s, exports from the region's countries grew at a two-digit rate, and the corresponding index for South Korea in 1963-1973 was an incredible 52 percent a year.[16] Towards the end of the 1980s, the ratio between export-import operations and the GNP was 347 percent in Singapore; 282 percent in Hongkong; 109 percent in Malaysia; 90 percent in Taiwan; 66 percent in South Korea; 42 percent in Indonesia; it is worth recalling that over the same period the analogous index for Japan constituted 11 percent and for the United States, a mere 6 percent.[17] As a result, in the first half of the 1990s, Taiwan and Korea alone accounted for about 8 percent of the world's export volume while Mexico, comparable with them in the size of the population and the wealth of natural resources and affiliated with the North American Free Trade Association, for a just 0.5 percent.[18]

It was not so much the export orientation of the economy as such that was fraught with the threat of a crisis as the fact that the exports flow was fairly narrow and targeted on the United States for the most part. From 1960 to 1985, the volume of US-bound exports from Asian countries (including Japan) increased almost 60-fold,[19] with South Korea and Taiwan sending to the United States from 38 to 45 percent of their total exports; from 12 to 20 percent of their export products went to Japan only to be given finishing touches there and to proceed to the United States.[20] So it is safe to claim that over the past thirty years the United States consumed no less than a half of Asia's total export (or at least 30-40 percent of the Asian nations' entire GNP). Characteristically, it was only the more developed "new industrial nations of Asia"—Hongkong, Taiwan and South Korea—that reduced somewhat the share of their US-targeted exports over the 1970-1992 period, with the rest of those nations steadily increasing it.[21]

Even the massive export of goods manufactured in Southeast Asian cannot fully explain the phenomenon of an extremely fast economic growth of the region's countries. Maintaining it required extra investment which could be obtained either through overaccumulation of funds or government intervention in the economy, or drawn from the outside.

In the 1950s–1960s, at the first stage of industrial growth, a squeeze on public consumption (the 1991-1992 savings rates were: in Taiwan, 24 percent; in Hongkong, 30 percent; in Malaysia, Thailand and South Korea, 35 percent each; in Indonesia, 37 percent of the gross national product)[22] and foreign economic aid were the main sources of accumulation. Foreign aid was hardly ever mentioned but there is no ignoring the fact that the West generously subsidized the Asian economies regarding them as outposts against the spread of the communist threat. Over the 1950s, in particular, the United States and its allies actually subsidized 40 percent of their imports from Taiwan and over 80 percent, from South Korea. Until the early 1960s, such subsidies financed up to 70 percent of all capital investment made in Korean industry (in case of Taiwan, the figure was somewhat lower).[23] It was only in the mid-1960s that government subsidies and commercial bank loans—also mostly connected with the government or big corporations—became critical sources of capital investment although artificial cost reductions were also practiced on a large scale: in 1960-1975, nine national currency devaluations were carried out in South Korea, one of them halving the won (in 1960).[24]

With the passage of time, the concentration of production and the policy of protectionism pursued by the government to helped "its own" manufacturers became the chief means of assuring fast growth. Over a decade, from 1974 to 1984, the share of the gross national product generated by one, five and ten leading South Korean corporations (*chaebols*) grew, respectively, from 4.9 to 12.0, from 11.6 to 52.4 and from 15.1 to 67.4 percent.[25] In the mid-1990s, five major companies were responsible for 53 percent of the GNP; 30 companies, for 80 percent; and 70 companies, for over 95 percent of the entire gross national product.[26] Conversely, in Taiwan, which is known to have suffered the least from the Asian crisis, the ten largest companies maintained a volume of sales almost one-seventh that in Korea; employed a sixth of the latter's workforce; and accounted for only 9.3 percent of the GNP.[27] The governments of the Southeast Asian nations—and of Japan, for that matter—encouraged the national companies in every way to purchase new patents and technologies abroad, with the result that, owing to the government-maintained stability of national currency, the balances of payment of many Asian countries—Thailand, Indonesia, Malaysia and the Philippines, in particular—became unfavorable beginning with 1990; South Korea joined them in 1992. Thailand, Singapore and Hongkong were the only three countries, which could by no means be regarded as typical of Southeast Asia, to keep their balances of trade favorable.[28] In 1995, amid a decline in exports, the aggregate commodity imports of the ten new industrial nations of Asia surpassed those of the European Union as a whole and amounted to $748 billion.[29]

Under the circumstances, the economies of the region's countries came to depend for their further development on monetary injections from domestic banks and financial companies and on foreign capital investment. Their fast economic growth could not but attract foreign investors' attention, and in the 1980s, the stock indices skyrocketed in the East Asian exchanges. Capital accessibility was one of the chief reasons why the Asian nations' economies failed to embark on intensive development producing. Instead of developing new technologies of their own, national corporations avidly bought up patents and know-how licenses abroad unmindful of the likely prospect of the Western market's demand for their products falling off and their national currencies depreciating against the US dollar and the Japanese yen. For their part, the governments took growth stimulating measurers with emphasis on subsidies and credits. They sought to stimulate economic growth and to increase the export volume through the strengthening of financial institutions built around the biggest corporations (as was the case in Korea) or around individual ruling clans (as in Indonesia) and through direct credits provided by government-owned banks. Having cheap credits within their easy reach, however, industrial companies lost all interest in raising production efficiency. Back in 1998, thirty leading Korean corporations drew credits to the amount of $65 billion which constituted at the moment 39 percent of the country's GNP;[30] by 1997 interest on the credits surpassed those companies' aggregate profits, and payments could only be made out of more loans.[31] In Malaysia, the amount of credits extended to companies grew from 85 percent of the GNP in the late 1980s to 160 percent of the GNP on the eve of the financial crisis.[32] In Indonesia, aggregate investment in government-approved industrial production and infrastructure development programs amounted to $78 billion with most of the funds provided by government-owned banks overburdened as they were with debts.[33]

The crisis would have bracken out much earlier hadn't financial institutions received substantial funds as private deposits; a define role was played by the fact that a large proportion of foreign portfolio investment was channeled into the shares issued by financial companies and banks (in 1996, for example, the moneys spent on acquiring banks' and other financial institutions' shares accounted for over 57 percent of the total investment in Thai companies' shares[34]). Short-term credits (which constituted 43.3 percent of all foreign investment in Malaysia in 1996 as against 13.2 percent in 1995[35]) added up to a pyramid which was inevitably bound to collapse sooner or later. Yet they did not solve the problem because the further incorporation of the region's states into the club of the developed countries called for unheard-of outlays. In 1995, the World Bank estimated that Vietnam's expenses on the construction of a modern industrial infrastructure would cost it $20 billion in the next decade,[36] that Indonesia, Thailand, Malaysia and the Philippines would need about $ 440 billion for the purpose,[37] while in case of China the figure would run into $500 billion.[38] In a situation, however, where South Korea's balance of trade and investment deficit was estimated at $23 billion[39] and where Taiwan's foreign debt increased from 4 to 14 percent of the GNP over the period of 1990-1994 alone,[40] drawing such amounts was already an unrealistic proposition.

By the mid-1990s it became obvious to all that the industrial countries of Southeast Asia were in for an acute economic crisis. It followed from the report J. Sachs submitted to the Brookings Institution Washington's in 1996 that most countries of that region had an extremely unsatisfactory balance of payments, that their export growth rates were slowing down and that their banking system was in a grave crisis owing to an inefficient use of borrowed funds.[41] In our opinion, the situation only went to confirm the fact that it is impossible to build a modern economy within a relatively short period through a massive mobilization of resources. The emphasis on accelerated industrialization compelled Asian countries to keep their populations' incomes relatively low, to restrain solvent demand at home and to seek foreign markets for their products. That, in turn, presupposed the dumping practice which depressed the efficiency of their national economies. The investment problems that arose were solved using the influx of foreign capital, the massive crediting of industry, and government subsidies. However, low living standards in those countries ruled out, first of all, the development of a system of post-materialistic motivations without which independent technological progress is impossible, thus dooming the nations to a continued expansion of import of production technologies and patents; second, it kept those countries dependent on foreign markets because domestic demand was inadequate. That was precisely why the Southeast Asian countries' economic progress could go on for as long as their successful year-in-year-out performance kept investors confident that they would go on making superprofits there. Any setback the region might receive in its economic development would produce a series of problems capable of dashing to the ground the radiant hopes which the Asian "tigers" and "dragons" nursed so fondly and which, to all appearances, were already coming true.

The Crisis and Its Lessons

The Asian crisis of 1997, which turned out to be wider-spreading and more dramatic than the 1990 Japanese upheavals, was a stern warning to all the countries adhering to the "catching up" development model.

There is no denying the importance of financial factors which exerted a serious influence on the course of the crisis, but its basic component—the intrinsic imperfection of the Asian model of industrialization, should be borne in mind, either.

Evidence indicating a deterioration of the economic situation in the Southeast Asian countries first manifested itself back in 1995: the GNP and export growth rates began to slow down, the balance of trade was getting increasingly unfavorable, the credit mass which artificially kept the market up was increasing. The world capital market situation remained unfavorable then: the Mexican collapse of 1994-1995 revealed the outflow of capital to the United States and Europe; whereas in 1993-1994 the dynamics of stock indices in the basic Western markets and in Southeast Asia was relatively uni-directional, by the fall of 1997 the Dow Jones index went up almost 50 percent, with the summary index indicating the state of developing markets being well below the 1994 figure, and with Thailand, Mexico and South Korea taking the lead in its fall rate.[42] The funds invested in the more liquid shares of Thailand, the Philippines, Malaysia, Singapore, South Korea and Indonesia in 1994 returned no profit three years later—on the contrary, the investors sustained losses which, in some cases, amounted to 35 percent and over[43]. Capital outflow from the region sent the dollar up against the yen and temporarily gave the Japanese economy a competitive edge on those of other Asian countries,[44] which led to a steady reduction in share prices at all the Asian stock exchanges in the first half of 1997.[45]

It was than that an investment crisis in the Asian countries became a harsh reality obvious to one and all. As the placement of shares was becoming more and more of a problem, the leading industrial companies began to shift the emphasis to massive borrowing taking advantage of the fact that close contacts between big corporations and the state gave creditors the illusion of their investments being safe.[46] As interest rates inevitably climbed up, the companies began to resort to foreign credits and to cut credit periods. Although most Asian countries continued to run surplus budgets, the burden of growing debt was more than they could endure. South Korea is a graphic illustration of that. Whereas in 1970 the size of its foreign debt did not exceed $ 2.2 billion, by 1980 it reached $ 27 billion, with a half of the funds intended for financing heavy and chemical industries development programs obtained in the shape of foreign loans.[47] Over the period of 1992-1996 alone, the amount of such loans grew 158 percent, and interest charged on them exceeded a quarter of all the international liabilities of the Southeast Asian nations taken together. Short-term borrowings constituted 63 percent of total loans and amounted to triple the nation's gold and foreign exchange reserve.[48] The real state of affairs was carefully concealed from the investors: in the spring of 1997, South Korea's debt was officially declared to be $40 billion but as the crisis unfolded the amount was "corrected" to 60, then to 100 and, by the end of 1997, to $119.7 billion.[49] Nevertheless, the largest South Korean companies actually went bankrupt in the early months of the crisis when the market value of such corporations as Kia Motors, Hanbo and Jinro turned out to be 6 times, 20 times and 35 times less than their debt liabilities, respectively.[50] Toward the end of 1997, about 20 percent of all bank credits had to be dismissed as hopeless, and riding the nation's financial system of out the crisis could cost $60-100 billion, at a most conservative estimate.[51] For fairness sake, it should be noted that the other countries of the region were in a similar position: in Thailand, about 70 percent of all the large industrial companies were in default of their credits or repudiated their liabilities; in Indonesia, 200 out of 228 companies listed at the stock exchange were declared technically bankrupt by the end of 1997.[52]

By the summer of 1997, the Asian countries had treaded in Japan's footsteps also in the sphere of real estate business: at the end of the 1990s, real estate prices there were among the world's highest (to illustrate, in 1999 a small apartment in Seoul cost $225,000, which corresponded to the maximum real estate prices charged in California where the per-capita GNP was five times that of Korea[53]). Later, the prices went down, but until the mid-1990s the investors behaved as if they had no idea of the Japanese precedent. In 1996-1998, ground was broken in Jakarta, Bangkok, Singapore and Manila for office blocks the total floorspace of which surpassed 1.5 times that commissioned in 1993-1995 although in 1996 alone the number of unsold immovables in those cities increased 50 percent[54]; the funding of real estate projects (the economic efficiency of which had never been calculated accurately enough, in most cases) constituted 25-30 percent of the total amount invested in the economy of Indonesia; up to 30-40 percent, of Singapore, Thailand and Malaysia; and an unprecedented 40-55 percent in Hongkong.[55]

The curtailment of foreign investment and a decline in the volume of export (in 1995-1997, it diminished 6 percent in Thailand; 11 percent in Indonesia and the Philippines; 13 percent in Taiwan and 18 percent in South Korea) led to a recession and mounting financial pressures. In Thailand, a 6 percent GNP increase in 1996 was followed by stagnation in 1997, with a 5 percent decline forecast for 1998; in Indonesia where a 7 percent growth had been observed in the third quarter of 1997, a 15 percent decline was expected as early as 1998.[56] In 1997 and in the first half of 1998, IMF experts revised their Asian economies' growth rate estimates eight(!) times—downwards each time.

The scale of the crisis became obvious after it had spread to the financial and stock markets. On July 2, 1997, after Thailand's currency reserves had shrunk from $40 billion to under $30 billion within three months, the Bank of Thailand devaluated the baht with the result that the latter became 20 percent cheaper within one day and fell to less than a half of its pre-1997 value in six months.[57] On July 11, the Bank of the Philippines, having spent over one billion dollars on maintaining the national currency, finally abandoned the attempts to keep up the peso which shared the fate of Thailand's baht.[58] Over the second half of 1997, practically all Asian currencies were devaluated, many of them drastically (in Indonesia, the rupiah fell from 2,430 to 17,000 to the US dollar over the period from July, 1997 to January 1998[59]); Singapore, Taiwan and Hongkong were the least affected by that spate of devaluations. Characteristically, the developments which had formally unleashed the crisis passed practically unnoticed in the world markets; the share price decline in Asia did not prevent the European and American stock exchange indices from reaching new highs in the spring and fall of 1997. The US dollar was rising smoothly against the yen while the Japanese index was going down slowly losing 20 percent of its value in 1997. It took a stock market crash in one of the region's nerve centers for the Asian crisis to send a shockwave through the world. In Hongkong, share prices kept falling steadily on October 20, 21, 22 and 23 by 630; 568; 765 and 1,211 points, respectively, which meant a 23 percent decline overall.[60] On October 27, the Dow Jones index fell over 300 points; trading was interrupted for the first time since the news of President Kennedy's assassination had come in on November 22, 1963; following the resumption of trading, the index went 254 points further down, and trading was suspended in accordance with the stock market regulations adopted in 1987. On the following day, the index jumped up over 300 points, but in Europe share prices fell sharply. The world markets' imbalance became a reality.[61]

The above circumstances revealed the scale of the developed nations' involvement in Southeast Asia's economic problems proportional to the fast-growing volume of their pre-crisis investment (in the period of 1993-1996 alone, for example, direct foreign capital investment in Hongkong, Singapore, Indonesia and Thailand increased more than 120 percent[62]). The chief problem in this case was that Japan stood out among the region's major investors, accounting for no less than a third of all capital investment in those countries and surpassing the United States by a factor of seven in that respect on the eve of the crisis;[63] in mid-1997, Japanese companies were responsible for 52 percent of total direct foreign investment in South Korea's economy; 37 percent, in Thailand's; 31 percent, in Singapore's; and 27 percent, in Taiwan's.[64] The chances of keeping the money invested looked slim under the consequences because at that time the region's foreign-debt-to-GNP ratio was almost as bad as that of the poorest African countries.[65] As a result, the investors hurried to save whatever they could, and the influx of investment to the region reversed. Whereas in 1996 the Southeast Asian nations attracted private credits in the amount of almost $80 billion, by the end of 1997 the figure was a mere $7.6 billion, and over $50 billion were withdrawn from their economies in the first half of 1998 alone. In 1997-1998, the outflow of capital amounted to over 10 percent of the crisis-stricken Asian countries' aggregate GNP.[66] By October 1998, the crisis swallowed up credits to the tune of one trillion dollars the retrieval of which seemed beyond hope; the local markets' capitalization decreased by almost $2 trillion, and the Southeast Asian countries' GNP losses came close to $3 trillion[67]. What looked particularly dangerous was the fact that Japan, the nation to which regional stability meant the most, was actually unable to take effective measures to rectify the situation what with the extent of its own involvement in the deepening crisis[68].

A dramatic depreciation of national currencies of most Southeast Asian countries' and the catastrophic crash of their stock markets (which amounted to 70 percent in Indonesia) exposed the state of their macroeconomic indicators for what they really were. It turned out shortly that most of the Bank's of Thailand: gold reserves had been sold in international markets back in August-October. It also transpired that over the same period the Bank of Korea had been actively selling dollars to commercial banks at a fixed rate thus making it easier for the latter to service their foreign debts[69] and, besides, had let them have $4.4 billion in the shape of direct aid made out as interbank credits as late as October when the insolvency of the credit institutions involved became obvious;[70] as a result of all these measures and thanks to persistent maintenance of the won's exchange rate the total volume of South Korea's currency reserves constituted \$7.3 billion as of November 21, 1997 and a mere \$5 billion as of December 4.[71] Seeking to put the situation right, Western governments and international financial institutions hastened to announce sweeping financial support for the crisis-stricken countries. During the second half of 1997, the International Monetary Fund approved the consecutive granting of \$17 billion to Thailand; \$23 billion to Indonesia (later the package was increased to \$45 billion) and, finally, \$57 billion to South Korea, which was the largest credit ever granted by that organization.[72]

The scale of the crisis was too large, however. In Indonesia, Malaysia, South Korea and Thailand, the amount of past-due and bad debts constituted about 60 percent of their GNP, and liabilities to foreign banks alone amounted to 30-45 percent of the GNP as of September 1997 (Malaysia's total debt exceeded 170 percent of the GNP, and Indonesia's, 190 percent of the GNP[73]). All the crisis-stricken countries did not have much room for maneuver because the currency reserves they had at their disposal constituted a mere fraction of their foreign debt liabilities. For example, Thailand's foreign debt, amounted to \$87.3 billion, and its reserves constituted no more than \$26.6 billion; for South Korea and Indonesia, the corresponding indices were \$152.3 and \$45.1 billion, \$136.4 and \$13.5 billion, respectively.[74] Therefore, most funds granted by the IMF as credit aid packages to those countries actually went into the rescheduling of their debts and had no substantial effect on the economic situation there.

The devaluation of national currencies and the stock market crash hit the real sector of the economy extremely hard. As banks channeled most of the credits into the investment sector, the financial crisis pushed loan interest rates far up (for example, by the early summer of 1998 loan interest rates amounted to 16 percent a year in the Philippines; 17 percent in South Korea; 23 percent in Thailand; and over 60 percent in Indonesia[75]). This reduced to naught the possibility of commodity price cuts which might have become the earliest effect of currency devaluation. There was a further decline in domestic consumption owing to a national currency exchange rate slump, banks going bust and wage cuts; as a result, devaluation depressed the export sectors of the economy instead of livening them up.[76] Production began to decline fast starting with the second quarter of 1997; as a consequence, industrial plant capacity utilization

factor dropped from 83 to 65 percent in April 1998.[77] The crisis
made Asian manufacturers' dependence on import all too obvious.
In the last quarter of 1997 and at the beginning of 1998, import
deliveries decreased 30 percent in Indonesia; 32 percent in Thailand; and 35 percent in South Korea.[78]

By mid-1998, the Asian countries had practically exhausted their
possibilities for reducing prices of domestic product price reduction
potentialities but the situation did not change for the better all the
same. Having spread to the sphere of production, the crisis caused
massive plant closures and business stoppages. Over the second half
of 1997, three out of South Korea's 30 largest *chaebols*—the Kia
Group, the Hanbo Group and the Sammi Group, were officially declared bankrupt, and 24 out of the remaining 27 were in the state of
technical bankruptcy.[79] By January 1998, South Korea, which, before the crisis, had ranked the world's 11th nation for the size of its
GNP (worth about $500 billion then), slid down to the 17th line of
the list with a $312 billion GNP and the per capita gross product
going down from $11,000 to $ 6,600.[80]

Experts estimated that by the end of 1998 the rate unemployment
in all the crisis-stricken countries surpassed the pre-crisis figure 2-
2.5 times;[81] anti-immigrant feelings began to run high in Malaysia
and Indonesia;[82] in the crisis-stricken countries, the standard of living fell by over 50 percent. The proportion of people living below
the official poverty line increased in all the Southeast Asian countries for the first time since the late 1960s: from 15.1 to 26.7 percent
in Thailand; from 15.7 to27.8 percent of the population in South
Korea; from 11.3 to 22.5 percent in Indonesia.[83]

The crisis resulted in the Asian companies practically losing their
influence in the international arena. The big corporations' enormous
debts caused a massive investor flight and the ensuing slump of share
prices. Whereas in the early- 1997 FT Global 500 rating the number
of Southeast Asian companies ranking with the world's 500 leading
firms in terms of capitalization constituted 37, by early 2000 it diminished to 21.[84]

It should be borne mind that in most cases capitalization is by no
means an exhaustive indicator of a company's financial status. In
the meantime, the state which had always played a crucial role in
Asian countries' economic life was not going to yield ground. As
government and business form an indivisible whole there, the terms

and conditions on which the IMF offered them financial aid, and the expediency of which was obvious, met with downright opposition, if not hostility. In case of Thailand, for example, an IMF credit was forthcoming only on condition that 57 large financial companies which were on the verge of bankruptcy but close to the powers-that-be would be closed down; in South Korea, the demand that a number of big conglomerates, including Hyundai, be dissolved and the petition for the winding up of some powerful companies such as the Kia Motors went against the grain. In Indonesia, an IMF delegation suggested that the members of the president's family should go out of business. Practice has shown that none of these demands stands any chance of being complied with. In Thailand, more than a half of the companies marked up for closure remain operative; the IMF's demands with regard to Malaysia elicited strongly-worded responses from Premier Mahathir and actually led to the self-isolation of that country; bargaining with President Suharto of Indonesia took months[85] and ended only with his overthrow; in South Korea, most of the terms were not fulfilled, either, and it is small wonder that following investment bidding the Kia Motors went not to the Ford Motor Co., which was the highest bidder, but to Korea's own Daewoo. Indicatively, in the process of acquiring the Kia Motors, Daewoo conducted active negotiations with its own creditors offering them to buy out its debts at no more than 40 cents per one dollar's worth of liabilities.[86] By the summer of 1998, all the aid-recipient countries violated agreements with the IMF as far as the need for balancing out the budget was concerned: whereas in the second half of 1997 the IMF had agreed with Thailand, South Korea and Indonesia on their budget surplus indices being one percent,[87] Thailand ran a 3 percent deficit as early as in May 1998; South Korea, 4 percent in June; and Indonesia, 8.5 percent. Although those breaches of the agreements were formally explained by the need to maintain a number of social programs, a substantial proportion of the funds had actually been injected into the industrial sector[88]. Despite the catastrophic state their economies are in, the Asian countries were plainly not inclined in 1997—any more than they are now, for that matter—to depart from the economic guidelines adopted way back in the 1980s even through it was the dogged adherence to these guidelines that had plunged the entire region into a disastrous crisis.

Now that the Asian crisis is a matter of the recent past and commonly believed to be over, it is hard to resist the temptation of explaining it by the fallacious policy of the Asian governments and by machinations of international financial speculators. "Why has such a successful model of economic development turned sour so soon?" G. Soros asks rhetorically in his latest book. His own answer to the question is as follows: "The root of instability lies in the international financial system itself.'[89] Each of the two basic schools of thought which took shape in Western literature by mid-1999 as to the causes of the Asian crisis emphasizes the financial aspect of the problem in some way or other. One attributes the crisis to excessive borrowing in the foreign and domestic markets, uncontrolled financing of ill-considered industrial and real-estate projects, deliberate overstatement of national currency exchange rates, balance of payment deficits, and so forth; each of the ten causes of the Asian crisis listed by M. Goldstein is connected with its financial aspects.[90] The adherents of this school of thought believe that the crisis will neither last long, nor bring any dangerous and persistent consequences.[91] The researchers who opt for the second school of thought pay attention to the organizational structure of the Southeast Asian countries' economies; they are of the opinion that the IMF and other international financial institutions are to suggest to those countries the following list of priorities: renunciation of direct government support for industry; demonopolization of most sectors; the encouragement and vigorous promotion of free enterprise.[92] Be that as it may, none of the authors puts in question either the Asian countries' achievements in the 1980s and the 1990s, or their ability to develop on their own.

We take a different stand on the matter; the message of this book is that the development of the Asian economies has never been natural and self-sustaining; over decades, their governments have provided supplementary investment de facto in five ways, at least: first, through the direct subsidizing of businesses in various forms; second, through protecting the interests of giant industrial-financial consortiums which mobilized internal resources via the banks under their control; third, through artificially maintaining their national currencies' exchange rates at a level which allowed importing high-tech equipment and components; fourth, through securing and guaranteeing credits for supporting the national industry; and five, through maintaining a relatively low manpower cost which made those countries' products competitive. High growth rates were maintained solely by massive injections of funds from abroad: in 1996 alone, foreign investment in Malaysia, Indonesia, the Philippines, Thailand and South Korea grew by $41 billion which constituted 5.9 percent of those countries' gross national product[93] (with the overall influx of foreign capital amounting to 13-17 percent of the GNP[94]); the Asian economies' instability can be illustrated by the fact that that the net outflow of investment in 1997 ($12 billion), which had truly catastrophic consequences, constituted no more than 1.3 percent of the aggregate gross national product of those countries[95]. No sooner had the pumping of foreign investment into these economies stopped than the Asian economic model collapsed. This goes to show that *the nations adhering to the "catching up" development strategy can make progress only for as long as the post-industrial world needs it.*

Life after Death

This statement does not contradict the fact of the Asian economies' rapid recovery from the ruinous crisis. Statistics show that the year 1999 was the best one for them over the past decade. Their gross national product growth rate turned out to be thrice as high as experts had predicted it to be in the fall of 1998. Malaysia's economic growth constituted about 6 percent, economic recession ended in Thailand, Indonesia entered the growth phase at the end of 1999. Mexico's economy grew 3.7 percent over the year, and even Brazil, hit by a financial crisis in January 1999, registered an almost four-percent increase of its GNP. Positive trends extended to Eastern Europe where the gross national products of Poland and Hungary grew 5 percent, and in Russia economic recession stopped. The Asian countries' foreign currency reserves were restored and even added to[96]. Most experts confidently predict that these positive trends will carry on in 2000.

Does that mean that the "catching up" development model has justified itself? To our mind, such a conclusion is not merely mistaken but downright dangerous in some respects. Let us try and ascertain the causes of the Asian countries' striking economic recovery in 1999-2000.

To begin with, a rise in exports was the decisive factor in rectifying the economic situation in all those countries without exception. The example of South Korea whose GNP diminished by 8 percent in

1998[97] only to grow 10.7 percent in 1999 shows that the volume of exports increased over those years by 16.3 percent (projections for 2000 put the figure at about 20 percent). Already by the end of 1998, its favorable balance of trade amounted to $ 40 billion—an all time high for the country's independent fifty years'.[98] Considering that in South Korea the worth of commercial transactions constitutes up to 80 percent of the GNP of which about 80 percent fall on exports and about 30 percent, on imports, one cannot but come to the conclusion that domestic economic processes account for only 1.5-2 percent of the overall 10.7-percent growth. An unprecedented increase in South Korea's foreign currency reserves which amounted to $83 billion[99] as of the end of March 2000, was due precisely to the livening up of export trade. Second, it is perfectly obvious that the lowering of the national currencies' exchange rates in all the countries which had gone through the crisis provided a strong stimulus to the development of production. Korea's won which fell to a half during the crisis remains 30 percent short of its pre-crisis value even today; Thailand's baht has frozen at half its former value; and Indonesia's rupiah has dropped almost 60 percent.[100] As a result, it became more profitable to use national manpower and materials, i.e. cost reduction re-opened the door to foreign markets for the nations of Southeast Asia—the door which had been slammed in their faces on the eve of the 1997 crisis.

Third, an enhancement of the Asian countries' investor appeal and the fact that their growing foreign currency reserves enabled them to prevent a default on their foreign debts caused a new influx of foreign capital accompanied by a surge of national investors' activity. In 1999, foreign investment in South Korea's fixed assets grew 4.1 percent and is expected to continue growing by 8 percent before this year is out and by 12 percent in 2001.[101] Charts showing the dynamics of foreign investment in Southeast Asia from all sources in 1999-2001, carried by *The Financial Times,* are a carbon copy of analogous charts for 1993-1995.[102] On the other hand, the Bank of Korea, having replenished its reserves, took a number of measures to reduce interest rates: back in 1998 they were cut from 33 to 22 percent in January; to 16 percent in June; to 7 percent at the end of September and to 4.5 at the end of the year.[103] An analogous trend is to be observed in the countries which have gone through the crisis—from Indonesia to Brazil, from Malaysia to Russia. The traditional practice used by the United States and Western Europe in 1999-2000, for example, is known to provide for a rise rather than a reduction in interest rates amid rapid economic growth.

Fourth, government support for national producers also remains strong enough. As early as 1998 when the end of the crisis was still a long way off larger banks resumed the crediting of South Korea's *chaebols* and offered ample credit facilities to Thailand's and Indonesia's companies in distress. In that year alone, the Korean *chaebols* drew about $9 billion against government guarantees in the domestic market, and the Daewoo Corporation received new credits in the amount of $1.9 billion.[104] Notably, all this is happening in a situation where, at the Deutsche Bank's estimates, the amount of overdue loans (extended for an indefinite period) adds up to 16 percent of the GNP in South Korea; 17 percent in Malaysia; 63 and 64 percent in Thailand and Indonesia, respectively.[105] If continued, such practice may, in our opinion, reproduce the problems the Asian economies came up against on the eve of the 1997 crisis.

Finally, the "catching up" economies' fundamental problem—their excessive dependence on the import of new technologies—remains unsolved. At one time, a reduction in local products' prices caused by a fall in the real incomes of the population and by the devaluation of national currencies made Southeast Asian products more competitive in world markets and temporarily obviated the need for supplementary investment previously indispensable for securing a competitive edge on the rivals. The assertions about a fast rise in exports in the crisis period ought in our view, to be taken cautiously: statistics show that in 1998-1999 the Asian countries' favorable trade balances were achieved primarily through a $80-120-billion cut in imports[106] (in relative terms, this constituted 19.5 percent in Singapore; 22.4 percent in Malaysia; 33.4 percent in Indonesia; 36.1 percent in South Korea; and almost 40 percent in Thailand[107]) rather than through an increase in export deliveries. As we already indicated, patents and technologies figured prominently in the Southeast Asian nations' pre-crisis import pattern. Therefore, we regard the current situation as temporary; the next few years will witness either a substantial rise in imports, or a dramatic reduction in the Asian nations' export potential.

To sum up, *the successes the nations of the Asia-Pacific Region achieved in early two post-crisis years were caused not by changes in their development paradigm but by a temporary restoration of the conditions under which alone the "catching up" economies can do relatively well.* The era of a turbulent expansion of mass consumer goods exports is back, labor costs are down, monetary injections into the economy have been intensified, and active government regulation of the industrial and financial sectors continues. This conclusion is corroborated by a comparison between Japan's economic predicament over the past few years and a rapid recovery of the Eastern Asian economies. Had the Japanese government allowed a similar crisis to happen, devaluated the national currency to a half of its value while keeping interest rates low, and let foreign investment in by liberalizing Japan's foreign trade legislation, it would have received the same effect which, however, would have been as short-lived as it appears to turn out to be in the rest of the "catching up" countries hit by the 1997-1998 crisis.

These assumptions began to gain substance in the spring and summer of 2000 when the economies of that region's countries started sending out alarm signals again. Although in 1999 their economic growth rates ran into two digits mostly (10.7 percent in South Korea; 11.7 percent in Malaysia; 14.3 percent in Hongkong), the first quarter of 2000 saw a sharp slowdown (to 3.2 percent in Indonesia and 3.0 percent in South Korea). There is no ignoring the fact that that economic surge was accompanied by a reduction of imports and a continued depreciation of national currencies (in April-May, 2000, alone Korea's, won fell by 3 percent; Thailand's baht, by 4 percent; the Philippines' peso, by 5 percent; and the Indonesian rupiah, by almost 12 percent). The inflation rate upswing in the first quarter of 2000 also indicates that the growth potential resulting from currency devaluation and the 1997-1998 crisis is beginning to fizzle out.[108]

By mid-2000, whatever optimism there had been at the end of 1999 about the Asian economies' further successes became much more cautious. An artificial slowdown of the US economic growth rate aimed at preventing an excessively rapid rise of stock market quotations brought with it a wave of Asian assets' depreciation. The prices of Korean high-technology companies' shares went down to a half or even a third of their value over the first four months of 2000 alone[109] while the losses sustained by the Korea Composite index at the Seoul stock exchange, which exceeded 30 percent, depressed it almost all the way to the 1997 mark.[110] Experts predict that in the second quarter of 2000 economic growth may slow down to 1.8 percent.[111] Still more alarming news is coming from Indonesia where the level of per capita income fell 16.2 percent in 1998 alone and no progress was made over the past two years.[112] President A. Wahid's new government is re-enacting the policy pursued by the previous administration with different "dramatis personae": today the companies which belong to the new President's relatives have unpaid debts to the tune of over $2 billion, and the Bank Restructuring Agency provides only formal guarantees for no more than $100 billion of problem bank liabilities[113]. The state debt swelled up from $ 51 billion in March 1998 to $147 billion in May 2000, and payments made by way of its reimbursement constitute 45 percent of all the current year's budget revenues.[114] Analogous trends are to be observed in most of the other countries which have gone through the 1997 crisis.

* * *

The chief reason why the difficulties the Asian nations have run into are now getting worse still is that they have failed to realize that their economic successes are of a transient nature. Regarding themselves as the developed countries' competitors (and actually being ones, to a certain extent) they have never grasped the degree of their dependence on the post-industrial world and still remain unaware of it. The import of technologies, the artificial cost depression, the massive injections of foreign capital and the building up of finished product exports—such were the main factors behind the Asian "prosperity". What interrupted that succession of achievements was by no means the financial crisis as such but the Western countries' entry into a new stage of their development. The formation in these countries of sustainable economies largely independent of external circumstances, a confident consolidation of the information sector of the economy and an explosion-like surge in the demand for individual benefits and specific custom-made goods and services—have combined to herald an end to Asian industrialization. The Western countries which sought, in the 1980s and early 1990s, to win a market for their technologies, software, knowhow and high-technology products through price competition have by now achieved a monopoly position in that market and asserted their "monopoly rights".

As the standard of living in the West is rising, so is the demand for top-quality products and services of domestic origin; in the meantime, high-income brackets solvent demand for Asian products is sagging; as to lower-income consumers, they are concerned with the price of the products which, as we have already pointed out, cannot be radically reduced owing to a large number of imported components they incorporate. The upsurge of business activity in the post-industrial countries naturally attracts substantial funds, and investors prefer to quit the developing markets the risk of getting involved in which is now exceeding all reasonable limits. All this suggests the conclusion, no matter how vehemently our opponents may deny it, that *the nations of Southeast Asia will never resume the positions they used to hold in the world economy in mid-1997.*

We are far from saying that the region's countries have no economic future; two important circumstances merit attention in this context. On the one hand, most observers agree that the model realized in Southeast Asian largely copies the Japanese model of industrialization[115]; it should be noted in this connection that it was quite some time before the purely financial troubles Japan had gotten into in 1990-1992 led to the near-hopeless stagnation persisting there since 1998 to this day. Therefore it is safe to predict that Southeast Asia's real economic problems are likely to manifest themselves in full in four or five years from now when the last potentialities of the conventional "catching up" methods are exhausted without bringing about a changeover to a new economic paradigm. On the other hand, the period of 1998-2000 has turned out to be among the most dynamic ones in the post-industrial world's progress record, and this circumstance should by no means be left out of account; the countries making up the post-industrial community have achieved steady economic growth rates thus helping the "catching up" countries along towards an early recovery. In the next few years this growth may continue and, consequently, the influx of investment to the more developed countries' markets will intensify to further detract from the developing countries' investor appeal. At the same time, there is no ruling out the outbreak of a local financial crisis provoked by excessively fast growth rates (some elements of which show in the instability of stock exchange indices particularly evident since April 2000) which can have a still more adverse effect on developing markets (at the beginning of May 2000, stock exchange index values in Hongkong and Tokyo were 25 percent short of the maxima reached two months before). So, no matter what course the development of the post-industrial powers will take, it will objectively have a restraining influence on the developing markets. In our opinion, therefore, there is no reason to expect either another fantastic rise characteristic of the 1970s and the 1980s, or a rapid economic recovery the signs of which manifested themselves right after the latest upheavals.

It is precisely in the context of the Asian countries' economic development being of a secondary and dependent nature, on the whole, that we shall discuss below the processes now under way in the region's second-largest, after Japan, economic system—in the People's Republic of China which many analysts see as the world's economic leader in the 21st century.

Notes

1. See Hobday, M. *Innovation in East Asia: The Challenge to Japan*, Edward Elgar, Cheltenham (U.K.)-Lyme (U.S.), 1997, p. 14.
2. See Dicken, P. *Global Shift: The Internationalization of Economic Activity*, Paul Chapman Publishing, London, 1992, p. 20.
3. See Hampden-Turner, Ch., Trompenaars, F. *Mastering the Infinite Game. How East Asian Values are Transforming Business Practices*, Capstone, Oxford, 1997, pp. 3, 2.
4. See Gough, L. *Asia Meltdown: The End of the Miracle?* Capstone, Oxford, 1998, p. 101.
5. See Yergin, D., Stanislaw, J. *The Commanding Heights: The Battle Between Government and the Marketplace That Is Remaking the Modern World*, Simon & Schuster, New York, 1998, p. 183.
6. See LaFeber, W. *The Clash: US-Japanese Relations throughout History*, W.W. Norton & Company, New York-London, 1997, p. 390.
7. See Huntington, S. P. *The Clash of Civilizations and the Remaking of World Order*, Simon & Schuster, New York, 1996, p. 103.
8. See Hiscock, G. *Asia's Wealth Club*, Nicholas Brealey Publishing, London, 1997, p. 112.
9. See Naisbitt, J. *Global Paradox*, Avon Books, New York, 1995, p. 339.
10. See Hatch, W., Yamamura, K. *Asia in Japan's Embrace: Building a Regional Production Alliance*, Cambridge University Press, Cambridge-New York, 1996, p. 180.
11. See Yip, G. S. *Asian Advantage: Key Strategies for Winning in the Asia-Pacific Region*, Addison-Wesley, Reading (Mass.), 1998, p. 119.
12. See Hobday, M. *Innovation in East Asia*, pp. 18-19.
13. See Amsden, A. H. *Asia's Next Giant: South Korea and Late Industrialization*, Oxford University Press, New York-Oxford, 1989, p. 328.
14. See Robinson, R., Goodman, D. S. G. (eds.) *The New Rich in Asia: Mobile Phones, McDonald's and Middle-Class Revolution*, Routledge, London-New York, 1996, p. 207.

15. See Hamlin, M. A. *Asia's Best: The Myth and Reality of Asia's Most Successful Companies*, Prentice Hall/Simon & Schuster (Asia) Pte Ltd., Singapore-New York, 1998, p. 14.
16. See Fieldhouse, D. K. *The West and the Third World: Trade, Colonialism, Dependence, and Development*, Blackwell Publishers, Oxford-Malden (Mass.), 1999, p. 325.
17. See *The World Bank Policy Research Report: The Asian Miracle: Economic Growth and Public Policy*, Oxford University Press for the World Bank, Oxford-Washington (D.C.), 1993, p. 39.
18. See Pempel, T. J. "The Developmental Regime in a Changing World Economy," in Woo-Cumings, M. (ed.) *The Developmental State*, Cornell University Press, Ithaca (N.Y.)-London, 1999, p. 148.
19. See Vogel, E. *The Four Little Dragons: The Spread of Industrialization in East Asia*, Harvard University Press, Cambridge (Mass.)-London, 1991, p. 9.
20. See Pempel, T. J. *The Developmental Regime in a Changing World Economy*, p. 177.
21. See Haggard, S. *Developing Nations and the Politics of Global Integration*, Brookings Institution, Washington (D.C.), 1995, p. 49.
22. See Robinson, R., Goodman, D. S. G. (eds.) *The New Rich in Asia*, pp. 205, 161, 47, 135, 183, 77, 17.
23. See Adams, N. A. *Worlds Apart: The North-South Divide and the International System*, Zed Publishers, London-Atlantic Highlands (N.J.), 1997, pp. 219-220.
24. See Amsden, A. H. *Asia's Next Giant*, p. 67.
25. See Amsden, A. H. *Asia's Next Giant*, p. 116.
26. See Cumings, B. "The Asian Crisis, Democracy, and the End of 'Late' Development," in Pempel, T. J. (ed.) *The Politics of Asian Economic Crisis*, Cornell University Press, Ithaca (N.Y.)-London, 1999, p. 38; Weiss, L. *The Myth of the Powerless State: Governing the Economy in a Global Era*, Polity Press, Cambridge, 1998, p. 60.
27. See Dunning, J. H., Hoesel, R. van, Narula, R. "Third World Multinational Revisited: New Developments and Theoretical Implications," in Dunning, J. H. (ed.) *Globalization, Trade and Foreign Direct Investment*, Elsevier Science Ltd., Kinglington (U.K.), 1998, p. 278.
28. See Eichengreen, B. *Globalizing Capital: A History of the International Monetary System*, Princeton University Press, Princeton (N.J.), 1996, p. 188.
29. See Plender, J. *A Stake in the Future: The Stakeholding Solution*, Nicholas Brealey Publishing, London, 1997, p. 224.
30. See Bello, W., Rosenfeld, S. *Dragons in Distress: Asia's Miracle Economies in Crisis*, A Food First Book, San Francisco, (Cal.), 1992, p. 71.
31. See Soros, G. *The Crisis of Global Capitalism [Open Society Endangered]*, Little, Brown and Company, London, 1998, p. 139.
32. See McLeod, R. H., Garnaut R. (eds.) *East Asia in Crisis: From Being a Miracle to Needing One?* Routledge, London-New York, 1998, p. 92.
33. See Robinson, R., Goodman, D. S. G. (eds.) *The New Rich in Asia*, p. 95.
34. See Phongpaichit P., Baker Ch. *Thailand's Boom and Bust*, Silkworm Books, Chaing Mai (Thailand), 1998, p. 101.
35. See McLeod R. H., Garnaut R. *East Asia in Crisis*, p. 89.
36. See Murray, G. *Vietnam: Dawn Of a New Market*, St. Martin's Press, New York, 1997, pp. 110-111.
37. See French, P., Crabbe, M. *One Billion Shoppers: Accessing Asia's Consuming Passions and Fast-Moving Markets—After the Meltdown*, Nicholas Brealey Publishing, London, 1998, p. 158.

38. See Kemenade, W. van. *China, Hong Kong, Taiwan, Inc.*, Alfred A. Knopf, New York, 1997, pp. 4, 6-7, 37.
39. See Moody, K. *Workers in a Lean World: Unions in the International Economy*, Verso, London-New York, 1997, p. 13.
40. See Rohwer, J. *Asia Rising: How History's Biggest Middle Class Will Change the World*, Nicholas Brealey Publishing, London, 1996, p. 16.
41. See Strange, S. *Mad Money*, Manchester University Press, Manchester, 1998, p. 109.
42. See *Economist*, February 22, 1997, p. 89.
43. See *Economist*, May 24, 1997, p. 79.
44. For details see *Economist*, March 1, 1997, pp. 23-25.
45. For details see McLeod, R. H., Garnaut, R. (eds.) *East Asia in Crisis*, pp. 14-16.
46. See Lee E. *The Asian Financial Crisis: The Challenge for Social Policy*, International Labour Office, Geneva, 1998, p. 19.
47. See Bello, W., Rosenfeld, S. *Dragons in Distress*, p. 58.
48. See McLeod, R. H., Garnaut, R. *East Asia in Crisis*, pp. 66-67.
49. See Henderson, C. *Asia Falling: Making Sense of the Asian Crisis and Its Aftermath*, Businessweek Books/McGraw-Hill, New York, 1999, p. 244.
50. See Hirch, M. "Cronyism Crashes," *Newsweek*, January 26, 1998, p. 21.
51. See *Economist*, November 29, 1997, pp. 23-25.
52. See Hirch, M. "Where is the Bottom?" *Newsweek*, January 19, 1998, p. 34.
53. See Bello, W., Rosenfeld, S. *Dragons in Distress*, p. 40.
54. See *Economist*, April 12, 1997, p. 82.
55. See Goldstein, M. *The Asian Financial Crisis: Causes, Cures and Systemic Implications*, Institute for International Economics, Washington (D.C.), 1998, p. 8.
56. See Lee, E. *The Asian Financial Crisis*, pp. 4, 6.
57. See McLeod, R. H., Garnaut, R. *East Asia in Crisis*, p. 58.
58. See Henderson, C. *Asia Falling*, pp. 115-116.
59. See McLeod, R. H., Garnaut, R. *East Asia in Crisis*, p. 42.
60. See Henderson, C. *Asia Falling*, pp. 146-147; for details see Spaeth, A. "Sinking Feeling," *Time*, June 22, 1998, p. 40.
61. For details see Powell, B. "Hiccup? Or Global Meltdown?" *Newsweek*, December 29, 1997, pp. 20-21.
62. See Hamlin, M. A. *The New Asian Corporation: Managing for the Future in Post-Crisis Asia*, Jossey-Bass Publishers, San Francisco (Cal.), 2000, p. 69.
63. See Delhaise, P. *Asia in Crisis: The Implosion of the Banking and Finance Systems*, John Wiley & Sons (Asia) Pte Ltd., Singapore-New York, 1998, p. 16.
64. See Kreinin, M. E., Lowinger, T. C., Lal, A. K. "Determinants of Inter-Asian Direct Investment Flows," in Dunning, J. H. (ed.) *Globalization, Trade and Foreign Direct Investment*, p. 197.
65. See *The World Bank Policy Research Report: The Asian Miracle*, p. 113.
66. See Rodrik, D. *The New Global Economy and Developing Countries: Making Openness Work*, Overseas Development Council, Washington (D.C.), 1999, pp. 89-90.
67. See Winters, J. A. "The Determinant of Financial Crisis in Asia," in Pempel, T. J. (ed.) *The Politics of Asian Economic Crisis*, pp. 88, 81.
68. For details see Hatch, W., Yamamura, K. *Asia in Japan's Embrace*, pp. 78, 159-160, 178.
69. See Solomon, R. *Money on the Move: The Revolution in International Finance Since 1980*, Princeton University Press, Princeton (N.J.), 1999, p. 132.

70. See Clifford, M. L., Engardio, P. *Meltdown: Asia's Boom, Bust and Beyond*, Prentice Hall Press, Paramus (N.J.), 2000, p. 212.

71. See McLeod, R. H., Garnaut, R. *East Asia in Crisis*, p. 78.

72. See Lacayo, R. "IMF to the Rescue," *Time*, December 8, 1997, p. 23.

73. For details see *Economist*, March 7, 1998, Survey "East Asian Economies," pp. 5-9.

74. See Emerson, T. "Asia's Agony," *Newsweek*, October 12, 1998, p. 26.

75. See Spaeth, A. "Sinking Feeling," *Time*, June 22,1998, p. 40.

76. See Soros, G. *The Crisis of Global Capitalism*, p. 149.

77. See McLeod, R. H., Garnaut, R. *East Asia in Crisis*, pp. 80, 81.

78. See Ignatius, A. "Asia's Bad News," *Time*, May 18, 1998, p. 33.

79. See Eichengreen, B. *Toward a New International Financial Architecture: A Practical Post-Asia Agenda*, Institute for International Economics, Washington (D.C.), 1999, pp. 151-152.

80. See Cumings, B. "The Asian Crisis, Democracy, and the End of 'Late' Development," in Pempel, T. J. (ed.) *The Politics of the Asian Economic Crisis*, p. 28.

81. See Lee, E. *The Asian Financial Crisis*, p. 40.

82. See Larimer, T. "No Place For Strangers," *Time*, April 6, 1998, p. 26.

83   See Emerson, T. *Asia's Agony*, p. 26.

84. Calculated from: *Financial Times*, FT 500, London, 1997, pp. 83-86; *Financial Times*, May 4, 2000, Survey FT 500, p. 3.

85. See McCarthy, T. "Indonesia on the Brink," *Time*, March 23, 1998, pp. 36-37.

86. See Sender, H. "Daewoo's Foreign Creditors Face Decision on Debt-Buyout Proposal," *Wall Street Journal Europe*, May 4, 2000, p. 6.

87. See Phongpaichit, P., Baker, Ch. *Thailand's Boom and Bust*, p. 124.

88. See Lee, E. *The Asian Financial Crisis*, p. 53.

89. See Soros, G. *The Crisis of World Capitalism: Open Society in Danger*, Infra-M, Moscow, 1999, pp. 155-156 (in Russian).

90. See Goldstein, M. *The Asian Financial Crisis*, pp. 65-67.

91. See Luttwak, E. *Turbo-Capitalism: Winners and Losers in the Global Economy*, Weidenfeld & Nicolson, London, 1998, p. 241.

92. See *World Economic Outlook: A Survey by the Staff of the International Monetary Fund, May 1998*, IMF, Publication Service, Washington (D.C.), 1998, p. 3; Gough, L. *Asia Meltdown*, pp. 106-107, 128.

93. See Clifford, M. L., Engardio, P. *Meltdown*, p. 212.

94. See *Economist*, March 7, 1998, Survey "East Asian Economies," p. 4.

95. Calculated from: *Economist*, April 11, 1998, p. 64.

96. See *Economist*, April 15, 2000, pp. 82-83.

97. See Miklethwait, J., Wooldridge, A. *A Future Perfect: The Essentials of Globalization*, Crown Business, New York, 2000, p. 46.

98. See Clifford, M. L., Engardio, P. *Meltdown*, p. 252.

99. See *Economist*, April 15, 2000, p. 83.

100. See Clifford, M. L., Engardio, P. *Meltdown*, p. 252.

101. See Schuman, M. et al. "Korea's Economy Expands by 10.7%," *Wall Street Journal Europe*, March 23, 2000, p. 10.

102. See Plender, J. "Emerging from the Gloom," *Financial Times*, April 11, 2000, p. 14.

103. See *Economist*, July 31, 1999, p. 63.

104. See Ihlwan, M. "Coddling the Chaebol — and Courting Disaster," *Business Week*, European Edition, September 21, 1998, p. 33.

105. See Clifford, M. L., Engardio, P. *Meltdown*, p. 257.

106. See *World Economic Outlook: A Survey by the Staff of the International Monetary Fund, May 1999*, IMF, Publication Service, Washington (D.C.), 1999, p. 43.

107. See Hamlin, M. A. *The New Asian Corporation*, p. 37.

108. For details see Montagnon, P. "Still no Miracle Alternative to Reform for Asian Economies," *Financial Times*, June 2, 2000, p. 4; Schuman, M. "South Korean Economic Surge Stokes Interest-Rate Debate," *Wall Street Journal Europe*, May 24, 2000, p. 8.

109. See Burton, J. "Broadband Demand Drives South Korea Internet Advances," *Financial Times*, May 23, 2000, p. 21.

110. See Kirk, D. "Sell-Off in Seoul Drags Stocks to 13-Month Low," *International Herald Tribune*, May 23, 2000, p. 16.

111. See *International Herald Tribune*, May 24, 2000, p. 17.

112. See Emmerson, D. K. "Indonesia's Problems Mount, and Jakarta Isn't Doing Much," *International Herald Tribune*, June 2, 2000, p. 6.

113. See Backman, M. "The New Regime in Jakarta Is Beginning to Look Like the Old," *International Herald Tribune*, May 25, 2000, p. 6.

114. See Baird, M. "Indonesia's Problems Force World Bank to Rethink Its Role," *International Herald Tribune*, May 17, 2000, p. 8.

115. See Kotler, P., Jatusripitak, S., Maesincee, S. *The Marketing of Nations: A Strategic Approach to Building National Wealth*, Free Press, New York, 1997, pp. 53-54.

6

China: Sharing the Fate of the Others or Going Its Distinctive Way

For a number of reasons, analysts who study the evolution of the "catching up" countries pay special attention to China. First of all, the history of that country, its size and its share in the world's population—all these factors make the sweeping economic and social transformations in the PRC a phenomenon having an immediate effect on the world economic situation and the world balance of political forces. Second, modern China is, so far, the only country which has made a successful transition from the agrarian socialist past to the capitalist present and achieved a medium level of industrial development. Finally, there is no ignoring the fact that the destructive crisis which put the Asian model to an acid test has not changed the rate and direction of China's economic progress.

The successes achieved by the Chinese economy over the past two decades are indisputable. The gross national product growth rate has averaged over 10 percent a year, with most of the fast-growing exports going to the post-industrial nations and the country becoming self-sufficient in supply food Today China is successfully becoming an integrate part of the world information economy. The People's Republic of China is turning into a mighty regional superpower rapidly superseding Japan as the leader of the Asia-Pacific Region. The country's steady advance goes to show that its leaders have learned much from their neighbors' experience and from the abortive attempts at reforming the Soviet economy. Nevertheless, in analyzing the forecasts whose authors are trying to guess whether the PRC takes five or ten years from now to surpass the United States in the volume of GNP, one ought to bear in mind that analogous projections were made in the early 1970s with regard to Japan and that the fact that the Land of the Rising Sun had emerged unscathed from the 1987 stock exchange crash was also regarded as an indicator of its unshakeable stability. However, Japan's former prosperity vanished into thin air a decade later, while the United States consolidated its lead in the world economy. Without belittling the importance of Chinese reforms, we should realize that China's social change is basically identical to the evolution of any country following the "catching up" development model and that, therefore, one should not expect China either to carry on its crisis-free progress for too long, or to take the lead in the 21st-century world economy. Nevertheless, before we review the Russian record of economic reforms, let us trace the path traversed by our Southeastern neighbor.

Reforms in Retrospective and the Economy's Current State

Economic reforms were initiated in China in 1978-1979 when the country was in the throes of an acute crisis following the "cultural revolution"; what the nation needed then was not really a full-scale economic modernization but rather a set of measures to assure the elementary survival of the majority of the population engaged in agriculture for the most part. At the time industry was in embryo, the gross national product constituted no more than 373 yuan per capita which, even at the artificial exchange rate of 1.55 yuan to one US dollar, did not exceed $250 per capita a year.[1] Realizing full well that such a level was much too low to be equal to the task of building up a developed industrial economy, Chinese leaders decreed that the per capital GNP index be quadrupled by the year 2000. It is noteworthy that the reforms emphasized, first and foremost, the development of agriculture to the extent sufficient for meeting the population's minimal food requirements—an objective which had never figured on other Southeast Asian nations' lists of priorities.

The phenomenon of fast economic growth became a distinguishing feature of the Chinese "economic miracle." It is precisely by extrapolating the current trends into the future that many experts have conjured up a picture of that formerly backward country as an economic superpower, the leader of the Asian region and a dangerous rival of the United States. Statistics show that throughout the 1980s and early 1990s, China's economy grew at the rate of 9.8 to 14.2 percent a year, or faster than that of any other Asian country;[2] the forecasts about China's economic growth rate slowing down should, in our view, be taken cautiously. China's economic growth is erratic rather than decelerating, and its reported unevenness can be explained, to a degree, by statistical accounting difficulties. Be that as it may, the PRC's gross national product increased 68.6 percent in 1991-1995, and in 1996-2000 its increase is likely to amount to an estimated 50.4 percent at least.[3] Notably, the growing mass of commodities was largely consumed by the domestic market while labor productivity, extremely low in the pre-reform period, grew at the rate of 2 to 3.8 percent a year and accounted for up to 43 percent of the national income increment.[4] At first glance, that was where the Chinese economy compared favorably to those of other Asian countries.

The industrialization drive concentrated mostly in the coastal regions where the Communist government had set up the so-called export product processing zones of which there were more than a dozen already in the early years of reforms and which attracted considerable foreign investment (for example, in 1984-1993, over $5 billion were invested in the free economic zone of Dalians[5]). The bulk of China's industrial production facilities was concentrated in those export-oriented regions the most important of which was the complex of free economic zones located in the immediate vicinity of Hongkong, its economic growth rate averaging 17.3 percent in the period of 1978-1993. In this case, positive factors (such as the prevalence of direct foreign investment over portfolio investment: as distinct from South Korea, for example, where the latter, along with foreign loans, surpassed direct foreign investments in the production sphere 15-fold, in China direct capital investment was double the amount of the loans obtained and tens times the amount of portfolio investment[6]) do not compensate in full for the negative consequences of the economy's regionalization (at the beginning of 1994, nearly a third of all Chinese exports came from the coastal regions with a population of 23 million which is less than 1.4 percent of the country's total[7]). The export-oriented industries as such accounted for 24 percent of the entire gross national product[8] in the first quarter of 2000 and constituted the basic sector marked by a fast rise in employment and employee incomes.

The fact certainly worth mentioning in the context of the Chinese reforms is not only that they were initiated amid an extremely low level of the country's development but also that this level remains rather modest to this day. Although the estimates of China's GNP size vary considerably, our guess is that at present its average per capita   index   does   not   exceed $500-600 a year. Some sources say that the GNP constituted 373 yuan per capita in 1978; 816 yuan in 1985; and 1,558 yuan in 1990; in terms of US dollars at the official average exchange rate for each respective year, the figures were: $239 for 1978; $268 for 1985; and $327 for 1990.[9] Such statistics putting China on a level with Haiti, Sudan or Tanzania, the world's poorest countries, are certainly an understatement but the attempts to blow Chinese GNP indices out of all proportion to reality are hardly trustworthy, either. Statistics based on currencies' purchasing power, made public back in 1984, put China's per capita GNP at $300 in 1950 and $1,135 in1980; in this case, taking the Chinese economy's post-1980 growth rate into account, the corresponding index can be put at $2,444 for 1985 and at $5,100 for 2000. The latter means that today's China has attained a higher development level than Ireland has in 1985 or Portugal in 1990, which is contrary to common sense.[10] Experts who base their calculations on the scale of energy consumption in the Chinese economy and the yuan exchange rate to the dollar in terms of these currencies' purchasing power in the food and primitive consumer goods market estimate the amount of China's GNP at $1,300 per capita as of 1988.[11]

In the meantime, regional domestic product indices are known to differ considerably from province to province: in 1990, the per capita worth of the GNP amounted to $5,700 in Shenzhen and $1,510 in Guangzhou[12] and surpassed the national average 17 and 5.5 times, respectively, proceeding from this year's estimate of the average per capita GNP worth of $327 a year. If we proceed from the index of $1,300 a year, it will turn out that in Shenzhen the regional domestic product's per capita worth was double that of Hongkong (which amounted to over $412,000 then), which obviously does not correspond to reality. Therefore, we are inclined to agree with the official estimate whereby the average per capita worth of China's GNP does not exceed $600 today; this is convincingly confirmed by the ratio between the wage level in China (90 cents per hour in a quite well-to-do Shanghai) and that in other countries of the region ($3 per hour in Jakarta; $4.6 per hour in Kuala-Lumpur; $5.2 per hour in Singapore; and $6.2 in Seoul[13]). From this standpoint, official government estimates look realistic enough; according to them, village dwellers—of whom there are 800 million in China—earn $190 per capita a year, on the average, with more than 65 million farmers living below the official poverty line set in the PRC by law at the equivalent of $64 a year.[14] Notably, while city dwellers' incomes grew 7 percent a year, on the average, in the late 1990s, in the countryside the increase constituted a mere 1 percent;[15] nearly 120 million people—a tenth of the total population—could barely make both ends meet doing odd jobs for a living, and the number of chronically or temporarily unemployed which amounted to 142 million in 1997 (of whom 12 million in towns and 120 million in the countryside)[16] may top 260 million toward the end of the year 2000.[17] In this context one cannot but agree with Zb.Brzezinski who thinks that "even if China avoids serious political upheavals and miraculously succeeds in maintaining its superhigh growth rates another twenty-five years, ... it will still remain a very poor country by international standards, which provides enough grounds for skepticism about China's ability to become a truly mighty world power within the next two or three decades."[18]

Sources of Accelerated Economic Growth

As we proceed to a more detailed analysis of the factors behind a rapid progress of the Chinese economy, we immediately find among them those familiar to us from previous chapters. We mean, above all, a high rate of accumulation, cheap labor, large-scale foreign investment, export orientation of the economy and vigorous stimulation of economic growth by the state.

The *first* factor predominated throughout the 1980s and early 1990s. During that period private savings kept growing steadily despite relatively low GNP indices per capita. Over the years of reforms their share in the gross national product increased from 33.2 percent in 1978 to 40.4 percent in 1991 and have been hovering over the 40 percent mark since then.[19] Proceeding from the record of most countries developing along the lines of industrialization, one can confidentially predict that in the next 10 to 15 years, i.e. until the per capita GNP has reached $1.5-2 thousand a year, no serious reduction in the rate of savings motivated by the urge to get rich quick is to be expected; consequently, the Chinese economy's growth rate will, more likely than not, remain high for the rest of the current decade. Remarkably, an extremely low family income level characteristic of the Chinese economy makes it highly competitive. Calculations made on the basis of 1995 statistics are graphic evidence that Chinese workers' efficiency, estimated at $5.09 per $1 of wages, is double the corresponding index for Malaysia and Taiwan ($2.62 and $2.60, respectively) and over 3.5 times that for South Korea ($1.47),[20] which explains the Chinese economy's strong investor appeal. As a result, private entrepreneurs have been particularly active of late: whereas in 1978 capital investments made in the economy along the budget lines accounted for 15.1 percent of the GNP, and private investment totaled a mere 1.1 percent of the GNP, in 1991 these indices reversed constituting 1.8 and 18.7 percent of the GNP, respectively.[21] This fact does not testify to a sharp decline in government influence on the economy but visually confirms the latter's going market. Thus, today's China possesses a substantial inner investment potential, and the above-quoted statistics pertaining to the standards of living in its individual regions and to the scale of overt and covert unemployment show that "China has larger free manpower resources than its Asian neighbors do,"[22] which is an important condition of successful competition with other countries on their way to industrialization.

The *second* factor manifested itself in China even more vividly than in any other "catching up" country. We have already pointed out that direct capital investments in the sphere of material production and construction accounts for most of the foreign capital present in the Chinese economy; according to official statistics, $194 billion or 78 percent of $250 billion invested in the Chinese economy in 1993-1997 were channeled directly into production, with only 22 percent arriving in the shape of private or interstate credits.[23] In 1983-1994, the volume of direct foreign investment in the Chinese economy increased 18 times[24] and this has certainly served as a major catalyst of China's economic growth in the first half of the 1990s. By 1994, more than 22,700 foreign-owned enterprises were registered in China; they employed 23 million workers and accounted for 37 percent of all the export products the aggregate worth of which increased from $13 billion to $47 billion in 1991-1995;[25] in the second half of the 1990s, about 20,000 foreign companies opened their branches or representative offices in China *every year*.[26] In 1993 alone, the government approved the drawing of investment in the amount of over $111 billion which surpassed the level attained over the previous 13 years; in 1994 it went up another 44 percent.[27] That was how the Chinese economy gained a broad access to foreign capital channeled into the production sphere.

When examining a growing influx of foreign investments in China, it is easy to trace the stages of the Chinese economy's liberalization. Their impressive dynamics as such came from a change of course effected at the end of the 1970s; the process gained momentum following Deng Xiaoping's famous "southern tour" of 1991. Before the early 1990s, joint ventures in which the Chinese party owned, as a rule, the controlling interest had been the most common form of foreign participation. Whereas 83 such ventures were registered in the country in 1979-1982, in 1991 alone the number of new joint ventures constituted 8,395.[28] In the 1990s, emphasis was shifted to a mass registration of companies with a 100 percent foreign participation, which offered investors entirely new business opportunities and was supposed to intensify the influx of capital sharply. The move lived up to the hopes pinned on it: whereas in 1991 direct capital investment did not exceed the $4 billion limit, in 1992 it reached $11 billion, climbing up to $26 billion in 1993 and topping $40 billion in 1996,[29] despite the fact that about 80 percent of the businesses set up with foreign participation still have the form of joint ventures and that only slightly over 20 percent of them are under foreign capital's undivided control. The total volume of capital investment declared in the newly-formed companies' Articles of Association exceeded $400 billion by then.[30]

An observer should bear in mind a number of specific features characteristic of capital investment in the Chinese economy the most prominent of them being a *strongly pronounced ethnic character of investment*. As distinct from most Asian countries for which Japan is the principal source of foreign investment, the bulk of capital invested in the Chinese economy comes from the countries in which the Chinese either make up a majority of the population, or are the principal economic players. Whereas in 1985, investment made by companies based in Hongkong or Macao—territories which reverted to China in 1997 and 1999, respectively—constituted 49.9 percent of the foreign capital influx into the country, in 1989 their share amounted to 62.1 percent, and in 1993 (including Taiwan the population of which consists of the ethnic Chinese only and which may also be reunited with main land China in the foreseeable future), 76.2 percent.[31] Before coming under China's control Hongkong had not only invested nearly $93 billion in the PRC but also set up 50,000 companies there which had over 4 million employees, thus transferring practically all of its industry to China. (It is a well-known fact that by the mid-1990s only nine percent of Hong Kong's GNP was generated by its industrial sector).[32] By 1997, investment coming in from Hong Kong accounted for about 5 percent of China's GNP and remained a pledge of the prosperity of the coastal provinces which produced (and still do) most of China's exports.[33] Hong Kong, Macao and Taiwan still have a crucial role to play; although their estimates vary somewhat,[34] most experts agree that these three sources are responsible for over three-quarters of foreign investment in the Chinese economy.[35] In the meantime, the role of other investors in financing the Chinese economy is diminishing steadily; over the period of 1985-1993, the share of US investment, for example, shrank from 18.3 percent to 7.4 percent, and that of Japan's, from 16.1 to 4.9 percent.[36]

Now that Hongkong and Macao reverted to China (in 1997 and 1999, respectively), and in the event of Taiwan following suit, the PRC will depend for most of foreign capital investment on other Asian countries which have strong and influential ethnic Chinese communities and which are now responsible for about 15 percent of all the foreign capital investment in Chaina. In the mid-1990s, there were about 25 million ethnic Chinese in Southeast Asia (not counting Hongkong, Macao and Taiwan), whose shares in the populations of Malaysia, Thailand, Indonesia and the Philippines constituted 32; 15; 4; and 1 percent, respectively.[37] As of 1990, they owned industrial, trading and service companies, immovables and commodity reserves worth an estimated $450 billion which amount surpassed mainland China's GNP by a quarter.[38] Accumulation rates in the companies they owned were no lower than those in the PRC and constituted from 25 to 45 percent. As a result, this part of the "Chinese" economy was estimated at $700 billion in 1996—an amount which almost equaled the PRC's gross national product at that time.[39] Even these statistics do not convey a full notion of the influence the ethnic Chinese wielded in Southeast Asian countries. Back in 1990, the Chinese diaspora controlled, through its companies, liquid assets (not counting shares and other industrial securities) to an amount

about 3 to 4 times the worth of its own property. Some experts estimate that amount at $1.5 to 2 trillion,[40] other regard $3 trillion as the
point of departure to be used in such calculations.[41] The maximum
assessment of the worth of the Chinese supranational economic
empire belongs to D.Landes who estimated it at $2.5 trillion.[42]

These statistics suggest that in the early 1990s the Chinese
economy outside the limits of China proper constituted about 60
percent of the GNP of Japan, the world second-biggest economic
superpower. Chinese emigrants and their heirs have created giant
financial empires in Asia: 39 out of 100 Asian billionaires are of
Chinese origin, with 12 families "worth" over $5 billion each.[43] As
of mid-1994, ethnic Chinese entrepreneurs owned controlling interests in 517 out of 1,000 large industrial companies—front runners
of the stock exchange listings in Seoul, Taipei, Shanghai, Shenzhen,
Hongkong, Bangkok, Kuala-Lumpur, Singapore, Jakarta and Ma-
nila.[44] In Malaysia and Thailand they owned over 62 and 80 percent
of the leading companies' shares' respectively.[45] Their presence was
particularly conspicuous in Indonesia where ethnic Chinese, constituting by various estimates 3.6 to 4.2 percent of the population, owned
70 percent of all the businesses outside the public sector, 240 out of
300 largest companies, and 14 out of 15 leading industrial and financial conglomerates of the country.[46] As to Singapore's economy,
most experts consider it to be under the Chinese diaspora's practically undivided control. Such an influential position of the ethnic
Chinese has been attracting ever closer attention over the past few
years; Western analysts are gravely apprehensive of the likely political consequences of their economic expansion. In the early 1990s,
P.Drucker coined the term "non-Communist Chinese societies"[47]
which now has come to be increasingly associated with Hongkong,
Taiwan, Singapore, South Korea, Malaysia and, partly, Indonesia;
over the past few years, Zb.Bzezinski has repeatedly pointed to the
danger of puppet pro-Chinese governments coming to power in a
number of South Asian countries.[48]

We have dwelt on this problem in such detail for two reasons. On
the one hand, an analysis of foreign investment in the PRC economy
from the angle of where it comes from suggests that China is Asia's
only country which has benefited from the destructive 1997-1998
crisis. In a situation where Chinese businessmen in Southeast Asia
have either become *personae non gratae* as is the case in Malaysia

and Indonesia, or (at best) can no longer invest their capitals as profitably as they used to, the PRC can expect an avalanche of investment while the rest of the Asian countries are critically short of it. On the other hand, enormous capital investment in China's economy (often seen by Russian analysts as a confirmation of the theory that a post-communist country on its way to a market-oriented economy becomes a highly attractive investment medium) is of a specific nature, and there is absolutely no reason to believe the phenomenon to be typical, to project it onto the Russian reality and to try and use it as the basis for totally unrealistic forecasts about the Russian economy's investor appeal.

The *third* of the factors under consideration is also of tremendous importance. China's economic growth, like many other Asian countries', largely depends on the expansion of export trade. Moreover, the highest growth rates have been shown either by the industries manufacturing traditional Chinese exports (mass produced industrial goods), foreign companies engaged in the assembly of primarily electronic goods out of western-made components, or construction firms active in coastal regions and large cities and geared to foreign investors or Chinese exporters, above all. A rapid rise in Chinese exports (averaging 16 percent a year throughout the post-reform period)[49] led to an increase in Chinese commodity shipments from $9.8 billion in 1978 to $121 billion in 1993, which corresponds to 0.6 and 2.5 percent of the world export volume, respectively.[50] In 1997, the volume of China's foreign trade constituted about $320 billion, with exports accounting for about $180 billion; imports, for slightly under $140 billion; and the favorable balance of trade exceeding $40 billion.[51] Although the latter decreased to $25 billion over the period of 1998-1999, the structure of imports changed in favor of cheaper commodities from the newly-industrialized countries of Asia, while import from the United States and Europe is stagnating.[52]

When analyzing the state of China's export trade today it is important, on the one hand, not to overstate its present scale and, on the other, to take a realistic approach to the question of the Chinese economy's growth potential. It is quite obvious that the country the GNP of which is comparable with the gross output of the New York State and falls far short of California's cannot be the leader of world trade even in absolute value indices let alone export structure. In the second quarter of 1997 which can be regarded as the last representative period preceding the onset of the Asian crisis, the volume of China's export ($46.1 billion) was smaller than that of Hongkong ($47.8 billion), surpassing 1.3-1.5 times only the relevant indices for South Korea ($35.8 billion), Singapore ($32.1 billion) and Taiwan ($30,7 billion).[53] By accounting for about 2.3 percent of the world trade turnover in 1992, China thus just went back to the level it had achieved in 1928(!).[54] On the leading exporters' list compiled on the basis of gross export worth estimates, China is now under Belgium (pop. 10 million)[55] and far below the Netherlands and Switzerland. Over the past few years researchers have been stressing the scale of Chinese export to the United States—and with good reason too: whereas in 1984 China's favorable balance of trade with the United States constituted $100 million,[56] by the year 1988 it reached $3.4 billion, and seven years later the figure increased tenfold jumping to $33.8 billion. Since June 1996, the United States' trade deficit with China began to surpass its trade deficit with Japan ($3.3 billion as against $3.2 billion a month). At the same time, the scale of China's export to the United States surpasses that from America fourfold while the corresponding index for Japan is a mere 1.6.[57] It should be borne in mind, however, that almost 60 percent of Chinese exports are manufactured not by Chinese companies, strictly speaking, but by 100 percent foreign-owned ones belonging to international corporations which actually makes the marketing of these products part of US or Japanese domestic trade.[58] Also, there is no ignoring the fact that even in the mid-1990s the entire volume of China's export to the United States did not exceed, in terms of value, 0.12 percent of the latter's GNP,[59] and although it has doubled since then, there is no reason to regard Chinese economic expansion as a serious threat to the United States. Finally, restricting trade with China will be no problem at all for American manufacturers because in terms of value US exports to China constitute almost a fourth of what the United States imports from that country[60], so the loss of such a market will have no fatal consequences for the United States.

At the same time, it should be noted that China compares favorably to its neighbors, if we may say so, in a most moderate degree to which it promotes its foreign trade. Over the 1980s and 1990s, its export trade grew only 1.5-1.8-fold faster than its GNP did, which made it possible to maintain an acceptable relationship between the domestic and foreign markets as catalysts of economic growth. The volumes of export did not exceed 20 percent of the GNP which is far short of the corresponding figures for other countries of the region. The fact that China exports less high technology products than South Korea, Taiwan or Japan helps retaining competitiveness of its goods on the foreign market because the PRC's dependence on the purchases of technologies and accessories is much lower than that of other countries. Whereas South Korea or Indonesia depend heavily for their growth on the world market demand for their products (the Asian region's current gradual emergence from depression is due, above all, to an increase in export deliveries to the United States and Europe), the Chinese economy's reliance on export for dynamic progress is much lower which makes its outlook for the future a bit brighter.

The *fourth* factor is connected with the influence of the state on the country's economic growth. For all the obvious liberalization of China's economic life, the central government still has a more substantial role to play in mapping out the country's development strategy than is the case in Japan or South Korea. Over the past few years the share of private and mixed enterprises which now account for 13.5 and 38 percent of the gross national product has been growing against the background of the giant public sector the share of which in the GNP was in excess of 50 percent until as recently as four years ago.[61]

For all that, state enterprises provide jobs for an overwhelming majority of the workers—125 out of 170 million of those employed in industrial production—which in itself testifies to their low efficiency. In the mid-1990s that giant industrial sector employing more than 70 percent of the nation's industrial workforce and using almost 75 percent of all the fixed assets and raw materials available, could do no better than produce a mere 32 percent of the total industrial output (according to the latest projections, this index is to diminish to 30 percent in 2000 and to constitute no more than 18 percent in 2010)[62], and its share in the aggregate profit of all the Chinese enterprises taken together did not exceed 1 (one!) percent.[63] In 1995, China's state-run enterprises first showed an aggregate loss estimated at 3 billion yuans (about $400 million),[64] and already in the following year half of 118,000 public enterprises showed losses in their balance sheets which totaled $7.2 billion—15-plus times the previous year's figure.[65] By the close of the year 1996, the worth of unrealised commodity stocks in the economy ran into over $65 billion. As a result, state companies raised enormous loans the total amount of which increased from $86 billion to $120 billion within the space of just three years, from 1993 to 1996, constituting today from 80 to 90 percent of all the loans extended by state-controlled banks and other financial institutions.[66]

As we have already pointed out above, the need for borrowed funds is growing as the budgetary financing of state companies is being cut down. As a result, the ratio between such companies' aggregate liabilities and their market value amounts to 500 percent today, and the state-owned banks' profit earning capacity has declined to 0.5 percent.[67] Analysts are divided on the magnitude of the problems facing the Chinese banking system. Chinese banks are certainly not in danger of an immediate loss of liquidity as was the case in Thailand, Indonesia and even South Korea in 1997 because the government control exercised over the banking system may prevent that. In the meantime, most Western experts believe that loans unlikely to be ever repaid constitute about 25 percent of the Chinese banks' total assets.[68] Some analysts insist that the figure is larger still, 25-30 percent of the credit portfolio, dismissing 20 percent of them as utterly hopeless.[69] In absolute terms, this may amount to $250 billion. Characteristically, the government's emphasis on the accelerated development of the economically backward western regions of the country will inevitably cause a rise in irrecoverable loans issued by state-owned banks: these loans may add up to a total of $600 billion by as early as 2002.[70] Even without looking too far ahead it is plain that a write-off of problem credits would be equivalent to a loss of 18-20 percent of the GNP[71] or to an actual rollback of the economy 2.5-3 years backwards (Chinese experts, however, are inclined to estimate the irrecoverable debts run up by China's banks at no more than 6-8 percent of their loan portfolio)[72]. Be that as it may, the danger of the current situation also consists in that private savings are snowballing: within the period of 1986-1996 this index increased over 15-fold,[73] and today Chinese banks hold deposits of over $600 billion.[74] Under the circumstances, the potentialities of the government which has allocated $33 billion to four largest state-owned banks to help them maintain their current liquidity look limited and, in the event of a crisis, will have no determining role to play.[75]

In the spring of 1998, the 15th Congress of the Communist Party of China put the task of reforming the public sector high on the list of priorities for the next few years. The following vital aspects of this task were singled out: transforming the management system of state-owned enterprises; improving the state of the banking system's financial health; putting the black market under control; cutting back on the capital outflow from the country; fighting corruption. At the same time, measures are being taken to stimulate production whose growth rates has been slowing down since 1992 when the GNP's growth rate reached an all-time high of 13.4 percent. In 1999, growth rate constituted a mere 7.1 percent, with many experts regarding this figure as an overstatement. Characteristically, since the onset of the Asian crisis the Chinese government has been annually financing various programs supposed to accelerate economic growth rate which cost it at least $30 billion a year—almost 3 percent of the GNP. Those programs brought no tangible results, however (experts have estimated that a $3 credit injection into China's economy brings a production increment worth only $2).[76] Most of the other administrative measures taken by the government have been of little avail, either.

Summing up, it must be admitted that China has achieved impressive successes in a catching up effort: it has solved some vital problems (achieved self-sufficiency for food, in particular, today it has surpassed the United States in egg, pork and grain consumption)[77] and built up an industry which does not only meet the domestic market's requirements but maintains a steady favorable balance of trade and a continuous increase of currency reserves (from $2.26 billion in 1980[78] to $130 billion in 1997[79] and $159 billion in January 2000[80]). Despite these successes, optimism about China's outlook for the future, displayed by many Western and Russian analysts, seems premature to us.

Problems and Prospects

So the successes of the Chinese economy stem from a near-optimum ratio between domestic and external investment sources, and a tested reliance on national and international markets. Nevertheless, economic progress still rests on extensive factors—extremely cheap labor and truly inexhaustible manpower resources (China's population is over 1.25 billion today and is expected to grow to an estimated 1.43-1.53 billion by 2020-2025).[81] Such "advantages" are fraught with a number of acute problems which may pose a danger both to China and to human mankind at large.

A drive for maximizing production indices leads to a rapacious consumption of natural resources. In 1957-1988 alone, China lost over 16 million hectares of arable land which constituted almost 14.5 percent of the entire sawn area as of the late 1950s[82]. The area under grain crops shrank from 105.2 to 96.6 million hectares in 1961-1990 (a more than 50 percent reduction per capita)[83]. About 40 percent of the fertilizers applied to rice fields are wasted because of their inefficient use.[84] It is small wonder, therefore, that whereas in the 1980s the agricultural sector's gross output grew at an average rate of 5.7 percent a year, in the 1990s this index barely reached 3.3 percent,[85] falling in some years to 1.9 percent a year. Most experts agree that by the year 2020 the PRC will become the world's leading food importer. Over the past thirty years China has lost three-quarters of its forest cover;[86] over the 1980s, tree felling rates exceeded by 40 percent the maximum permissible limit beyond which the felling-renewal balance is upset.[87] The volume of aggregate losses connected with the destruction of forests and the subsequent destruction of soils is estimated by experts at 5.5 to 9.5 percent of the nation's GNP.[88]

These, however, are not the most alarming tendencies. After all, the foregoing statistics have to do with the country's domestic problems. Seeking to minimize their products' cost with a view to enhancing their competitiveness, Chinese businessmen and the state are displaying a flagrant disregard for modern ecological standards. Coal production has increased forty-fold in the country over the past forty years: whereas in 1949 China produced slightly over 30 million tons of coal a year, by 1976 the figure rose to 500 million tons, and in 1990 China became the world leading coal producer (1.1 billion tons a year)[89]. In 1995, the government approved a sweeping national program for the expansion of the network of coal-burning power stations and other power generation plants[90] the implementation of which will bring coal consumption in the PRC up to 15 procent of the world's.[91] Coal combustion efficiency is extremely low: 15 to 25 percent for most household turnaces (to compare, heating systems burning diesel fuel have an efficiency of 50-60 percent, and gas-burning systems, 80-95 percent); steam locomotives, common in China, have an efficiency of 6-8 percent, at best, as against 25 percent and over featured by modern diesel engines.[92] As a result, it has turned out that "the coal China is burning adds more sulfur dioxide and nitrogen oxide discharges to the atmosphere than improved environment pollution control systems detract from it in all the OECD countries taken together".[93]

International comparisons in this sphere look dismal. In the period from 1950 to 1989 China led the world in the amount of CO_2 discharges into the atmosphere which increased 30 fold since then, from 0.08 to 2.4 billion tons per year.[94] As a result, China became the world's third worst CO_2 polluter of the atmosphere responsible for 11.2 percent of its total discharge (which is in excess of the relevant indices for Japan, Germany and the UK taken together), with the USSR accounting for 15.8 percent and the US, for 21.8 percent. In 1996, amid the deepening economic crisis in the former Soviet constituent republics which caused a sharp drop in energy consumption, China moved to the second line on that list of dubious "credit standings". Since 1992, the PRC has been firmly maintaining the lead for the volume of CO_2 discharges per unit of the gross national product (5.2 tons per $1,000 worth of the GNP[95]). Expert calculations inspire no hope for a radical change in the situation; the accelerated economic development programs now being implemented in China will lead to the share of coal in the overall pattern of energy carriers used worldwide increasing from 42 percent in1985 to 53 percent in 2020.[96] By about the same year, China will take over from the United States not as the world's largest economy but as the world's worst polluter of the atmosphere.[97]

Over the last few years the Chinese government has given the go-ahead to a rapid development of chemical production facilities including extremely hazardous ones thus giving rise to a multitude of problems. Having declined to join in important international agreements on the protection of the environment (the well-known Montreal Protocol, in particular) China has doubled, over the past five years alone, the output of ozone-destroying substances and taken the lead in this sphere: today it produces more such substances than all the industrialized countries and Russia do taken together.[98] Such are only some of the aspects of the accelerated industrialization policy being pursued as part of "building socialism Chinese-style".

As it enters the 21st century, China is cherishing high hopes of becoming a new Pacific superpower. Although its defence budget is an estimated one-seventh of that of the United states,[99] the PRC is, without a doubt, one of the strongest countries in Asia militarily. From this angle, Z.Brzezinski's words to the effect that the US policy in that region should boil down to devising a stratagem towards channeling Japan's energy into solving international problems and restricting China's might to regional confines[100] sound reasonable enough. China's economic growth rate is much higher than these of the other Asian countries. Unlike most of them, China emerged from the 1997 crisis practically unscathed. In that year, its GNP increased 10 percent, by early 2000 its currency reserves grew to almost $160 billion, direct foreign investments which increased more than 15 percent—from $37 billion to $42.3 billion—in 1996, amounted to $43 billion (another record high) in the post-crisis year of 1998.[101] At the beginning of 2000 there appeared strong indications of the coming rise in the growth rate because by the end of the first quarter the GNP showed an increase by 8.1 percent as against a 7-percent growth in 1999.[102] In January-March of the current year, the volume of export was 39 percent up on the last year's figure, and the total worth of the contracts signed jumped 27 percent. The government keeps the national economy and prices under strict control, taking every measure to prevent the devaluation of the yuan and retaining the ownership of 68 percent of shares of all the 1007 listed Chinese companies.[103]

In our opinion, there is every reason to believe that the Chinese economy is capable of avoiding the crisis which has hit the rest of the Asian countries. There are several factors to support this assumption: the reasonable evolutionary way of development the Chinese government has opted for, its well-balanced policy in the sphere of international trade and currency reserve buildup and, besides, certain specifics ranging from a populous diaspora abroad to a low standard of living of the population making it possible to keep Chinese products competitive. All that does not mean, though, that China embodies an ideal model of society capable of attaining the post-industrial countries' standard some time—even in the distant future.

Comparisons between the United States and China have become ideologized in the extreme over the past few years. The adherents of accelerated modernization theories and practices are emphasising

China's achievements and overstating the volume of the its gross domestic product. This is particularly true of the works by those Russian authors who hold China up as an example of a successful transition to the market economy with the central government retaining its influence on and control over the economy. Such attitudes are backed by over-inflated estimates of the Chinese GNP putting it at 80 percent of the United States' GNP as of early 1999; if that were true, one would expect the PRC to surpass the United States in the volume of the gross national product by as early as 2006[104]. As a matter of fact, such estimates derive from comparisons made between parities of currencies' purchasing powers and, owing to extremely low prices in China's home market, turn out to be overstated several-fold. As W.Greider pointed out, with good reason, the use of hard currency, the world economy's only objective criterion, as the unit of measurement will reveal the utter absurdity of the view that China ranks third or fourth among the countries capable of catching up with the United States in 10-15 years from now[105].

The researchers who presume that China can overtake the United States generally ignore the numerous differences between these nations' real economic potentials at the threshold of the new millennium. In 1999, only six Chinese companies found themselves on the list of the world's top 500 corporations owing chiefly to the size of their assets (the Sinopec oil company, for example, employs 1.2 million). In the meantime, the total assets and sales volumes of China's 500 biggest companies average a mere 0.9 and 1.7 percent of the corresponding indices of the companies meeting the *Financial Times* 500 rating qualifications.[106] Besides that, most of the authors drawing such comparisons fail to estimate capitalized values of Chinese and US stock markets and, finally, to take per capita income and GNP indices into account. It is quite obvious, however, that given the US economic growth rate of 3 percent a year (actually it has been much higher of late), the GNP increases by $950 per capita, on the average, while in case of China, with its economic growth rate of 9 percent a year, the corresponding index increases by only $300, at most. So, even if China succeeds in keeping up its superhigh growth rate for years at a stretch, every average Chinese citizen will be getting $600 poorer than his American counterpart[107] every year—such is the simple arithmetic of the "catching up" development strategy today. Other facts not to be overlooked either are that the PRC imports at least 3 billion dollars' worth of computer software and technologies annually and that 95 percent of Chinese students receiving education abroad never return home. Therefore, those who maintain that the prospect of China ever becoming the world's research and development center is highly unlikely may not be too far from the truth. In terms of the present-day reality this is tantamount to saying that China will hardly ever assume the dominating position in the world economy.[108]

Although Western experts are not inclined to underestimate China's successes today, most of them agree that the PRC may be more of a political and military threat to the post-industrial world rather than its dangerous economic rival. A dramatic acceleration of the Western countries' progress as they enter the era of the information economy, and the amount of the wealth produced in the sphere of the new economy add weight to L.Thurow's prediction that even in a hundred years from now, in 2100, China will be able to guarantee its population an average per capita income constituting 70 percent of that of Japan, in terms of the yuan's purchasing power, and only 20 percent of the same in terms of the yuan's value against the US dollar.[109]

China largely depends on its steadily favorable balance of trade for the stability of its economic advance. The former manifests the fact that China can practically manage without importing high-technology products and information systems from the US and Europe a high cost of which retards the crisis-stricken countries' economic progress. In other words the successes achieved by China are, to a certain extent, reminiscent of the situation in Japan which had shown how effectively an industrial country can operate in world markets in the midst of post-industrial ones. Therefore, presuming that the PRC, which is now at the active industrialization stage, is capable of striding into the post-industrial world means nursing a hope which is as illusory as the myth of the Asian economies' likely domination in the 21st century.

* * *

For all the specific features of its development, the Chinese economy shares most of the trends discernible in the economic progress of most countries which have opted for the "catching up" development strategy. Naturally enough, Chinese reformers may (and do) learn from the experience of the PRC's Asian neighbors, of the former Soviet republics and, partly, of Japan. Admittedly, however,

China has not as yet come up against any of the problems the said countries have failed to offer a satisfactory solution for. This is due not so much to the Chinese leaders' wisdom as, above all, to the fact that China, for all its achievements, has actually not advanced too far towards a developed industrialized society. Although the ideology underlying the Chinese reforms is basically sound, it nevertheless presupposes making the most of the advantages offered by the current situation in the country and objectively geared to the use of intensive growth factors. At the same time, this ideology is far more geared to the nation's ambition to gain a special place in the world economic system than other Asian countries' programs were. Historical experience shows, however, that the wider the gap between this or that strategy's objectives and their feasibility, the more likely—and painful—its failure becomes. China will hardly stop at the stage where it is destined to stop for it will never content itself with being just a steadily developing country with a relatively high standard of living. Its urge to assert itself as the chief economic force may reduce to naught many of the achievements awaiting the nation in the near future. An extrapolation of Japan's and other Southeast Asian countries' "catching up" development trends—both past and present—discussed in previous chapters suggests the conclusion that a major crisis may hit the PRC after it has achieved the level of economic development comparable with that of today's Thailand, Malaysia and, possibly, even South Korea. It is precisely at that level that the advantages stemming from manpower cheapness are lost, and if a failure to start designing modern technologies of its own and to use them for a massive retooling of its production facilities, declining demand in Western market may bring the Chinese industry's triumphant advance to a halt. In another scenario, China may become Asia's No.1 industrial country with the bulk of its output swallowed up by the nearby markets (the Japanese one included to a certain extent) and by domestic consumers. In that case a crisis would be less likely, but such a scenario presupposes the abandonment by China, in some form or other, of its attempts to become a key player in the worldwide economy "game," which is highly improbable. Summing up, although its economy will hardly fall prey to a crisis comparable to that of 1997, China—and other embodiments of the "catching up" development concept, for that matter—will never succeed in approaching the post-industrial nations' level.

Notes

1. See Ayres, R. U. *Turning Point: An End to the Growth Paradigm*, Earthscan Publications Ltd., London, 1998, p. 57.
3. Calculated from: *East Asian Institute. China's Economy and the Asian Financial Crisis*, Occasional Paper No. 4, Singapore University Press, Singapore, 1998, pp. 8-9; Kynge J. "China Hopes to Turn Corner on Growth," *Financial Times*, February 29, 2000, p. 6.
4. See Chai, J. C. H. *China: Transition To a Market Economy*, Clarendon Press, Oxford, 1997, p. 150.
5. See Ohmae, K. *The End of the Nation-State: The Rise of Regional Economies*, Free Press, New York, 1995, p. 86.
6. See Mitchell, J., Beck, P., Grubb, M. *The New Geopolitics of Energy*, Royal Institute of International Affairs, London, 1996, p. 100.
7. See Yergin, D., Stanislaw, J. *The Commanding Heights: The Battle Between Government and the Maketplace That Is Remaking the Modern World*, Simon & Schuster, New York, 1998, p. 208.
8. See Roberts, D. "China's Wealth Gap," *Business Week*, European Edition, May 8, 2000, p. 28.
9. See Dent, Ch. M. *The European Economy: The Global Context*, Routledge, London-New York, 1997, p. 152.
10. For details see Smil, V. *China's Environmental Crisis: An Inquiry into the Limits of National Development*, An East Gate Book/M. E. Sharpe, Armonk (N.Y.)-London, 1993, p. 71.
11. See Smil, V. *China's Environmental Crisis*, pp. 71-73.
12. See Ohmae, K. *The End of the Nation-State*, p. 82.
13. See Spaeth, A. "Big Kid on the Block," *Time*, September 29, 1997, p. 35.
14. See McGeary, J. "The Next China," *Time*, March 3, 1997, p. 24.
15. See Roberts, D. "China's Wealth Gap," *Business Week*, European Edition, May 8, 2000, p. 28.
16. See Serril, M. S. "Can This Man Fix China?" *Time*, March 16, 1998, p. 29.
17. See Gray, J. *False Dawn: The Delusions of Global Capitalism*, Granta Books, London, 1998, pp. 188-189.
18. Brzezinski, Zb. *The Grand Chessboard: American Primacy and Its Geostrategic Imperatives*, Basic Books, New York, 1997, p. 163.
19. See Chai, J. C. H. *China: Transition To a Market Economy*, p. 118.
20. See Marber, P. *From Third World to the World Class: The Future of Emerging Markets in the Global Economy*, Perseus Books, Reading (Mass.), 1998, p. 99.
21. See Chai, J. C. H. *China: Transition To a Market Economy*, p. 118.
22. Henderson, C. *Asia Falling: Making Sense of the Asian Crisis and Its Aftermath*, Business Week Books/McGraw-Hill, New York, 1999, p. 268.
23. See Naughton, B. "China: Domestic Restructuring and a New Role in Asia," in Pempel, T. J. (ed.) *The Politics of the Asian Economic Crisis*, Cornell University Press, Ithaca (N.Y.)-London, 1999, p. 206.
24. See Li, C. *China: The Consumer Revolution*, Singapore-New York, 1998, p. 29.
25. See *Economist*, March 8, 1997, Survey "China," p. 10.
26. See Li, C. *China: The Consumer Revolution*, John Wiley & Sons (Asia) Pte Ltd.-Deloitte & Touch Consulting Group, 1998, p. 29.
27. See Chai, J. C. H. *China: Transition To a Market Economy*, p. 160.
28. See Goldman, M. *Lost Opportunity: What Has Made Economic Reform in Russia so Difficult?* W.W. Norton & Co., New York-London, 1996, p. 206.

29. See Dent, Ch. M. *The European Economy: The Global Context*, p. 152; *Economist*, March 8, 1997, Survey "China," p. 10.
30. See Pearson, M. *China's New Business Elite: The Political Consequences of Economic Reform*, University of California Press, Berkeley (Cal.)-London, 1997, p. 10.
31. See Chai, J. C. H. *China: Transition To a Market Economy*, p. 160.
32. See Vines, S. *Hong Kong: China's New Colony*, Aurum Press, London, 1998, p. 182.
33. See Rosecrance, R. *The Rise of the Virtual State: Wealth and Power in the Coming Century*, Basic Books, New York, 1999, p. 113.
34. See Pomfret, R. *Asian Economies in Transition: Reforming Centrally Planned Economies*, Edward Elgar, Cheltenham (U.K.)-Brookfield (U.S.), 1996, p. 41.
35. For details see On-Kwok, L., So, A. Y. "Hong Kong and the Newly Industrializing Economies: From Americanization to Asianization," in Postiglione, G. A., Tang, J. T. H. (eds.) *Hong Kong's Reunion with China: The Global Dimensions*, M. E. Sharpe, Armonk (N.Y.)-London, 1997, pp. 112-113.
36. See Hajari, N. "High Seas Diplomacy," *Time*, April 21, 1997, p. 57.
37. See Yergin, D., Stanislaw, J. *The Commanding Heights*, p. 189.
38. *Economist*, July 18, 1992, pp. 21-22.
39. See Gray, J. *False Dawn*, p. 59.
40. See Hobday, M. *Innovation in East Asia: The Challange to Japan*, Edward Elgar, Cheltenham (U.K.)-Lyme (U.S.), 1997, p. 22.
41. See Yergin, D., Stanislaw, J. *The Commanding Heights*, p. 189.
42. See Landes, D. *The Wealth and Poverty of Nations: Why Some Are So Rich and Some So Poor*, Little, Brown and Company, London, 1998, p. 478.
43. See Hiscock, G. *Asia's Wealth Club*, Nicholas Brealey Publishing, London, 1997, p. 29.
44. See Naisbitt, J. *Megatrends Asia: The Eight Asian Megatrends That Are Changing the World*, Nicholas Brealey Publishing, London, 1996, p. 3.
45. See *Drucker on Asia: A Dialogue Between Peter Drucker and Isao Nakauchi*, Butterworth-Heinemann, Oxford, 1997, p. 7.
46. See Moreau, R., Nordland, R. "After Suharto," *Newsweek*, June 1, 1998, p. 39.
47. Drucker, P.F. *Managing in Turbulent Times*, Butterworth-Heinemann, Oxford, 1993, p. 136.
48. See Brzezinski, Zb. *The Grand Chessboard*, pp. 167, 168 note.
49. See Dent, Ch. M. *The European Economy: The Global Context*, p. 153.
50. See Neef, D., Siesfeld, G. A., Cefola, J. (eds.) *The Economic Impact of Knowledge*, Butterworth-Heinemann, Boston-Oxford, 1998, p. 9.
51. See *East Asian Institute. China's Economy and the Asian Financial Crisis*, p. 11.
52. See Jonquieres, G. de. "Beijing's Hard Bargain," *Financial Times*, May 26, 2000, p. 14.
53. See Spaeth, A. "Big Kid on the Block," *Time*, September 29, 1997, p. 35.
54. See *Economist*, April 8, 2000, Survey "China," p. 14.
55. See *Economist*, April 12, 1997, p. 119.
56. See Brahm, L. J. *China as No 1: The New Superpower Takes Central Stage*, Butterworth-Heinemann Asia, Singapore, 1996, p. 100.
57. See Bernstein, R., Munro, R. H. *The Coming Conflict with China*, Alfred A. Knopf, New York, 1997, pp. 131, 132.
58. See Gilpin, R., with Gilpin, J. M. *The Challenge of Global Capitalism: The World Economy in the 21st Century*, Princeton University Press, Princeton (N.J.), 2000, p. 283.

59. See Brockway, G. P. *Economists Can Be Bad for Your Health: Second Thoughts on the Dismal Science*, W. W. Norton & Company, New York-London, 1995, p. 104.

60. See Jonquieres, G. de. "Beijing's Hard Bargain," *Financial Times*, May 26, 2000, p. 14.

61. See McGeary, J. "The Next China," *Time*, March 3, 1997, p. 23.

62. See Cumings, B. *Parallax Visions: Making Sense of American-East Asian Relations at the End of the Century*, Duke University Press, Durham (N.C.)-London, 1999, p. 163.

63. See *China's Futures: Scenarios for the World's Fastest Growing Economy, Ecology, and Society*, Pharo Books, San Francisco (Cal.), 2000, p. 22.

64. See Lam, W. W-L. *The Era of Jiang Zemin,* Prentice Hall/Simon & Schuster (Asia) Pte Ltd., Singapore-New York, 1999, p. 291.

65. See Dorn, J. A. "China's Future: Market Socialism or Market Taoism," in Dorn, J.A. (ed.) *China in the New Millennium: Market Reforms and Social Development*, Cato Institute, Washington (D.C.), 1998, p. 102.

66. See Burstein, D., Keijzer, A. de. *Big Dragon: China's Future: What It Means for Business, the Economy, and the Global Order*, Simon & Schuster, New York, 1998, pp. 196-197, 200-201.

67. See *Economist*, May 2, 1998, p. 79.

68. See Hayes, D. *Japan's Big Bang: The Deregulation and Revitalization of the Japanese Economy*, Tuttle Publishing, Boston (Mass.)-Tokyo, 2000, p. 185.

69. See *Hong Kong Economic Journal*, April 7, 1998, p. 6.

70. See Roberts, D. "China's Wealth Gap," *Business Week*, European Edition, May 8, 2000, p. 32.

71. See Naughton, B. "China: Domestic Restructuring and a New Role in Asia," in Pempel, T. J. (ed.) *The Politics of the Asian Economic Crisis*, p. 206.

72. See Lam, W. W-L. *The Era of Jiang Zemin*, p. 383.

73. See Li, C. *China: The Consumer Revolution*, p. 172.

74. See *Economist*, October 24, 1998, p. 23.

75. See *Economist*, May 2, 1998, p. 79.

76. For details see Leggett, K. "China Tries Reforms of Its Private Sector in Bid to End Slump," *Wall Street Journal Europe*, March 13, 2000, p. 2.

77. See Brown, L. R., Flavin, Ch., French, H. et al. *State of the World 1998: A Worldwatch Institute Report on Progress Toward a Sustainable Society,* Earthscan Publications, New York-London, 1998, p. 12.

78. See Brahm, L. J. *China as No. 1*, pp. 63-64.

79. See Wolf, Ch., Jr. "China: An Emerging 'Economic Superpower'?" in Dorn, J. A.(ed.) *China in the New Millennium: Market Reforms and Social Development*, p. 22.

80. See *Economist*, May 6, 2000, p. 122.

81. See Smil, V. *China's Environmental Crisis*, pp. 34-35.

82. See Smil, V. *China's Environmental Crisis*, pp. 55-56.

83. See Taylor, J. "Sustainable Development: A Model for China?" in Dorn, A. (ed.) *China in the New Millennium: Market Reforms and Social Development*, p. 395.

84. See Kennedy, P. *Preparing for the Twenty-First Century*, Fontana Press, London, 1994, p. 69.

85. See *The World in 2020: Towards a New Global Age*, OECD Publications, Paris, 1997, p. 116.

86. See Meadows, D. H., Meadows, D. L., Randers, J. *Beyond the Limits: Global Collapse or a Sustainable Future?* Earthscan Publications Ltd., London, 1992, p. 181.

87. See Smil, V. *China's Environmental Crisis*, p. 63.
88. See Ayres, R. U. *Turning Point: An End to the Growth Paradigm*, p. 144.
89. See Smil, V. *China's Environmental Crisis*, p. 10.
90. See Weizsaecker, E. U. von. *Earth Politics*, Zed Books, London-Atlantic Highlands (N.J.), 1994, p. 66.
91. See Garten, J. *The Big Ten: The Big Emerging Markets and How They Will Change Our Lives*, Basic Books, New York, 1997, p. 97.
92. See Smil, V. *China's Environmental Crisis*, p. 124.
93. McRae, H. *The World in 2020: Power, Culture and Prosperity: A Vision of the Future*, Harper Collins Publishers, London, 1995, p. 135.
94. See Smil, V. *China's Environmental Crisis*, p. 135.
95. See *The World in 2020: Towards a New Global Age*, p. 59.
96. See Dent, Ch. M. *The European Economy: The Global Context*, p. 391.
97. See Mitchell, K., Beck, P., Grubb, M. *The New Geopolitics of Energy*, pp. 169-170.
98. See Brown, L. R., Flavin, Ch., French, H. et al. *State of the World 1997: A Worldwatch Institute Report on Progress Toward a Sustainable Society*, W.W. Norton & Company, New York-London, 1997, p. 166.
99. See Burstein, D., Keijzer, A. de. *Big Dragon*, p. 116.
100. Brzezinski, Zb. *The Grand Chessboard*, p. 185.
101. See Henderson, C. *Asia Falling*, p 257.
102. See Kynge, J. "Chinese GDP Data Raise Growth Hopes," *Financial Times*, April 17, 2000, p. 3.
103. See Smith, C. S. "Chinese Expansion Is Sharp but Uneven," *International Herald Tribune*, April 18, 2000, p. 19.
104. See Li, C. *China: The Consumer Revolution*, p. 4.
105. See Greider, W. *One World, Ready or Not: The Manic Logic of Global Capitalism*, Simon & Schuster, New York, 1997, p. 32.
106. See *Economist*, April 8, 2000, Survey "China," p. 14.
107. See Cox, W. M., Alm, R. *Myths of Rich and Poor: Why We're Better Off Than We Think*, Basic Books, New York, 1999, p. 106.
108. See Callan, B., Costigan, S. S., Keller, K. H. *Exporting U.S. High Tech: Facts and Fiction about the Globalization of Industrial R&D*, Council on Foreign Relations, Washington (D.C.), 1997, p. 30.
109. See Koch, R. *The Third Revolution: Creating Unprecedented Wealth and Happiness for Everyone in the New Millennium*, Capstone, Oxford, 1998, p. 112.

7

Russia: Pipe-Dreams and Realistic Objectives

Research into problems of the "catching up" development concept cannot be considered complete without an analysis of an extremely rich (but, unfortunately, not quite successful) experience accumulated in that sphere by Russia. Over the past 300 years, this country has gone through several consecutive waves of modernization, most of them connected, in some way or other, with the improvement of the existing economic system after the Western pattern. At the beginning of the eighteenth century, in the epoch of Peter the Great, a backward country practically unknown in Europe managed an unheard of stride forward as a result of which, without actually reforming social and economic relations, it became one of the leading European powers, built up an enormous army, gained access to the sea and secured a firm foothold in the foreign market. The impulse of that first wave of modernization died down by the early nineteenth century when a radical social reform became a pressing need but was never carried out by the powers-that-were. At the end of the nineteenth century Russia made another attempt to break through into Europe where it could no longer claim a leading position with Britain, Germany, and France firmly in control. Nevertheless, that was a period of Russia's rapid economic progress accompanied by its active integration with other European states. In the twentieth century, the Soviet Union made two vigorous attempts—in the 1930s and in the 1950s-60s—at proving the historic advantages of the socialist system along the lines of accelerated industrialization—and to a certain extent succeeded in accomplishing the latter.

A close look at this country's 300-year economic history will show that Russia has always tried to join the great powers' community "its own way," ignoring the historical experience of other states which had found themselves in the van of progress. Even when we came level with Europe economically and technologically, we always remained behind it from the angle of civil liberties and human potential buildup, and that inevitably forced the nation back and depreciated all its previous successes. The history of Russia corroborates, better than any other nation's, the fact that genuine social progress is actually impossible in a situation where people are fenced in with political and ideological dogmas and where the "national idea," now being much talked about, is formulated in terms of the "catching up" development policy. In any case, as the post-industrial society was taking shape in the West, the Soviet Union and the Russian Federation after it stood ever-slimmer chances of occupying in the modern world a place worthy of their history.

The Specific Features of the USSR as an Industrial Power

At he beginning of the twentieth century, the Russian Empire was one of Europe's most backward states in terms of production structure and labor productivity. It was not by chance that the 1917 revolution proclaimed accelerated industrialization of the country one of its priorities. Having suppressed whatever political opposition had been offered to them, the Bolsheviks got down to the implementation of their reformatory lans in the late 1920s. In the history of Soviet industrialization, an unbiased researcher may find (and in a hypertrophied form) most of the important elements later reproduced in the majority of the other "catching up" countries: an extremely low standard of living for the bulk of the population, a disproportionately large part of the national income used for investment purposes, reinforcement of the working-class ranks by the peasantry, overemphasis on the development of heavy industry which made for the nation's relatively autonomous progress. Experts stress today that Soviet industrialization coincided, fortunately for its ideologists, with the period of catastrophic economic crisis in the West "which assured for decades to come the intellectual respectability, so to say, of the socialist recipes for solving development problems, made them an object of close attention and a model worthy of imitation in countries confronting the challenges of 'catching up' industrialization."[1]

As a result of massive industrialization which changed the gross national product and employment structure entirely, the Soviet Union found itself in a class with the world's major industrial powers for the time being. The victory in the Second World War, rapid postwar reconstruction, the development of nuclear weapons and space rockets, confrontation with the United States in the arms race, indisputable achievements in space research—all that was believed to be evidence that the country's economy was at the stage of mature industrialism complete with all its attributes such as job engineering, a steady rise in investment and accelerating economic progress.[2] Over the period of 1945-1980, steel production increased in the USSR from 12.3 to 148 million tons; electric energy output, from 43.2 to 1,294 million kW; car output, from 74,000 to 2.2 million, and so on.[3] From 1960 to 1985, the gross national product and national income increased 3.87 times in the USSR; industrial production, 4.85; and total production assets, almost sevenfold.[4] According to Soviet statistics, the USSR's industrial output constituted 85 percent of that of the United States; the country led the world in the production of gas, steel, coke, mineral fertilizers, tractors, ferroconcrete structures and a number of other raw materials and manufactured goods.[5] Since the mid-1950s, all the indices characterizing the development of science and education were rising steeply: the number of students increased from 1.25 million in 1950 to 3.86 million in 1965; R&D spending increased almost sevenfold over the same period to constitute about 7 percent of the total accrued national income.[6] Using modern terminology, it looked as if all the necessary prerequisites had been provided for a changeover to the post-industrial phase of development.

However, in the 1970s and particularly in the 1980s, which were marked in the Western world by rapid progress of new production technologies, it became obvious that the Soviet economy was falling behind the dynamism of the West and could not act as an equal rival in the notorious "competition between the two systems" announced by the ideologically myopic Soviet leaders.

The difficulties the Soviet economy came up against were caused by a variety of factors.

First of all, there was a tangle of problems generated by the Communist regime's short-sighted (and sometimes criminal) policy. We mean, in particular, the aftermaths of the elimination of the middle class in the countryside and of wholesale reprisals against the "differently minded"; an extremely inefficient foreign trade; support for unpopular and essentially anti-democratic pro-Communist regimes in the Third World countries; and finally, over-militarization of society which exploited the nation's intellectual and labor resources and largely contributed towards the collapse of the Soviet system. At various estimates, the USSR's military spending over the period of 1960-1987 alone amounted to about \$4.6 trillion or 15[7] to 30[8] percent of the gross national product, which is 3.5-4 times the corresponding U.S. figure and almost forty times that of Japan's. Here is a comparison to give the reader a notion of the magnitude of these figures: the USSR's and Russia's foreign debt which we are now straining in vain to reimburse to our Western creditors constitutes \$150 billion—just 4 percent of the unproductive and wasteful cold war arms race spending.

Second, the Soviet economic system was not intended to maximize ultimate consumption. Throughout the post-war period, the share of the fixed capital in the structure of national wealth was growing steadily, reaching 65.8 percent by the year 1990 while citizens' personal property constituted no more than 20 percent of its total volume.[9] Whereas in the U.S. the share of wages in the gross domestic product constituted 59 percent in the early 1990s, in Russia the figure was a mere 23; for aggregate monetary incomes, the respective indices were 85 and 58 percent.[10] Owing to the ever-unsatisfied consumer demand, the industry had no incentive to improve its products, and new sectors were geared to military or political needs, for the most part. The result was monstrous monopolism (towards the end of the 1980s, about 80 percent of all manufactured items were produced by one or two plants, the share of factories employing over 1000 constituted 73.3 percent as against 26 percent in the United States),[11] and the industrial system rejected innovations instead of adopting them and suppressed elements of competition. In agriculture to which 30 percent of all productive investment was channeled and which employed over 20 percent of the total workforce, the situation was worse still. Direct and indirect subsidies provided for the agrarian sector at the end of the 1980s were estimated by Western experts at \$28 billion a year.[12]

Third, a kind of a "production efficiency depression mechanism" took shape in the country in the 1970s and the 1980s. The technological revolution in the more advanced countries made the products of the Soviet industry absolutely non-competitive, and rising raw material prices triggered an accelerated development of the primary sector. By 1982, the share of machines and equipment in Soviet exports was down to 12.9 percent from 21.5 percent in 1970, and the share of fuel and electric energy up from 15.6 to 52.3 percent. Characteristically, an increase in the export of energy carriers was accompanied by their excessive use inside the country thus perpetuating the structure of production which existed then. In the 1970s and in the first half of the 1980s when oil export earned the USSR over $170 billion,[13] per capita energy consumption more than doubled, rising from 3.16 to 6.79 tons of conventional fuel.[14] As a result, the Soviet economy consumed more energy in 1988 than Japan, France, the U.K. and Switzerland combined, but spent sixteen or eighteen times more energy on making a unit of the gross national product than Japan or Switzerland did, and eight or eleven times more than the United Kingdom and France.[15] The "malignant" nature of the processes then under way in the Soviet economy is best illustrated by the degraded economic system's inability to solve the food supply problem: throughout the 1980s the country which had the world's largest sown areas imported about 375 million tons of grain and exported about 12 million tons. In the second half of the 1980s and in the early 1990s, amid a rise in world prices for oil, the lopsidedness of Soviet export structure became even more striking.

Fourth, the USSR's scientific and technological advances were grossly exaggerated. At the end of the 1980s the number of college students per 1,000 of the population was about eighteen in the USSR as against nearly fifty-five in the United States. The proportion of those who went to college for at least a year within five years of leaving school constituted about 20 percent in the USSR while in the United States the corresponding index exceeded 63 percent.[16] Notably, research workers were employed either in advanced sectors which, however, had no substantial effect on ultimate consumption, if not reduced it, or found jobs at plants where no attempts were made at technological innovation and product range renewal. Therefore, a gap in the top-skilled specialists' utilization efficiency was even wider than that in their numbers.

What really caused the final collapse of the Soviet economy was its failure to create and use intellectual capital—the vital resource of the post-industrial type of economy. Although an essentially meritocratic system was emerging in the USSR, and most workers began to display a tendency towards non-materialistic motivations, even though of a specific kind, those processes were artificial by nature. Instead of having been provoked by a substantial rise in consumption standards, they occurred in spite of it. The renumeration for intellectual work was grossly devalued in comparison to that for unskilled labor, and consumer preferences had no effect on the structure of production and on the distribution of society's resources. Seeking to prevent the model they had created from being shaken loose, the Soviet leaders minimized economic and humanitarian contacts with the outside world thus impeding the progress of the information sector. To sum up, the Soviet economy had a number of objective prerequisites for a transition to the post-industrial phase of development. These prerequisites, however, obtained only in a few sectors of the economy and, besides, were not backed by subjective factors, which caused a collapse of the previous system of motivations in the early years of reform. The processes that followed in the second half of the 1980s and in the 1990s proved beyond doubt the case of the theoreticians of post-industrialism who had warned, back in the 1970s, that *an industrial model not based on a mass consumption society cannot serve as the basis of a successful post-industrial transformation and that the post-industrial society cannot be built—it emerges in the process of natural social evolution.*

The End of a Superpower: The First Stage of Reforms (1985-1995)

In the mid-1980s, the Gorbachev government initiated radical economic reforms which have been in progress for fifteen years now. Their objectives were proclaimed to be integration into the world community, an open dialogue with the West, democratization of public life, and a transition to a socially oriented market economy. As of now, the chief results of reforms are the abandonment of the state-controlled economy model, free competition, the groundwork for the market economy, and—what merits a special note—a more sober-minded vision of Russia's real role in the modern monopolar world.

Despite the illusion harbored in 1986-1987 that the reforms were off to a good start, the Soviet economy found itself in a grave crisis by the late 1980s. The crisis was caused, first of all, by a growing imbalance in the financial sphere where a higher degree of business entities' independence filled the gap which had previously existed between the centrally planned and market spheres of the economy with the result that the amount of money in circulation increased but the mass of commodities did not. Second, the raw material sector attained the natural "ceiling" of its development (over the period of 1985-1991, oil production within the Russian Federation fell by almost 13 percent—from 542 to 462 million tons, and the total worth of Soviet export was shrinking steadily since 1983).[17] Despite the inflation hazard, the Soviet government was compelled to keep up high budgetary expenditures financed in the second half of the 1980s, to an ever greater extent, through growing deficit which increased from 13.9 billion rubles (or 1.8 percent of the gross domestic product) in 1985 to 80.6 billion rubles (or 9.2 percent of the GDP) in 1998. At the same time, owing to the policy of international openness, announced by Gorbachev, and a change of attitude to the USSR in the West, external borrowings began to grow fast, bringing Soviet foreign debt up to $43.8 billion by 1989 as compared with $18.3 billion in 1985. At the end of 1989, there appeared precedents of Soviet debtors defaulting on interest payments the total amount of which topped $6 billion by 1991.[18]

In 1990, practically all essential commodities were in short supply in the country, the inflation rate was rising steadily, and the restructuring of the economy existed only in words. An epoch of inner conflicts began culminating in the Baltic republics' withdrawal from the USSR and the subsequent breakup of the Soviet Union at the end of 1991. The years 1990-1992 proved to be the hardest ones in the Soviet economy's postwar history. In 1990, the GDP of the Russian Federation diminished by 5 percent; in 1991, by 10 percent; and in the first half of 1992, by 17 percent. In 1991-1992, the cost of living soared 20-25 times while the wages of those employed in the national economy rose a mere 7-8 times.[19] In 1991-1994, real per capita incomes reduced to less than a half which made the Russian "reforms" more catastrophic than the U.S. Great Depression had been.[20]

Such results were only natural and could have been predicted. Disintegration of the Soviet economy was caused, chiefly, by a premature transition to average world price parities in the absence of a free competition mechanism and in a closed economy (although the volume of trade between the USSR and the CMEA member-states was quite large, amounting to 17.9 percent of the Russian Federation's gross national product as of 1990)[21] and by the government's extremely inefficient policy which boiled down to a primitive version of "monetarism." The leveling of domestic and world prices laid bare the fact that in most cases the Russian industry reduced rather than increased the cost of the feedstock and raw materials it processed because its finished products often cost much less, in world prices, than the materials which had gone into making them.[22] As a result, in a situation where manufactured products accounted for 80 percent of Chinese exports' total worth, in Russia the figure was 27 percent in 1997 which puts it slightly above Mozambique, Cameroon, Mongolia, and Bolivia but way below Senegal, Morocco and Egypt let alone the developing countries of Asia.[23]

It is small wonder, therefore, that under the circumstances Russia and other post-Soviet states began to pin special hopes on increasing the export of energy carriers and raw materials—contrary to all the post-industrial trends. By the early 1990s, Russia's share in the world output of oil constituted 12 percent; of rare and non-ferrous metals, 13 percent; potassium salts, 16; natural gas, 18; of apatites, 55 etc. Notably, minerals and other primary raw materials constituted 80 percent of its exports. While the post-industrial world preferred to export information products which, by definition, do not fall into the "rare" category, Russia exported 90 percent of the aluminum it produced; 80 percent of copper; 72 percent of mineral fertilizers; 43 percent of crude oil; and 36 percent of natural gas[24] thus drawing heavily on its finite resources. Similarly, even though not as strongly pronounced, tendencies are observed in all the former Soviet republics without exception: in Azerbaijan, the share of the mining industry in overall industrial production grew from 49.1 to 63.8 percent; in Kazakhstan, from 28.2 to 38.7; in Georgia, from 5.7 to 21.3; in Kirghizia, from 6.6 to 18.5 percent.[25]

Such a state of affairs resulted in an obvious de-industrialization of the Russian economy. A rise in world and, consequently, domestic prices of raw materials made industry and agriculture non-competitive. According to statistics, the ratio between raw materials and farm product prices in Russia was more than double the corresponding index in Western markets. As a result, the bulk of the investments were shifted to the raw materials production sector and to the metallurgical industry, and the country began to import consumer goods and food on a large scale. Whereas in 1991-1996 the GNP diminished by 42 percent and the production of consumer goods and services, by 58 percent, the overall public consumption went down only 18 percent. The share of imports in trade resources increased more than fourfold (from 12 percent in 1991 to almost 54 percent in 1995).[26] In larger cities, over 80 percent of food products were either imported or made from imported raw materials.[27]

The economic crisis of the first half of the 1990s was further aggravated by the financial shocks which were both its causes and its effects. Beginning with 1987, Soviet state budget deficit came close to 7 percent of the GDP, and national currency depreciation assumed catastrophic proportions. In an attempt to counter this process, Russian reformers called off price control at the beginning of 1992 and effected massive privatization of public property in 1992-1994, the idea being to put the market competition mechanism into play. The moves had both positive and negative consequences. On the one hand, privatization created a substantial stratum of property-owners (at an official estimate, about 44 percent of the public held industrial shares as of the end of 1993)[28] and turned many state-run enterprises into joint-stock companies most of them controlled by their managers (the number of such companies reached almost 60,000 by the summer of 1993).[29] Having stepped up economic efficiency and intensified competition, the above-mentioned measures helped beat inflation rate down to a quite acceptable 15-20 percent a year. On the other hand, the reformers' attempts to enforce a rigid monetarist policy which, in its Russian version, amounted to the government's actual default on its pecuniary obligations to the public sector employees and to a number of industrial plants (at experts' estimate, non-payments by the state were responsible for 60-70 percent of all the other defaults in the economy)[30] led to a squeeze of demand, a decline in industrial production and to a catastrophic plummeting of the standard of living amid growing social inequality.

The impoverishment of a large section of the population was accompanied by a crisis of the social security and public health systems. By the mid-1990s, the average life expectancy among men was down to 58 years, and natural depopulation began in the country.[31] Nearly 20 percent of Russian citizens regularly do not get enough to eat, about 4 percent are alcohol and drug addicts, and almost 1 percent are serving prison sentences.[32] In 1990, there were

251 mental cases per 100,000 of the population; in 1996, the proportion changed to 386 per 100,000. In Russia, there were 4 million people suffering from chronic mental disorders, and among children under 10, their share amounts to 10-12 percent.[33] Western experts estimate that by the year 2050 the population of the Russian Federation may decrease from 145 million today to 80 million. In the mid-1990s, the U.N. classification put the Russian Federation in the *lower-middle income economies* category where it was sandwiched between Peru and Namibia.[34]

At the same time, the reforms provoked an unprecedented polarization of what had previously been a relatively egalitarian society. The World Bank's experts estimated that the number of the poor in the Russian Federation (in this particular case the poverty-level income was taken to be $4 a day, at most) had increased more than thirtyfold over the period of 1989-1996—from 2 to 60 million[35]; Russian experts also predict that by the year 2002 the share of those in the lower income bracket will exceed 50 percent of the country's population.[36] In the meantime, the figures released by the RF State Committee for Statistics show a reduction in the share of the poor from 33.5 to 22 percent of the population in 1991-1996.[37] A fast rise in the incomes of the well-to-do brought the gap between the poorest and the wealthiest fifths of the population to 1,100 percent.[38] The corresponding index for the nation's wealthiest and poorest 10 percent amounted to 3,100 percent. Already now, only African and Latin American countries are ahead of the Russia in the value of the Gini coefficient. Today the people spend over 70 percent of their real incomes buying food and paying their public utilities bills, with other nations (not counting the former Soviet republics—now the CIS member-states) "lagging far behind" in this index.

The first half of the 1990s was a period of an ever-steeper decline for the Russian economy. The GNP fell by 12.8 percent in 1991, 18.5 percent in 1992, 12.0 percent in 1993, and 15.0 percent in 1994 in fixed market prices. Gross industrial output diminished at a still faster rate: by 8.0, 18.8, 16.2, and 20.9 percent in the respective years. By the end of 1995, real wages constituted no more than 35 percent of the index registered in December 1991. Unemployment hit 8 percent of the able-bodied population. Towards the end of 1995, arrears of wages exceeded 15 trillion ruble (over $3 billion), and non-payments by enterprises, 134 trillion rubles (over $30 billion).[39]

Public finance was in a sorry plight: the budget deficit amounted to about 6-7 percent of the GNP, and a substantial proportion of taxes was collected in money surrogates or on a mutual offset basis. By 1996, the constituent entities of the Russian Federation and industrial enterprises had run up debts which exceeded the aggregate debt of the federal government.[40] The share of barter or offset settlements (which come not so much of hyperinflation as of the impotence of the central government, as American experts point out with good reason) in the payment for products supplied by manufacturing plants increased from 6-8 percent in July 1992 to over 50 percent in 1996.[41]

Against this background the government actually did not intervene in the processes which were going on and remained their passive onlooker. Privatization resulted in the loss of government control over enterprises' activities with all the ensuing consequences: an unrestrained decline in investment, a reduction in tax revenues, and a sharp rise in crime in the economic and financial spheres. The reduction in investment and the liberalization of the hard currency exchange rate caused an outflow of capital from Russia which intensified in 1995-1996 following the formation of the modern banking system in the country. At that time, capital outflow rate amounted to $ 5-6 billion a quarter; in the fourth quarter it rose to $10 billion which amounted to 5-8 percent of the gross domestic product.[42] The maximum estimates of the flight of capital from the country in 1992-1996 is $165 billion.[43] The balance could be restored only by medium- and short-term borrowings which finally led to the grave crisis of 1998. Having renounced direct state regulation Soviet-style, the Russian leadership failed to find the economy control levers adequate to the market environment. This was due not only to the fact that those at the helm of the state were wanting in competence, but also to the growing corruption at practically all the levels of state power. As a result, it was the action of the state machinery that caused, to a greater extent than anything else, the exacerbation of the crisis. By its own actions, the Russian government provoked non-payments, tax dodging, capital outflow, and an unprecedented criminalization of society. It is perfectly safe to claim that what we had in Russia in the 1990s was an "anti-developmental state" as distinct from the "developmental state" of Japan or those in Southeast Asia.

The first decade of the reforms brought in their wake a steep decline in the basic economic indices, the actual de-industrialization of the economy, a fall in the nation's standard of living, an unprecedented dependence on import and the Russian Federation's external insolvency thinly camouflaged by continuous borrowings from the world capital markets and international financial organizations. When radical economic reforms were in their fifth to sixth year, the Eastern European countries' gross national product approached the pre-crisis level. In Russia it remained, in 1996, almost 60 percent short, or less than a half of, the 1989 figure.[44] As a result, Russia went down to the 23rd line of the world classification of countries for the GNP value in current market prices. While occupying 11.47 percent of the planet's territory, the Russian Federation accounted for only 1.63 percent of the world GNP and for 1.37 percent of world exports.[45] In Russia's industrial sector, efficiency was under 20 percent of America's efficiency,[46] and in agriculture remained 1.2 percent of the world's maximum level (the Netherlands).[47] The country regarded until a short while back as the most dangerous rival of the U.S. found itself on a level with Illinois—the United States' ninth-richest state—for the volume of the gross national product.[48]

Absence of Prerequisites for "Catching Up" Development in the 1990s

The second half of the 1990s was marked, on the one hand, by relative financial stabilization, a reduction in industrial recession rate—and by Russia arousing interest in the world capital markets. Demand for Russian stocks rose appreciably (total market capitalization exceeded $200 billion), the country floated several Eurobond issues (with a yield some 200-300 basic points exceeding the advanced countries' liabilities), the Finance Ministry's securities were much sought after by foreign investors (who accounted for up to 30 percent of the overall demand for them), Russia was accepted (from political considerations mostly) to the industrialized nations' club and appeared to be on its way to economic recovery.[49] Despite the fact that the process was interrupted by the financial crisis of 1998, the relatively fast industrial upturn of 1999-2000 and an early enough financial stabilization confirm that Russia is past the most dramatic period of its reforms. As the twenty-first century begins, the nation is vigorously looking for avenues of further progress.

Most Russian economists, whatever their ideological and theoretical views, agree that Russia is the next candidate for joining the group of the countries committed to the "catching up" development strategy. In our opinion, however, Russia does not have what it takes to follow in the footsteps of the Asian "tigers" and will hardly be able to find a quick remedy for the economic hardships it is now experiencing. Neither is it likely to become, within the next few decades, a country the post-industrial world will reckon with from economic considerations rather than for reasons of its having a huge arsenal of nuclear warheads or being politically unpredictable.[50]

First of all, the accomplishment of the "catching up" development strategy requires, as it follows from the previous chapters, enormous investment resources. Russian experts are quite right in saying that the adherence to this strategy "rules out any alternatives to the restoration of the manufacturing industry."[51] Nevertheless, the share of industrial plant aged under five years constitutes less than 10 percent as against 65 percent in the United States, while over 70 percent of the investments made in the industry go into developing export-oriented raw materials or metallurgical sectors. In the meantime, the share of savings in personal incomes has reduced from 20-25 percent to 5-7 percent over the reform years. The net share of accumulation has been negative since 1993 in the production sector and since 1995 in the economy in general, while in 1998 gross investments in fixed capital constituted a mere 22 percent of the 1990 level in comparable prices.[52] The possibility of fixed assets renewal are immediately linked up with the ruble's exchange rate to the U.S. dollar. The fall of the latter in 1998-1999 made the likelihood of extra investments most problematic. Symptomatically, even in case of Gazprom, the more successful production monopoly, the sum total of productive investments went down from $9 billion to less than $2.5 billion a year in 1996-1999.[53] In the meantime, the state remains a net recipient rather than a net donor of investments because budgetary funds are going into financing the administrative machinery, repaying foreign debt, or meeting the expenditures connected with regional conflicts. On the eve of the 1998 crisis, for example, the Russian government spent 1.4 times more funds monthly on servicing the internal debt than the state budget actually received in revenues.[54]

Direct foreign capital investments which accounted for a lion's share of the funds channeled by Asian nations, for example, into the development of their national industries also remain insignificant here. Over the period of 1991-1996, they added up to no more than $6 billion, increasing to $12 billion towards the end of 1997.[55] The upward trend in investment was blocked, however, first by the Asian crisis and then by Russia's default on its foreign debt. As a result, the overall influx of foreign investments into Russia did not exceed 2 percent of its annual GDP.[56] Foreign investments in Russia amount to no more than $80 per capita which is one-fifteenth of the corresponding figure for Hungary. In order to come abreast with most of the emergent markets in the level of capitalization, Russia must draw capital investments to an astronomical amount of $1 trillion which is absolutely unrealistic. Therefore, new Western technologies will hardly become available to Russia within the next fifteen to twenty years.

Second, Russia remains critically dependent on the import of consumer goods, food and most of modern information technologies. In the Russian Federation, the world's leading companies have actually no assembly plants of the kind found in other developing countries—plants capable of saturating the domestic market with competitive products, increasing tax revenues and creating new jobs. Russia produces no computer accessories, microchips, software, mobile phones, satellite communication systems and many other indispensable attributes of post-industrial civilization. The presence of Russian-made audio and video equipment on the home market is infinitesimal; televsion sets, refrigerators, washing machines, and most of the other domestic appliances are assembled from imported components. Not a single major motor company is manufacturing its products in the Russian Federation on a scale significant for the market. A country so heavily dependent on the import of most high-technology products and advanced knowhow and supplying nothing but raw materials to the world market can hardly ever become a model of a successful "catching up" development strategy.

Third, the record of many nations committed to the "catching up" development strategy shows that the latter requires a favorable investment climate in the country which, among other things, encourages export. In Russia, the ruling upper crust is constantly impeding this process, whether unwittingly or by design. It is common knowledge that in most Asian countries currency exchange rate is maintained at the level of 20-40 percent of the purchasing power parity (PPP) whereas in China where export and currency reserve are growing particularly fast, this rate is under 20 percent of the PPP.[57] In the meantime, the ruble's real purchasing power more than doubled over the period from January 1994 to mid-1995 and then doubled again by mid-1997.[58] As a result, in the Russian market the U.S. dollar's purchasing power was almost 40 percent of that in the United States. Naturally such a policy of financial "stabilization" has a catastrophic effect on Russian companies' export potential and reduces the relative cheapness of its manpower to naught thus eliminating one of the Russian economy's competitive advantages—its relatively low production costs.

Fourth, the past decade was marked in Russia by total neglect of national science and intellectual potential in general, although in the post-industrial epoch "catching up" development is possible given a full-scale enlistment of skilled labor's services. In the United States, unskilled labor constituted no more than 3.9 percent of the total workforce in 1995; in Russia, its share does not fall below 25 percent.[59] In the U.S. budget (which is twenty times in excess of Russia's) allocations for education and public health surpass those in Russia 2.5 and almost six times, respectively. By the year 1997, R&D expenditures were down to one-seventh compared with 1990, and constituted 0.32 percent of the GDP, the threshold limit value of this index being 2 percent. In the period of 1985-1997, as many as 2.4 million people abandoned scientific careers thus confirming the obvious fact that non-materialistic motivations, so widespread in Soviet society, did not amount to a solid system which had evolved naturally and gave way to exclusively utilitarian stimuli on contact with economic reality. The number of researchers working in their lines is now at the early post-war years' level, and the annual number of researchers leaving the country amounted to 300,000 in some years. The estimates of the losses caused by the brain drain range from $60-70 billion over the entire period of reforms to 45-50 billion a year.[60] Even amid such a reduction in human potential, fixed capital per scientist in Russia remains 8-9 percent of that in America and Germany. Notably, Russia is still ahead of the United States in the number of research workers per 1 million of its population (4,350 as against 3,730). In the meantime, the shares of high-technology products in Russian and U.S. exports constitute 3 and 44 percent, respectively.[61] Russia's R&D spending is five times, on the average, that of the other countries making up the group of the lower-middle income economies, but in the per capita share of the GNP Russia surpasses those countries' average by a mere 30 percent.[62] In mid-1997, Russia was behind Colombia and Egypt in the number of international telephone calls made,[63] and the proportion of the Internet users to the population in Russia was one-eightieth that in the United States.[64] All this makes the hopes of Russia's likely breakthrough into a "neoindustrial" future using whatever high technologies are available to it look absolutely unrealistic.[65]

Fifth and finally, in most "catching up" countries the state has had a positive role to play getting the national priorities right. In Russia, the state is demonstrating its total inability to carry on such a constructive policy. In Japan and South Korea the state, on the one hand, stimulated the acquisition of foreign technologies and patents by the local companies as the groundwork on which to build up those countries' own industries and, on the other, backed the effort to promote the sales of the national industry's products in foreign markets. The Russian government is doing neither. The World Bank experts put Russia at the bottom of the list in five "nominations"—corruption, unpredictable changes in legislation, government instability, lack of property safeguards, and the absence of an effective judicial system—right below the states of tropical Africa.[66] In the period of reforms, special privileges were granted to companies which imported popular consumer goods, alcoholic drinks included, and exported natural resources, such as oil or aluminum. The state renders no support to foreign companies which transfer their production facilities to the territory of Russia; it grants preferential treatment to domestic manufacturers who turn out products known to be of poorer quality. In other words, national interests are regarded in our country as interests of the group which is in office at the moment, and this is hardly a factor in making the "catching up" development policy a success.

The above is best illustrated by the ripening, progress, and consequences of the 1998 crisis. Having set itself the aim of keeping inflation in check, the government artificially induced money famine in the country which, rather than creating a high demand for money, reduced the monetization of the economy to an unprecedented 10-12 percent of the GNP (with lower level registered in 1998 only in Armenia, the Democratic Republic of the Congo and Guinea-Bissau) and increasing non-payments to the public-sector enterprises and organizations.[67] A low U.S. dollar exchange rate suited government bureaucracy and the financial upper crust, above all, which cashed in on securities market speculations and took capital out of the country. However, the pressure on the ruble increased—first in the fall of 1997 and then in the summer of 1998—and rising interest rates on government short-term liabilities required ever-larger payments. As early as at the end of 1997, the foreign currency reserves of the Bank of Russia went down by a third, from $18.4 to 12.2 billion[68] (which, in itself, is surprising for a country having a favorable trade balance of $30-35 billion a year). Under the circumstances, the only correct move would be "to devaluate the ruble at an accelerated rate, that is, to change over from stabilization based on currency exchange rate fixing to monetary stabilization based on a low price of the ruble and a restrictive monetary policy."[69] That was not done: at the end of 1997 export declined (for the first time since 1992), the more liquid shares fell by 40-45 percent from the October 1997 high, and the yield on short-term government liabilities constituted 60 percent per annum.

In the summer of 1998, the Russian government received from the International Monetary Fund a large stabilization credit, spending a substantial part of it on reimbursing short-term government liabilities early in August which could no longer remedy the situation where the Central Bank's reserves, most of them represented by the gold reserve stock, fell below the $9 billion mark. The situation was further aggravated by a fall of the world energy carrier prices which told on the Russian budget revenues. From August 8 to 17, the Russian financial system was in "death throes" whereupon the government devaluated the ruble and defaulted most of its financial obligations.[70] The consequences of the August crisis were most painful. As early as in September, industrial production fell by 14.5 percent compared with the corresponding period of 1997; in the following year, prices more than doubled, investments went down by over 40 percent with the result that the GNP diminished by 5.5 percent at the end of 1998.[71] The basic RTS stock index fell to 37 point, and the overall capitalization of all the Russian companies listed at the stock exchange constituted less than a half of the capitalization of the Amazon.com Internet bookstore.[72] Over the period of 1998-1999, the ruble fell by a factor of four not only cutting, for the umpteenth time, the international estimates of Russia's gross product but detracting from the state's investment potential and the volume of funds redistributed by the federal government. In 2000, the Taxes and Dues Ministry proposes to collect about 560 billion rubles in tax payments which is regarded as a major achievement. It is worth noting here that this amount (slightly less than $20 billion) is comparable with the capitalized value of companies like Seagram Records (Canada) and Nintendo TV Game Decks (Japan).[73]

There is no denying the fact that in 1999-2000 the Russian economy experienced one of the highest upturns over the past few decades.[74] This improved performance can be explained by the same factors that had caused the industrial boom in the East Asian countries in 1998-1999. The Russian industry gained access to extremely cheap raw materials which, with the wages practically frozen, made it possible to minimize labor costs. Notably, in 1999 the prices of oil and other energy carriers jumped nearly threefold; as a result, foreign currency flooded into the country, replenishing budget revenues. The successive Primakov, Stepashin and Putin Governments went over to a relatively mild monetary policy with the result that the money mass almost tripled over the period from August 1998 to May 2000, and industrial production grew almost 8 percent[75] (the GNP growth constituted, at Western estimates, about 5 percent in 1999 and almost 7 percent in the first quarter of 2000).[76] It looks, however, that by early 2000 the government went back to its former policy of financial "stabilization" at a new level of ruble exchange rate to the dollar. The exchange rate actually froze in the corridor between 28 and 29 rubles to the dollar, which spells an inevitable gradual rise in industrial production costs and subsequent price increases (characteristically, March and April inflation indices were twice as high as the monthly average for the first quarter of 2000). Besides, it should be borne in mind that the production of exports commodities such as oil, gas, aluminum, rare-earth metals, etc., was responsible for a substantial proportion of industrial output growth (almost 76 percent). The recently established Russian Aluminum group intends to produce almost 2.4 million tons of aluminum in 2000 which will make it the world's second–biggest producer of that metal after America's Alcoa.[77] Besides that, the heavy and defense industries are livening up; their recovery, however, will inevitably come to an end as soon as government orders are again curtailed. Growth achieved by the expansion of the domestic market cannot be stable in a situation where the population's incomes remain lower than they were in the pre-crisis period. Therefore, one can agree with the view that the government's policy remains unchanged, on the whole, and that the beneficial effects of devaluation and high oil prices in 1999 will be short-lived.[78] Russian analysts say that a slowdown in industry bordering on recession has been observed since as early as April-May 2000, and that inflation is running at double the January-March rate.[79]

To sum up, today's Russia is a country having a sufficiently diversified but hopelessly outdated production potential, enormous natural wealth, a high-capacity home market and skilled enough labor. It is capable of producing only a very limited range of goods although it is axiomatic for the modern economic theory that a competitive economy is supposed to change easily from manufacturing conventional products to high-technology goods and vice versa in line with market demand fluctuations.[80] Regrettably, whatever merits Russia has as a promising economic system stem from its past record of industrial achievement while the root cause of its defects is not so much a shortage of investments as lack of post-industrial experience. The conclusion to draw from the situation is unequivocal: *in the immediate future* Russia should concentrate *on becoming a developed industrialized country; it has practically no real chance of promptly joining the post-industrial community.*

* * *

The current crisis in Russia is something worse than a conventional financial crash or an ordinary slump in industrial production. It has not merely thrown the country many decades back. Today Russia has little to show for the pains it has taken over the past century to acquire the great power status. It is distressing for the Russian public to realize that the country is becoming not even a third World, but "Fourth World" state, copying the worst models of corrupt Asian capitalism and is being represented, one might say, by mistake at the G-7 summits because it does not deserve it in the least.[81] This is not so much a matter of steep decline in the country's economy potential as the attending implication that "Russia no longer has development prospects acceptable from the standpoint of its own public consciousness."[82]

The nation can ride out the current crisis if its basic characteristics are clearly identified. We are of the opinion that in the 21st century Russia ought to work towards becoming a mature industrial nation with principles of freedom and democracy deeply ingrained in its public mind. We are to launch products competitive with foreign makes, to actively build up and use our intellectual potential. Russian society is to get rid of its imperial complex and to arrive at the realization of the fact that it is one of the equal nations making up the human race. In the 21st century Russia is to accomplish a historic industrial break-through which presupposes, among other things, economic openness and drawing foreign investors into the country—not merely as extrac-tors of local mineral wealth but as builders of new production facili-ties which offer people jobs, pay taxes to the state and hand down priceless work experience to the growing generation.

Giving every encouragement to entrepreneurial activity in the sphere of production should become an important function of the state. Before domestic and foreign investors are put on an equal foot-ing we shall neither achieve a substantial rise in tax revenues, nor cut the criminal bond between those in high places and the manage-ment of major national companies. We are to work toward the country's natural integration into the world economic system through reducing the share of mining and processing sectors and increasing that of the consumer goods industries. It is precisely the emphasis on the pro-duction of competitive consumer commodities rather than building up the munitions industry or the practice of awarding government contracts to unprofitable production plants that can set into motion the natural reproduction mechanism based on the citizens' solvent de-mand. Given a relative saturation of the consumer market, a rise in real incomes does not stimulate inflation but provides an impulse to the development of production. Cuts in imports will make it possible to gradually reduce the rubles' exchange rate to the dollar without provoking inflation and to build up the nation's export potential. In the near future, mass-produced commodities of Russian manufacture are to supersede raw materials as the chief export items.

As far as the heavy industry is concerned, the production of capi-tal goods non-competitive in the world market is to be slashed dras-tically. The state should by no means finance the development of equipment already mass-produced abroad. Financial support should be rendered only to projects which promise technological priority (i.e. those in the spheres of space research, nano-technology, computer software etc.). The practice of keeping unprofitable Russian companies afloat by awarding them government contracts is impermissible. It is necessary to change over from subsidizing farms regardless of their production efficiency to the policy of centralized purchases of agriculture produce at prices guaranteeing the profitability of the agrarian sector, with the said produce subsequently sold to processing plants at market prices.

Apparently, such a policy would turn the Russian Federation, within two or three decades, into an industrialized country with a medium level of development and a gross national product worth about $8,000 per capita. Such a policy would cut the share of energy resources and raw materials in the gross national product and increase the share of the consumer products sectors. The pursuance of such policy would enable the Russian Federation to retool its production facilities, to introduce new technologies in the industry and agriculture and to put an end to the humiliating dependence on the import of consumer goods. It is only in the more distant future that the economic complex of Russia and of most East European countries will be able to proceed to the post-industrial stage.

This avenue of progress is by no means tragical and detracts nothing from Russia's historical role and its national dignity. In our opinion, the way out of the current crisis lies in the country's natural integration into the world community and in a gradual improvement of the nation's welfare standard without any nostalgia for the great-power trappings lost. We think that having gone through several revolutions, two world wars and innumerable internal conflicts in the 20th century, this nation has earned the right to evolutionary advance as part of real economic and social progress.

Russia has got used to being one of the poles of international confrontation. The fallacy of the talk about the need to prevent the formation of a unipolar world consists in that the new civilization now in the making will have, and already has, the opposite pole— the pole of poverty and decay. The worst mistake this nation may commit in the new century would be to opt for that pole just in order to set itself apart from the "rest of them." It is our hope that the arguments and facts set forth above will bring it home to the reader that such a step, if it is ever made, will be the last one in the history of this once great and powerful nation.

Notes

1. *Gaidar, Ye. Anomalies of Economic Growth.* M.,1997. P.106.
2. For details, see: *Aron R.* Politics and History. New Brunswick, 1984. P. 122-138.
3. See: *Kennedy P.* The Rise and Fall of the Great Powers. Economic Change and Military Conflict from 1500 to 2000. N.Y., 1988. P. 554-555.
4. Even attempts at a revision of such indices undertaken at the end of the 1980s (the one that had the farthest-reaching repercussion was made by *V. Selyunin* and *G. Khanin* in the article Deceptive Figures//Novy Mir. 1987. No. 2. P. 194-195) furnish no grounds for denying the Soviet economy's impressive achievements in the 1950s and the 1960s.
5. See: The National Economy of the USSR over 70 years. An Anniversary Statistical Bulletin. M., 1987. P. 49, 13, 12.
6. See: *Krasilschikov V.A.* In Pursuit of the Past Century. M., 1998. P. 129-130.
7. Human Development Report 1999. N.Y.–Oxford, 1999. P. 189.
8. *Schaeffer R.K.* Understanding Globalization. The Social Consequences of Political, Economic, and Environmental Change. Lanham—N.Y., 1997. P. 23-24.
9. See: A Road to the 21st Century. Strategic Problems and Prospects of the Russian Economy. Ed. Lvova D.S. M., 1999. P. 222.
10. See:*Krasilschikov V.A.* In Pursuit of the Past century. P. 196-197.
11. See: *Goldman M.* Lost Opportunity. What Has Made Economic Reform in Russia So Difficult. N.Y.–L., 1996. P. 13.
12. See: *Kennedy P.* The Rise and Fall of the Great Powers. P. 633.
13. See: *Goldman M.* What Went Wrong with Perestroika. N.Y.–L., 1992. P. 49.
14. See: *Gaidar Ye.* Anomalies of Economic Growth. P.120, Table 8.
15. See: Human Development Report 1999. P. 201-202.
16. See: The Road to the 21st Century. Strategic Problems and Prospects of the Russian Economy. P. 305.
17. See: *Gaidar Ye.* Anomalies of Economic Growth. P.172.
18. See: *Oslund A.* Russia: Market Economy Is Born. M., 1996. P. 68, 71.
19. See: *Bogomolov O.T.* My Chronicle of the Transition Period. M., 2000. P. 173-174.
20. See: *Simes D.* After the Collapse. Russia Seeks Its Place as a Great Power. N.Y., 1999. P. 146.
21. See: *Solomon R.* ?oney on the Move. The Revolution in International Finance Since 1980. Princeton (N.J.)., 1999. P. 102.
22. See: *Andrianov V.D.* Russia in the World Economy. M., 1999. P. 23.
23. See: Human Development Report 1999. P. 27.
24. See: *Andrianov V.D.* Russia: Economic and Investment Potential. M., 1999. P. 194.
25. See: *Pavlenko F., Novitsky V.* Restructuring Tendencies and Industrial Policy in the CIS Member-States//Problems of Economics. 1999. No. 1. P. 116.
26. See: *Grigoryev L.* Seeking Ways of Economic Growth//Problems of Economics. 1998. No. 8. P. 40.
27. See: *Glazyev S.* The Central Bank Versus the Russian Industry//Problems of Economics. 1998. No. 1. P. 21.
28. See: *Oslund A.* Russia: Market Economy Is Born. P. 312.
29. See: *Goldman M.* Lost Opportunity. What Has Made Economic Reform in Russia So Difficult. ?. 133.
30. See: *Shmelev N.* A New Stage of Russian Reforms: Limits and Possibilities // Problems of Economics. 1998. No. 1. P. 4.
31. See: *Blasi J.R., Kroumova M., Kruse D.* Kremlin Capitalism. Ithaca (N.Y.)–L., 1997. P. 24.

32. See: *Delyagin M.G.* Ideology of Revival. Looking for Ways Out of Poverty and Decay. M., 2000. P. 50.

33. See: *Usher R.* Ivan the III // Time. 2000. February 21. P. 64-65.

34. See: The State in a Changing World. World Development Report 1997. Wash.—Oxford, 1997. P. 197.

35. See: *Stiglitz G.* Whither the Reforms? // Problems of Economics. 1999. No. 7. P. 6.

36. See: *Lvov D.* Russia's Economic Progress and the Tasks of Economic Science. M., 1999. P. 40-412.

37. See: *Ovcharova L., Turuntsev Ye., Korchagina I.* Poverty: Where Is the Threshold?/ / Problems of Economics. 1998. No. 2. P. 65-66.

38. See: *Friedman T.L.* The Lexus and the Olive Tree. N.Y., 2000. ?. 320.

39. See: *Blasi J.R., Kroumova M., Kruse D.* Kremlin Capitalism. P. 190.

40. See: *Grigoryev L.* Seeking Ways to Economic Growth. P. 52.

41. See: *Woodruff D.* Money Unmade. Barter and the Fate of Russian Capitalism. Ithaca (N.Y.)—L., 1999. ?. 110-111, 147-148.

42. See: *Bulatov A.* Export of Capital from Russia: Regulation Problems // Problems of Economics. 1998. No. 3. P. 56.

43. See: *Abalkin L.* Capital Flight: Nature, Forms and Ways of Combatting It // Problems of Economics. 1998. No. 7. P. 39.

44. See: *Blanchard O.* The Economics of Post-Communist Transition. Oxford, 1998. ?. 19.

45. See: *Illarionov A.* How Russia Has Lost the 20th Century/ Problems of Economics. 2000. No. 1. P. 6.

46. See: *Kudrov V, Pravdina S.* Comparative Labor Efficiency Levels in the Industries of Russia, the USA and Germany in 1992// Problems of Economics. 1998. No. 1. P. 131-132.

47. See: *Andrianov V.D.* Russia in the World Economy. P. 26.

48. See: *Schwartz P., Leyden P., Hyatt J.* The Long Boom. A Vision for the Coming Age of Prosperity. Reading (Ma.), 1999. ?. 134.

49. For details, see: *Granville B.* Problems Involved in Stabilizing Currency Circulation in Russia // Problems of Economics. 1999. No. 1. P. 26-27.

50. For details, see *Rosensweig J.A.* Winning the Global Game. A Strategy for Linking People and Profits. N.Y., 1998. P. 156.

51. *Lvov D.S.* Russia's Economic Progress and the Tasks of Economic Science. M., 1999. P. 66.

52. See: *Volsky A.* Innovation Factor of Providing for Sustainable Economic Development // Problems of Economics. 1999. No. 1. P. 12.

53. The Wall Street Journal Europe. 2000. April 12. P. 3.

54. See: *Lyasko A.* Stabilization Program Implementation Will Not End Crisis // Problems of Economics. 1998. No. 9. P. 7.

55. See: *Brady R.* Kapitalizm. Russia's Struggle to Free Its Economy. New Haven (Ct.)–L., 1999. P. 186.

56. See: *Montes M.F., Popov V.V.* The "Asian Virus" or the "Dutch Disease"? The Theory and History of Currency Crises in Russia and Other Countries. M. 1999. P. 11.

57. See: *Montes M.F., Popov V.V.* The "Asian Virus" or the "Dutch Disease"? P. 42

58. See: *Woodruff D.* Money Unmade. P. 162-163.

59. See: *Bushmarin I.* Russia's Labour Resources: Development and Utilization Concept //World Economy and International Relations. 1969. No. 9. P. 54.

60. See: *Ushkalov I., Malakha I.* The Brain Drain: Scale, Causes, Consequences. M., 1999. P. 86-87.

61. See: Knowledge for Development. World Development Report 1998/99. Wash.–Oxford, 1999. ?. 227.

62. See: Knowledge for Development. World Development Report 1998/99. ?. 2.

63. See: Human Development Report 1999. P. 28.

64. See: Knowledge for Development. World Development Report 1998/99. ?. 227.

65. The more active proponents of such views include the Russian scientists Yu.M.Osipov, Yu.V.Yakovets, E.G.Kochetov (see: On the Way to Post-Industrial Civilization. Ed. Yu.V.Yakovets. M., 1996; *Yakovets Yu.V.* The Formation of the Post-Industrial Paradigm: Sources and Prospects// Problems of Philosophy. 1997. No.1; *Osipov Yu.M.* Fundamentals of the Economic Mechanism Theory. M.,1994; Economic Theory on the Threshold of the 21st Century. Ed. Yu. M. Osipov, V.T. Pulyayev. S-Pb., 1996; *Kochetov E.G.* Geoeconomics. M., 1998, etc.)

66. See: The State in a Changing World. World Development Report 1997. P. 35.

67. See: *Montes M.F., Popov V.V.* The "Asian Virus" or the "Dutch Disease"? P. 78.

68. See: Banking Crisis: Is the Fog Dispersing? // Problems of Economics. 1999. No. 5. P. 13.

69. See: *Popov V.* Lessons of the Currency Crisis in Russia and Other Countries // Problems of Economics. 1999. No. 6. P. 112.

70. The chronicle of this process was vividly described by G.Soros, one of the financial speculators worst hit by the Russian crisis (see: Soros G. The Crisis of Global Capitalism [Open Society Endangered]. N.Y., 1998. P. 152-168).

71. See: *Bogomolov O.T.* My Chronicle of the Period of Transition. P. 246.

72. See: *Castells M.* Information Technology and Global Capitalism // Hutton W., Giggens A. (Eds.) On the Edge. Living with Global Capitalism. L., 2000. P. 71.

73. See: Financial Times. 2000. May 4. Survey FT 500. P. 10.

74. For details, see: *Wines M.* Little by Little, Russia Claws Its Way Back // International Herald Tribune. 2000. June 3-4. P. 11.

75. See: *Delyagin M.G.* Ideology of Revival. Looking for Ways Out of Poverty and Decay. P. 43.

76. See: *Cullison A.* Russia's Economic Growth Tops 7% // The Wall Street Journal Europe. 2000. April 12. P. 1, 4.

77. See: *Whalen J.* Russia Aluminium Barons Will Unite Their Assets // The Wall Street Journal Europe. 2000. April 18. P. 9.

78. See: *Delyagin M.G.* Ideology of Revival. P. 34.

79. See: Gazette. 2000. June 2. P. 1.

80. See: *Porter M.E.* The Competitive Advantage of Nations. Houndmills–L., 1990. P. 164-165.

81. See: *Simes D.* After the Collapse. Russia Seeks Its Place as a Great Power. P. 105, 108.

82. See: *Delyagin M.G.* Ideology of Revival. P. 34.

Index

Accelerated development theories
approaches of, 3-4
industrial development importance
in, 4
modernization and, 5-8
technocratic approach in, 4
Airtouch Communications, 47
Akimatsu, K., 19
Amazon.com Company, 177
Amin, S., 9, 12, 13
Amoco Company, 47
Aron, R., 4
Attali, J., 18

Bank of Japan, 90-91, 99
Bank of Korea, 121
Bank of Philippines, 120
Bank of Thailand, 120-121
Baran, P., 9
Bauer, P., 3
Bauman, Z., 20
Bell, D., 34
Bendix, R., 16
Black, C., 5
Brookings Institution, 116
Brzezinski, Z., 141, 145, 153

Cardoso, F., 9, 12
"Catching up" development concept
accelerated development problems,
2-3
characteristics of, 1-2
conclusions on, 20-21
decline of, 14-20
development theories, 8-14
modern globalization failures, 21
modernization and, 8
origins of, 3
post-industrial changes and, 14-21
research origins of, 2
twentieth century revolutions and, 1

twenty-first century focus of, 20
vs socioeconomic realities, 20
Westernization accelerated theories,
3-8
Western vs Eastern blocs, 20-21
See also Accelerated development
theories
"Catching up" development internal
contradictions
capital importation and, 67-69
circumstances impacting, 75-76
countries unequal to tasks in, 75
development factor extensiveness,
65-67
development model types, 61
nonselfsufficiency factors, 69-71
one-sidedness as, 62-63
post-industrial world dependence,
71-72
public under consumption and, 63-
65
state role importance, 73-74
vs evolutionary development, 73, 76
"Catching up" development theory decline
"developmental state", 18-19
economic trends and, 14-15
human capital significance, 17
modernization concept improve-
ments, 17-18
1970-1980 era growth and, 16-17
self-sufficiency and, 15-16
Southeast Asian countries and, 19-
20
Westernization concept successes
and, 14
China
accelerated growth sources, 141-150
"catching up" development trends,
155-156
conclusions on, 155-156

problem avoiding by, 156
problems in, 150-155
reform retrospectives, 138-141
significance of, 137
successes achieved by, 137-138
China's capital investments
    characteristics of, 143-144
    economic liberation stages, 143
    ethnic Chinese communities and,
        144-146
    foreign investment capital, 142-143
China's economic reforms
    development levels and, 139-140
    economic growth origins, 138-139
    industrialization locations as, 139
    initiating of, 138
    regional domestic product levels,
        140-141
China's economic success factors
    banking system problems, 149-150
    capital investments in, 142-146
    export expanding as, 146-148
    private savings rates, 141-142
    state's influences, 148-149
    vs problem avoiding, 150-151
China's exporting
    economic growth from, 146
    scale of, 146-147
    types of, 146
China's governmental influences
    banking system problems, 149
    economic growth and, 148
    public sector reforms, 150
    state owned business size, 148-149
China's problems
    crisis avoiding, 153
    ecological standards disregarding,
        151-152
    natural resource losses, 151
    as political threat, 155
    vs other Asian countries, 153
    vs success factors, 150-151
    vs U.S., 153-155
Clark, C., 3

Daimler Chrysler Company, 47, 101
"Dependent development" concept
    changes within, 13-14
    economic isolationism, 13
    modernization theory criticisms, 11
    vs modernization advocates, 11-13
"Dependientism" concept

as anti-modernization, 9
author of, 8
goal of, 9
Development theories
    "dependent development" concept,
        9-14
    "dependientism" concepts, 8-9
    See also "Dependent development"
        concept
"Developmental state"
    "catch up" development linking, 19
    focus of, 18-19
    writings on, 18
Drucker, P., 145

Economic Journal, 2
Economist, 15
Eisenstadt, S., 5
European Union, 45-46

Faletto, E., 9
Financial Times, 127
"Flying geese vee formation" theory, 19
Ford Motor Company, 42-43, 124
Foster-Carter, A., 9
Frank, A. G., 9
Friedman, T., 51
Fukuyama, F., 72
Furado, S., 9

Galbraith, James K., 14
Giddens, A., 51
Goldstein, M., 125
Greider, W., 154

Hanbo Group, 123
Hardt, M., 51
Hirschman, A., 3
Hitachi Company, 74
Hokkaido Takushoku Bank, 95
Human capital, significance of, 17

Industrial development model
    characteristics of, 61
    countries adopting, 61
Inglehart, R., 34
International Monetary Fund (IMF), 98,
        122-124, 125, 177-178

Japan
    economic leadership of, 38
    U.S. balance of payments to, 39-40

U.S. response to, 38-39
Japan's banking system
  debt estimates of, 97-98
  economy and, 98
  interest rate suppression, 96-97
  investment risks, 97
  stock market crash and, 96
Japan's economic crisis
  economic growth rates declining, 89-90
  government borrowing practices, 90-91
  government preventive steps, 91-92
  stock market pressures, 89
  technology development lacking, 88-89
Japan's economic future
  current status of, 101-102
  economic recovery measures, 101
  GNP redistribution issues, 100-101
  government industrial production funding, 99
  vs inherited status, 98-99
Japan's economic miracle
  accomplishments of, 81
  "catching up" development limits, 102-104
  conclusions on, 102-104
  crisis threshold of, 88-92
  economic baggage, 98-102
  ending of, 92-98
  as industrial country model, 81
  multipole world theory, 82
  post-war economic progress, 102
  success in, 82-88
Japan's economic miracle ending
  Asian financial crisis, 95-96
  banking system problems, 96-98
  capital investments and, 94-95
  demand stimulation attempts, 92-93
  economic ranking of, 92
  financial problems origins, 96
  market shifting and, 93-94
  unemployment growing, 93
Japan's mobilizing development system
  export trade increases, 86
  investment levels in, 83-84
  state's participation in, 84-86
Japan's success model
  capital exporting, 87-88
  export trade increases, 86
  mobilizing development system for, 82-86

1989 economic crisis, 88
  reform environment for, 82
  trade surplus signals, 86-87
Johnson, C., 18

Kahn, Herman, 4
Kia Group, 123-124
Kodak Company, 42
Krugman, P., 67

Landes, D., 145
Levy, M. Jr., 5
Lewis, A., 3

Maslow, A., 33
Mitsubishi Company, 74, 101
Modernization
  "catching up" development from, 8
  country differentiation in, 7-8
  cultural aspects of, 7
  developing countries and, 6-7
  industrial development and, 5-6
  problems from, 5
  sociopolitical aspects of, 6
  vs "dependent development" concept, 9-14
  vs dependientistas, 11-14
Monteverde, A., 9
Multipole world theory, 82
Myrdal, G., 3, 8, 16

NEC Company, 74
Negri, A., 51
Nissan Company, 101
North American Free Trade Association (NAFTA), 113
Nurski, R., 5

Parsons, T., 5
Posenstein-Rodan, P., 3
Post-industrial change, vs economic freedom, 14-15
Post-industrial society development stages
  Asian countries economic leadership, 38
  circumstances characterizing, 41
  industrial society popularity, 35
  Japanese economy and, 39-40
  mass production opportunities, 37-38
  "new world economic order" preventing, 36-37

1999-2000 economic boom, 40
stages within, 35
vs "catching up" development strategy, 42
vs commodity-exporting countries, 36
Western countries response to, 38-39
world economy leadership, 41
Post-industrial society rise
industrial development connections to, 29-30
intellectual class importance, 30-31
intellectual's role in, 34
knowledge-based society developing, 31
knowledge-intensive industry profits, 31-32
material vs human need cultivating, 34
needs changing in, 33
technological breakaway origins, 32-33
Western nation's dynamism sources, 34-35
worker's qualification standards, 30
Post-industrial trends
conclusions on, 49-52
country's leadership characteristics, 28
development stages, 35-42
industrial phases, 50-52
industrial production limitations, 27-28
information and knowledge as monopolistic, 29
rise of, 29-35
self-sustaining modernization focus, 27
stable prosperity requirements, 28-29
Western self-sufficiency, 42-52
world economic progress, 49-50
Prebisch, R., 3, 8

Renault Company, 101
Rosenstein-Rodan, P., 2
Rostow, W., 3-4
Russia
capital goods funding criteria, 180-181
"catch up" development and, 172-179

conclusions on, 179-181
current crisis in, 179
entrepreneurial activity encouraging, 180
great powers' joining approaches, 161-162
industrial power features of, 162-166
modernization waves in, 161
success characteristics for, 180
superpower status ending, 166-172
vs international confrontations, 181
world economy integration, 181
Russia's advancement limitations
consumer goods importing, 174
favorable investment climate, 174-175
foreign capital investments, 173-174
intellectual potential neglecting, 175-176
investment resources, 173
state role inability, 176
Russia's "catch up" development
advancement limitations, 172-176
advances from, 172
economic upturn reasons, 178-179
future of, 179
government inflation checking, 176-177
IMF stabilization credits, 177-178
Russia's industrial power
economic difficulties reasons, 163-165
final collapse reasons, 165-166
as major industrial power, 162-163
1917 revolution and, 162
vs Western production technology, 163
Russia's reforms
de-industrialization of, 168-169
economic disintegration causes, 167-168
energy exporting, 168
financial shocks causes, 169
Gorbachev's economic reforms, 166-167
governmental non-intervention, 171
1980 crisis reasons, 166-167
outcomes of, 171-172
population impoverishing, 169-170
raw materials exporting, 168
reform polarizing, 170

Sachs, J., 116
Sammi Group, 123
dos Santos, T., 9
Schneider, B., 16
Sen, A., 102
Singer, G., 3
Sony Company, 74
Soros, G., 125
Southeast Asia
    as "catching up" development example, 109
    conclusions on, 130-132
    crises for, 117-126
    development contradictions in, 109-110
    economic future of, 131-132
    economic growth vs sociocultural environment, 16-17
    economic life for, 126-130
    individual nations categories, 110-111
    industrialization of, 111-117
    post-industrial world dependent, 130-131
    success as transient, 130
Southeast Asia economic crisis
    "catch up" development warnings, 117
    currency depreciation, 121-123
    developed nation involvement, 120-121
    export declining, 119
    financial factors important, 117
    foreign investment curtailing, 119
    government investment supplementing, 125-126
    IMF aid opposition, 123-124
    international influence loss, 123
    lessons from, 125
    origins of, 117-119
    production impact from, 123
    scale of, 120, 122
    stock market crash and, 122-123
    unemployment rates during, 123
Southeast Asia economic recovery
    causes of, 126-128
    reasons for, 128-130
    vs "catching up" development, 126
Southeast Asia industrialization
    Brookings report on, 116-117
    crisis vs financial support, 116
    economic growth factor, 111
    export focus dangers, 113-114

    foreign investment in, 115-116
    GNP growth rates, 111-112
    government protection of, 114-115
    as mass industrial production rivals, 112-113
    product export focus, 113
    Western foreign aid to, 114
Sprint Company, 42
Staley, E., 2
Sunkel, O., 9

Third World
    investment shrinking in, 43
    nineteenth century vs today's gap, 15-16
    self-sufficiency growing in, 15
Thurow, L., 155
Tinbergen, J., 3, 6
Toshiba Company, 74
Touraine, A., 17

UNCTAD, 9
United Nations Economic Commission for Latin American, 9

Volcker, P., 51

Wahid, President A., 130
Wallerstein, I., 10
Western nation self-sufficiency
    commodity concentrating, 44-45
    ecological situation in, 43
    economies importance, 45
    European Union economies, 45-46
    human flow migrations, 48-49
    investment flows importance, 47-48
    knowledge-based economy consequences, 42
    national corporate debenture investments, 48
    production and consumption knowledge, 42
    raw material utilization, 42-44
    Third World investments shrinkage, 43
Western post-industrial model
    characteristics of, 61-62
    countries adopting, 61
World Bank, 2, 170
World Economic Development, 2

Yamaichi Securities, 95

For Product Safety Concerns and Information please contact our EU
representative GPSR@taylorandfrancis.com
Taylor & Francis Verlag GmbH, Kaufingerstraße 24, 80331 München, Germany